RUSSIAN

in 10 minutes a day®

by Kristine Kershul, M.A., University of California, Santa Barbara

Third Edition

Special Consultant: Patricia Mueller-Vollmer, Ph.D.
Book Editor: Fran Feldman

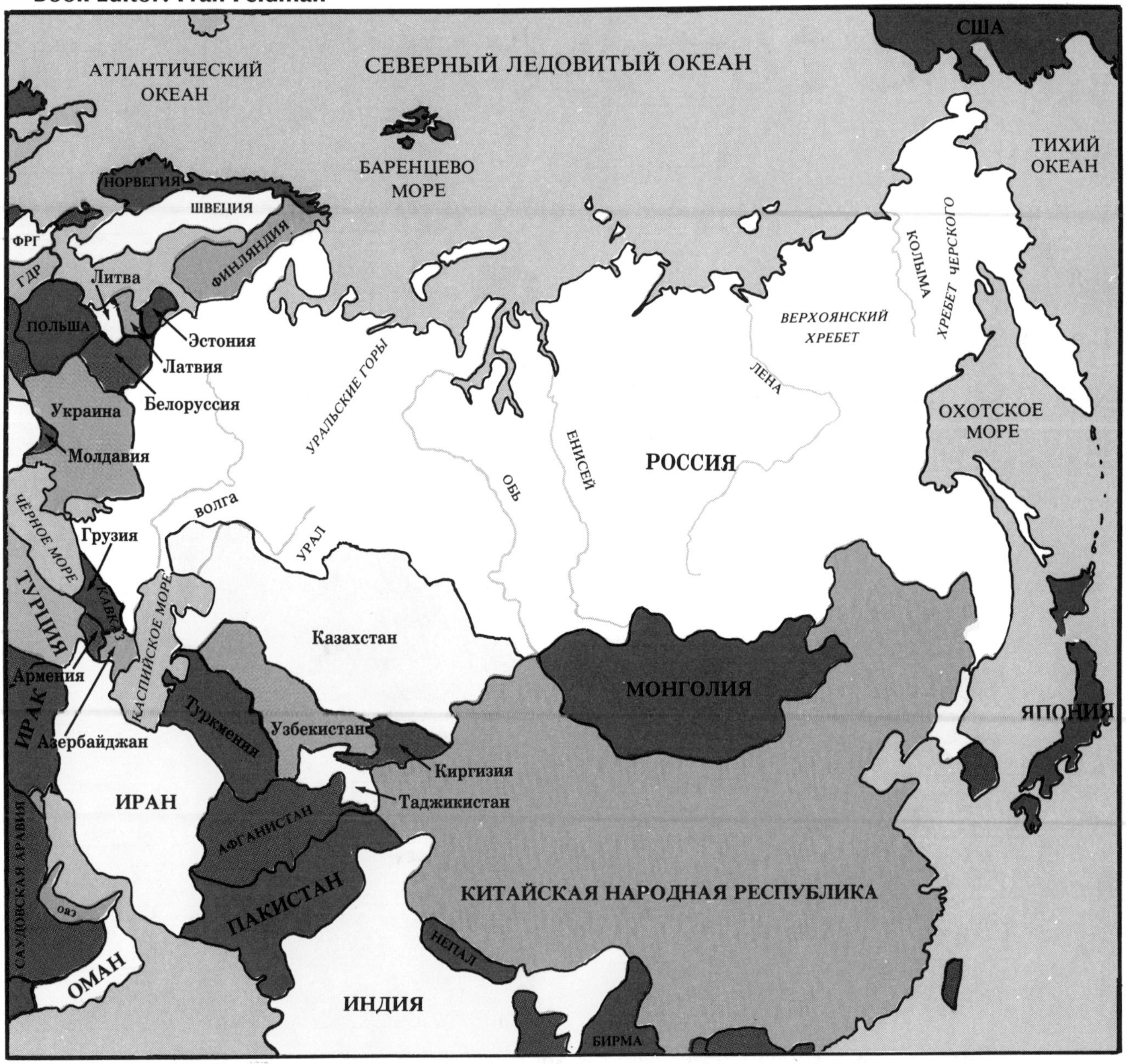

СЕВЕРНЫЙ ЛЕДОВИТЫЙ ОКЕАН
АТЛАНТИЧЕСКИЙ ОКЕАН
США
ТИХИЙ ОКЕАН
БАРЕНЦЕВО МОРЕ
НОРВЕГИЯ
ШВЕЦИЯ
ФИНЛЯНДИЯ
ФРГ
ГДР
Литва
ПОЛЬША
Эстония
Латвия
Белоруссия
Украина
Молдавия
КОЛЫМА
ХРЕБЕТ ЧЕРСКОГО
ВЕРХОЯНСКИЙ ХРЕБЕТ
ЛЕНА
ОХОТСКОЕ МОРЕ
УРАЛЬСКИЕ ГОРЫ
ЕНИСЕЙ
ОБЬ
РОССИЯ
ВОЛГА
УРАЛ
ЧЁРНОЕ МОРЕ
Грузия
ТУРЦИЯ
КАВКАЗ
КАСПИЙСКОЕ МОРЕ
Казахстан
Армения
ИРАК
Азербайджан
Туркмения
Узбекистан
Киргизия
Таджикистан
МОНГОЛИЯ
ЯПОНИЯ
ИРАН
АФГАНИСТАН
ПАКИСТАН
САУДОВСКАЯ АРАВИЯ
ОАЭ
ОМАН
КИТАЙСКАЯ НАРОДНАЯ РЕСПУБЛИКА
НЕПАЛ
ИНДИЯ
БИРМА

A Sunset Series Sunset Publishing Corporation
Menlo Park, CA 94025

First printing June 1993

 ISBN 0-944502-46-6.
Lithographed in the United States.

When you first see words like „машина“ and „когда,“ Russian can appear to be forbidding. However, it is not, when you know how to decode these new letters. To learn these new Russian letters, study the alphabet below. Note that when you write Russian, you use the cursive form, as shown. Some letters change their pronunciation depending on whether they are stressed or unstressed. The syllable that is stressed is indicated throughout the book by an accent mark at the end of the syllable.

	Russian letter	English sound	Practice here!		Russian letter	English sound	Practice here!
А а		ah		**П п**		p	
Б б		b		**Р р**		r	
В в		v		**С с**		s	
Г г		g/v		**Т т**		t	
Д д	or	d		**У у**		oo	
Е е		eh/ yeh		**Ф ф**		f	
Ё ё		yoh		**Х х**		h/hk	
Ж ж		zh		**Ц ц**		ts	
З з		z		**Ч ч**		ch	
И и		ee		**Ш ш**		sh	
Й й		oy/ay/ i/ee		**Щ щ**		shch/ sht/sh	
К к		k		**ъ**		no sound (called a hard sign)	
Л л		l		**ы**		ee/ih	
М м		m		**ь**		no sound (called a soft sign)	
Н н		n		**Э э**		eh/air	
О о		oh/ah		**Ю ю**		yoo	
				Я я		yah	

Notes: The three letters **ъ, ы** and **ь** never begin a word in Russian and have only lower-case forms. When the lower-case **л, м** and **я** follow another letter, add a tiny peak in front of them.

Example: ____________.

Seven Key Question Words

Step 1

When you arrive in a country where Russian is spoken, you will need to ask many different questions—"Where is the bus stop?" "Where can I exchange money?" "Where *(gdyeh)* **(где)** is the lavatory?" "*(gdyeh)* **Где** (where) is a restaurant?" "*(gdyeh)* **Где** (where) do I catch a taxi?" "*(gdyeh)* **Где** (where) is a good hotel?" "*(gdyeh)* **Где** is my luggage?"—and the list will go on and on for the entire length of your visit. In Russian, there are SEVEN KEY QUESTION WORDS to learn. For example, the seven key question words will help you find out exactly what you are ordering in a restaurant before you order it—and not after the surprise (or shock!) arrives. Notice that "what" and "who" are differentiated by only one letter, so be sure not to confuse them. Take a few minutes to study and practice saying the seven basic question words listed below. Then cover the *(roos'-skee)* **русский** (Russian) with your hand and fill in each of the blanks with the matching *(roos'-skeem)* **русским** (Russian) *(sloh'-vahm)* **словом.** (word)

1. *(gdyeh)* **ГДЕ**	=	WHERE	где, где, где, где, где
2. *(shtoh)* **ЧТО**	=	WHAT	________
3. *(ktoh)* **КТО**	=	WHO	________
4. *(kahk)* **КАК**	=	HOW	________
5. *(kahg-dah')* **КОГДА**	=	WHEN	________
6. *(pah-chee-moo')* **ПОЧЕМУ**	=	WHY	________
7. *(skohl'-kah)* **СКОЛЬКО**	=	HOW MUCH	________

Now test yourself to see if you really can keep these *(slah-vah')* **слова** (words) straight in your mind. Draw lines between the *(roos'-skee-mee)* **русскими** (Russian) *(ee)* **и** (and) English equivalents below.

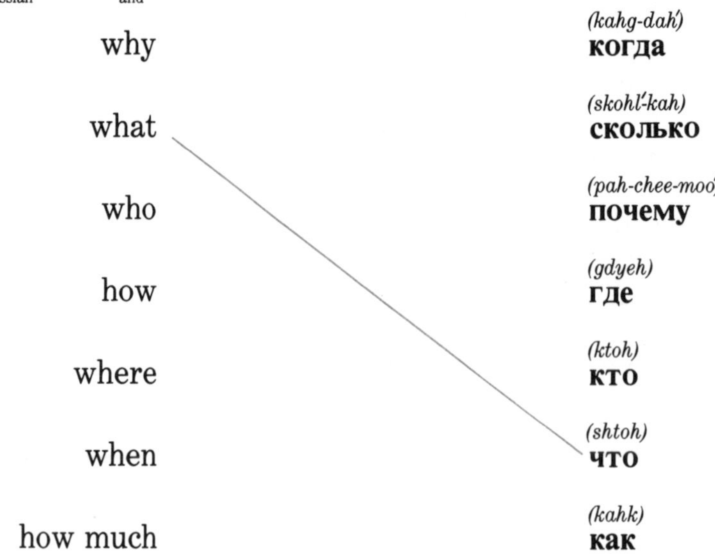

why	*(kahg-dah')* **когда**
what	*(skohl'-kah)* **сколько**
who	*(pah-chee-moo')* **почему**
how	*(gdyeh)* **где**
where	*(ktoh)* **кто**
when	*(shtoh)* **что**
how much	*(kahk)* **как**

Examine the following questions containing these words. Practice the sentences out loud *(ee)* **и** (and) then quiz yourself by filling in the blanks below with the correct question *(sloh'-vahm)* **словом.** (word)

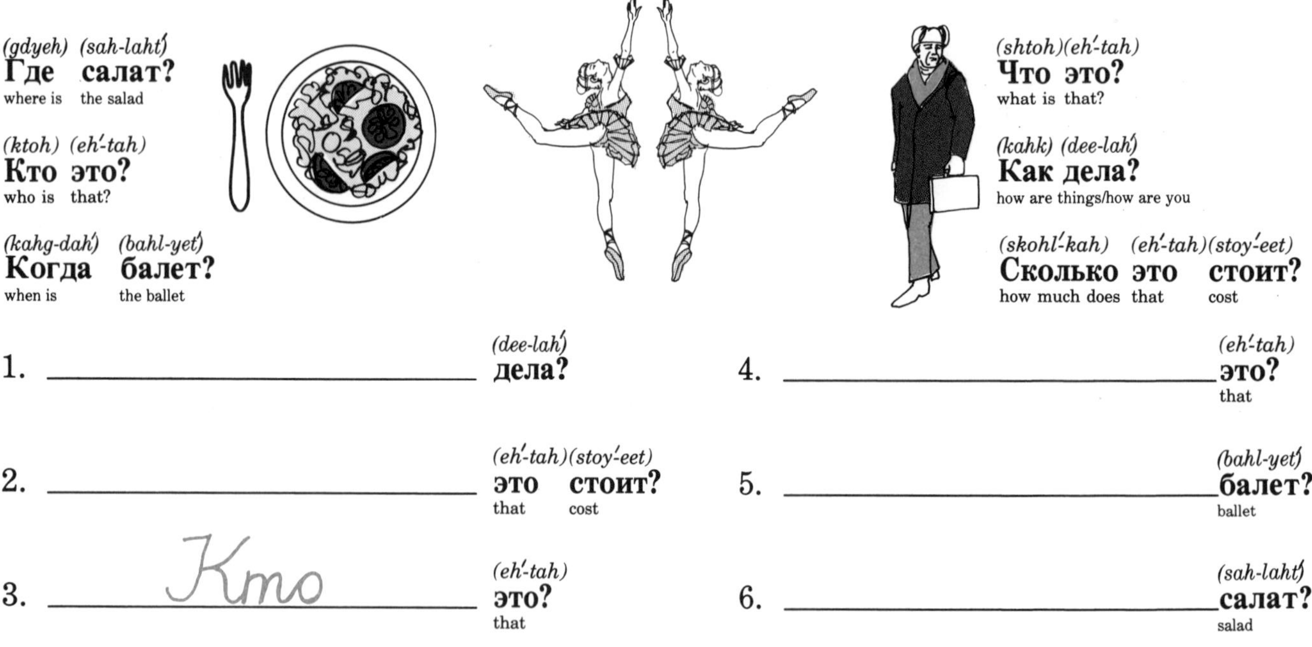

(gdyeh) (sah-laht') **Где салат?** — where is the salad

(ktoh) (eh'-tah) **Кто это?** — who is that?

(kahg-dah') (bahl-yet') **Когда балет?** — when is the ballet

(shtoh)(eh'-tah) **Что это?** — what is that?

(kahk) (dee-lah') **Как дела?** — how are things/how are you

(skohl'-kah) (eh'-tah)(stoy'-eet) **Сколько это стоит?** — how much does that cost

1. ______________ *(dee-lah')* **дела?**

2. ______________ *(eh'-tah)(stoy'-eet)* **это стоит?** (that cost)

3. ____Кто____ *(eh'-tah)* **это?** (that)

4. ______________ *(eh'-tah)* **это?** (that)

5. ______________ *(bahl-yet')* **балет?** (ballet)

6. ______________ *(sah-laht')* **салат?** (salad)

(gdyeh) **„Где“** (where) will be your most used question *(sloh'-vah)* **слово,** (word) so let's concentrate on it. Say each of the following *(roos'-skah-yeh)* **русское** (Russian) sentences aloud. Then write out each sentence without looking at the example. If you don't succeed on the first try, don't give up. Just practice each sentence until you are able to do it easily. Remember **„c“** is pronounced like an "s" *(ee)* **и „p“** is pronounced like an "r." Stress the syllable with the accent mark after it.

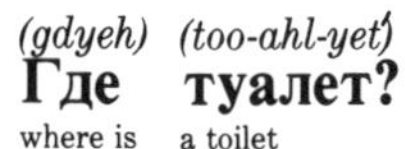

(gdyeh) (too-ahl-yet)
Где туалет?
where is a toilet

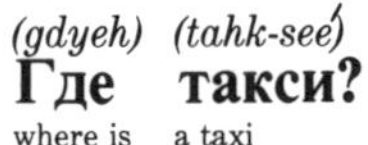

(gdyeh) (tahk-see)
Где такси?
where is a taxi

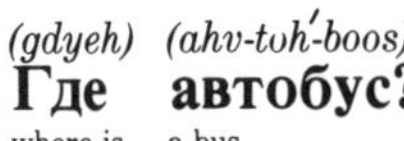

(gdyeh) (ahv-toh-boos)
Где автобус?
where is a bus

______________ Где такси? ______________

(res-tah-rahn)
Где ресторан?
a restaurant

(bahnk)
Где банк?
a bank

Где { *(ah-tyel)* **отель?** a hotel / *(gah-stee-nee-tsah)* **гостиница?** a hotel/an inn }

______________ ______________ ______________

Да *(dah)* (yes), you can see similarities between **русским** *(roos-skeem)* (Russian) **и** *(ee)* (and) **английским** *(ahn-glee-skeem)* (English), if you look closely. **Русский** *(roos-skee)* **и** *(ee)* (and) **английский** *(ahn-glee-skee)* are distantly related languages, so you will find that some words are similar. Of course, they do not always sound the same when spoken by a Russian, but the similarities will certainly surprise you and make your work here easier. Listed below are five "free" **слов** *(slohv)* (words) beginning with „**а**" *(ah)* to help you get started. Be sure to say each **слово** *(sloh-vah)* aloud **и** *(ee)* then write out the **русское** *(roos-skah-yeh)* (Russian) **слово** *(sloh-vah)* (word) in the blank to the right.

☑ **абрикос** *(ah-bree-kohs)*	apricot		______________
☑ **август** *(ahv-goost)*	August		______________
☑ **авиация** *(ah-vee-ah-tsee-yah)*	aviation	**а**	______________
☑ **Австралия** *(ahv-strah-lee-yah)*	Australia		______________
☑ **Австрия** *(ahv-stree-yah)*	Austria		______________

Free **слова** *(slah-vah)* (words) like these will appear at the bottom of the following pages in a yellow color band. They are easy—enjoy them! Don't forget to pronounce „**и**" as "ee."

Step 2

Odds 'n Ends

(roos'-skee) (yah-zik') (slohv)
Русский язык (Russian language) does not have **слов** (words) for "the" and "a," which makes things easier for you.

Russian **слова** (slah-vah') (words) also change their endings depending on how they are used, so don't be surprised! Learn **слова** (slah-vah') (the words) and be prepared to see their endings change. Here are some examples.

(sloh'-vah)
слово
word
(slah-vah')
слова
(sloh'-voo)
слову
(sloh'-vahm)
словом
(slohv)
слов
(slah-vah'-mee)
словами

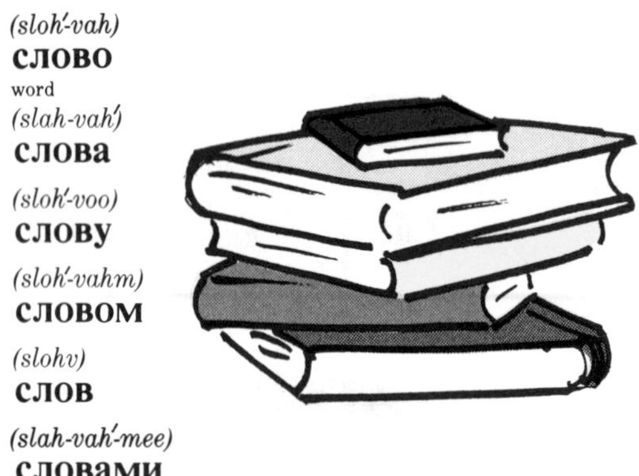

(knee'-gah)
книга
book
(knee'-gee)
книги
(knee'-geh)
книге
(knee'-goo)
книгу
(knee'-goy)
книгой
(kneeg)
книг

(stool)
стул
chair
(stoo'-lah)
стула
(stoo'-loo)
стулу
(stoo'-lohm)
стулом
(stool'-yeh)
стуле
(stool'-yah)
стулья

Just remember the core of **слова** (sloh'-vah) (word) doesn't change, so you'll always be able to recognize it. Nouns in Russian are grouped by gender. Most nouns ending in a consonant or **ь** are masculine; most ending in **а** or **я** are feminine, and nouns ending in **о** or **е** are neuter. When consonants are clustered in a syllable, as in **книга,** (knee'-gah) pronounce each one.

Step 3

Look Around You

Before you proceed **с** (s') (with) this step, situate yourself comfortably in your living room. Now look around you. Can you name the things that you see in this **комнате** (kohm'-naht-yeh) (room) in Russian? You can probably guess **лампа** (lahm'-pah) (lamp) and maybe even **диван.** (dee-vahn') (divan/couch) But let's learn the rest of them. After practicing these **слова** (slah-vah') (words) out loud, write them in the blanks below **и** (ee) (and) on the next page.

(kar-tee'-nah) (kar-teen'-kah)
картина/картинка picture ______________________

(pah-tah-lohk')
потолок = ceiling______________________

☐ **автобиография** (ahv-tah-bee-ah-grah'-fee-yah). autobiography ______________
☐ **автограф** (ahv-toh'-grahf)................. autograph ______________
☐ **автомат** (ahv-tah-maht)................. automat ______________
☐ **автомобиль** (ahv-tah-mah-beel')............ automobile ______________
☐ **автор** (ahv'-tar)......................... author ______________

а

(oog'ahl) **угол**	=	corner	____
(ahk-noh') **окно**	=	window	____
(lahm'-pah) **лампа**	=	lamp, light	____
(dee-vahn') **диван**	=	sofa	____
(stool) **стул**	=	chair	____
(kahv-yor') **ковёр**	=	carpet	____
(stohl) **стол**	=	table	____
(dvyair) **дверь**	=	door	____
(chah-sih') **часы**	=	clock	____
(zah'-nahv-yes) **занавес**	=	curtain	____
(styen-ah') **стена**	=	wall	____
(tee-lee-fohn') **телефон**	=	telephone	____

In Step 2, you learned that *(roos'-skee-yeh)* **русские** (Russian) *(slah-vah')* **слова** (words) vary. The correct form of each *(sloh'-vah)* **слово** (word) will always be given to familiarize you with the variations. Now open your *(knee'-goo)* **книгу** (book) to the sticky labels (between pages 48 and 49). Peel off the first 14 labels *(ee)* **и** (and) proceed around the *(kohm'-nah-tih)* **комнаты** (room) labeling these items in your home. This will help to increase your *(roos'-skah-yeh)* **русское** (Russian) *(sloh'-vah)* **слово** (word) power easily. Don't forget to say each *(sloh'-vah)* **слово** (word) as you attach each label.

Now ask yourself, „*(gdyeh)* **Где** *(kar-tee'-nah)* **картина?**" (the picture) and point at it while you answer, „*(tahm)* **Там** (there is) *(kar-tee'-nah)* **картина.**" (the picture)

Continue on down the list until you feel comfortable with these new *(slah-vah'-mee)* **словами.** (words) Say, „*(gdyeh)* **Где** *(pah-tah-lohk')* **потолок?**" (the ceiling) Then reply, „*(tahm)* **Там** (there is) *(pah-tah-lohk')* **потолок,**" and so on. When you can identify all the items on the list, you will be ready to move on. Now, starting on the next page, let's learn some basic parts of the house.

а

- ☐ **агент** *(ah-gyent')* .... agent ____
- ☐ **адвокат** *(ahd-vah-kaht')* .... advocate, lawyer ____
- ☐ **адрес** *(ah'-dres)* .... address ____
- ☐ **Азия** *(ah'-zee-yah)* .... Asia ____
- ☐ **академия** *(ah-kah-dyeh'-mee-yah)* .... academy ____

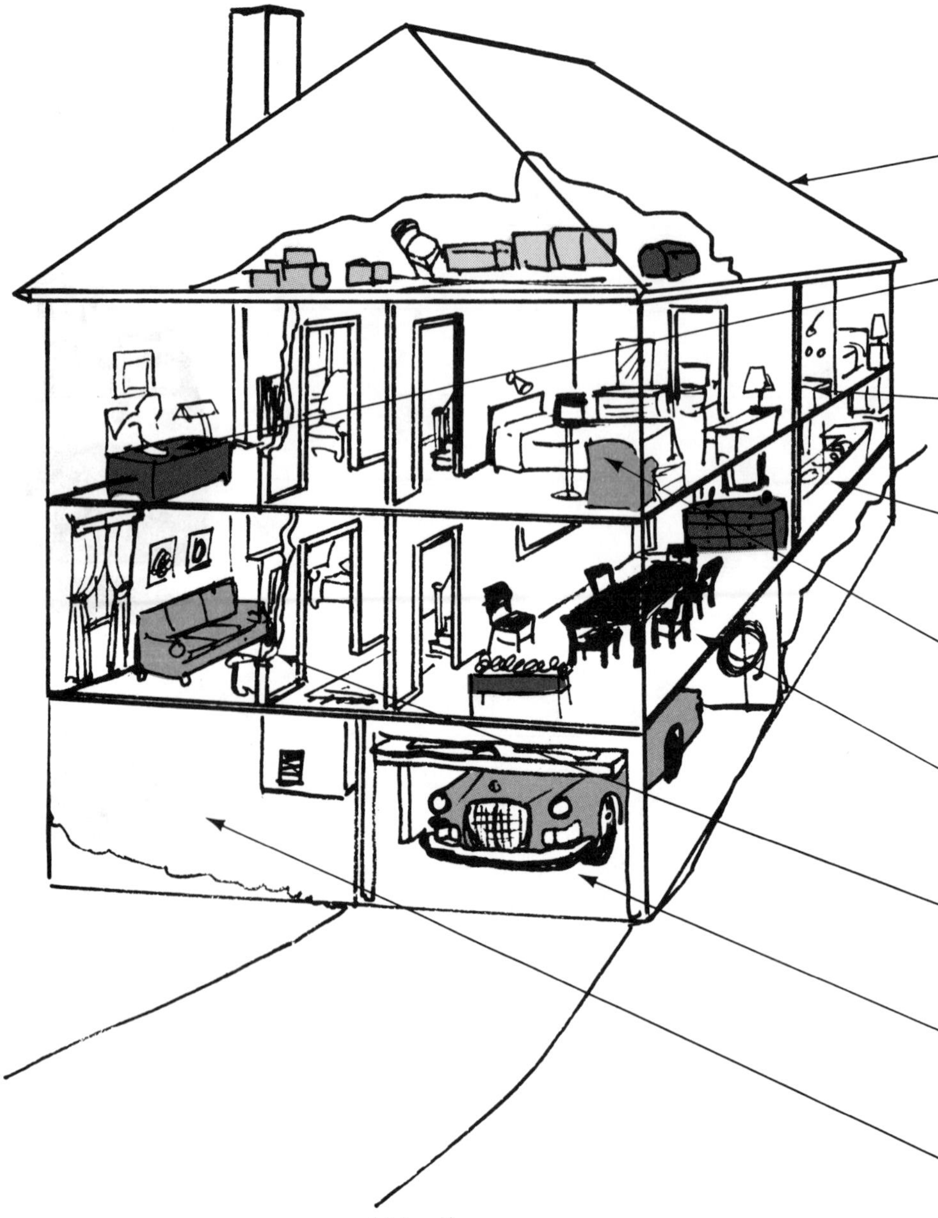

(dohm)
дом = house

(voht) *(dohm)*
Вот дом.
here is the house

(kah-bee-nyet')
кабинет
study

(vahn'-nah-yah)
ванная
bathroom

(koohk'-nyah)
кухня
kitchen

(spahl'-nyah)
спальня
bedroom

(stah-loh'-vah-yah)
столовая
dining room

(gah-stee'-nah-yah)
гостиная
living room

(gah-rahzh')
гараж
garage

(pahd-vahl')
подвал
basement

While learning these new *(slah-vah')* **слова,** (words) let's not forget

(ahv-tah-mah-beel') *(mah-shee'-nah)*
автомобиль/машина
automobile/car

(mah-tah-tsee'-kul)
мотоцикл
motorcycle

(sah-bah'-kah)
собака
dog

☐ **аккуратный** *(ahk-koo-raht'-nee)*............ fastidious, neat
☐ **акробат** *(ah-krah-baht')*.................... acrobat
☐ **акт** *(ahkt)*.................................. act
☐ **актёр** *(ahk-tyor')*........................... actor
☐ **акцент** *(ahk-tsyent')*........................ accent

а

(koht)
кот
cat

(sahd)
сад
garden

(poach'-tah)
почта
mail

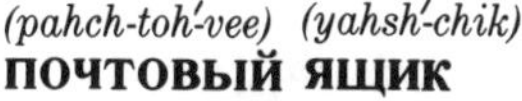

(pahch-toh'-vee) (yahsh'-chik)
почтовый ящик
mailbox

(tsveh-tih')
цветы
flowers

(zvah-nohk')
звонок
doorbell

Peel off the next set of labels *(ee)* **и** wander through your *(dohm)* **дом** learning these new *(slah-vah')* **слова** (words).

Granted, it will be somewhat difficult to label your *(koht)* **кот** (cat), *(tsveh-tih')* **цветы** (flowers) or *(sah-bah'-koo)* **собаку** (dog), but use your imagination. Again, practice by asking yourself, „*(gdyeh)* **Где** *(ahv-tah-mah-beel')* **автомобиль?**" (the car) and reply, „*(voht)* **Вот** (here is) *(ahv-tah-mah-beel')* **автомобиль.**"

Now for the following... **Где собака? Где...**

☐ **алгебра** *(ahl'-gyeh-brah)* .... algebra
☐ **алкоголь** *(ahl-kah-gohl')* .... alcohol
☐ **Америка** *(ah-myeh'-ree-kah)* .... America
☐ **—американец** *(ah-myeh-ree-kah'-nyets)* ...... American male
☐ **—американка** *(ah-myeh-ree-kahn'-kah)* ...... American female

а

Step 4

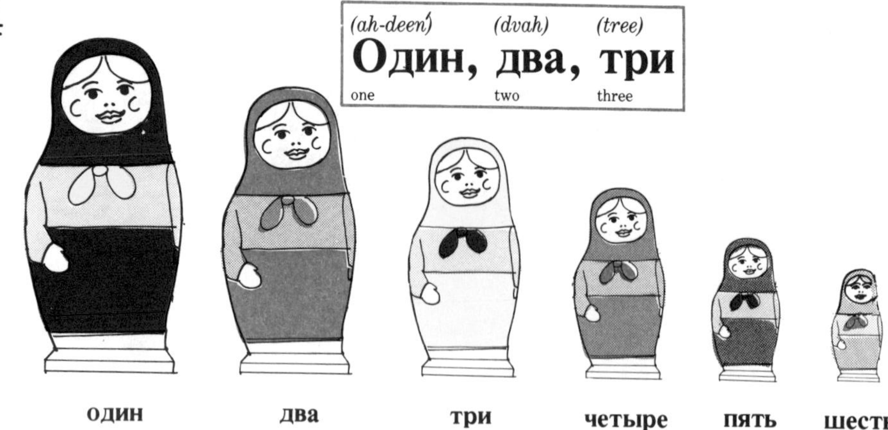

Consider for a minute how important numbers are. How could you tell someone your phone number, your address *(ee'-lee)* **или** (or) your hotel room if you had no numbers? And think of how difficult it would be if you could not understand the time, the price of an apple *(ee'-lee)* **или** (or) the correct bus to take. When practicing the *(chee'-slah)* **числа** (numbers) below, notice the similarities (underlined) between *(ah-deen')* **один** (one) and *(ah-deen'-nud-tset)* **одиннадцать** (eleven), *(tree)* **три** (three) and *(tree-nod'-tset)* **тринадцать** (thirteen), and so on.

0	*(nohl)* **ноль**			0	ноль, ноль, ноль, ноль
1	*(ah-deen')* **один**	11	*(ah-deen'-nud-tset)* **одиннадцать**	1	
2	*(dvah)/(dveh)* **два/две**	12	*(dveh-nod'-tset)* **двенадцать**	2	
3	*(tree)* **три**	13	*(tree-nod'-tset)* **тринадцать**	3	
4	*(cheh-tih'-ree)* **четыре**	14	*(cheh-tir'-nod-tset)* **четырнадцать**	4	
5	*(pyaht)* **пять**	15	*(pyaht-nod'-tset)* **пятнадцать**	5	
6	*(shest)* **шесть**	16	*(shest-nod'-tset)* **шестнадцать**	6	
7	*(syem)* **семь**	17	*(sim-nod'-tset)* **семнадцать**	7	
8	*(voh'-syem)* **восемь**	18	*(vah-sim-nod'-tset)* **восемнадцать**	8	
9	*(dyev'-yet)* **девять**	19	*(div-yet-nod'-tset)* **девятнадцать**	9	
10	*(dyes'-yet)* **десять**	20	*(dvahd'-tset)* **двадцать**	10	

- ☐ **алло!** *(ahl-loh')*............................ hello!
- ☐ **Англия** *(ahn'-glee-yah)*...................... England
- ☐ —where they speak **по-английски** *(pah-ahn-glee'-skee)*
- ☐ —**англичанин** *(ahn-glee-chah'-neen)*.......... Englishman
- ☐ —**англичанка** *(ahn-glee-chahn'-kah)*......... Englishwoman

а

Use these *(chee'-slah)* **числа** (numbers) on a daily basis. Count to yourself *(pah-roos'-skee)* **по-русски** (in Russian) when you exercise *(ee'-lee)* **или** (or) commute to work. Remove the next 10 labels and use them to practice. Now fill in the following blanks according to the *(chee'-slahm)* **числам** (numbers) given in parentheses.

Note: This is a good time to start learning these two *(oh'-chen)* **очень** (very) important phrases.

(yah) (hah-choo') (koo-peet') **я хочу купить**	= I want to buy	____________________
(mwee) (hah-teem) (koo-peet') **мы хотим купить**	= we want to buy	____________________

(yah) (hah-choo') (koo-peet') (eh'-tah)
Я хочу купить это.
I want to buy that

(yah) (hah-choo') (koo-peet')
Я хочу купить __________ (1) .
I want to buy

Я хочу купить __________ (7) *(mah'-rahk)* **марок.** (stamps)
I want

Я хочу купить __________ (8) *(mah'-rahk)* **марок.** (stamps)

Я хочу купить пять (5) .

(mwee) (hah-teem') (koo-peet')
Мы хотим купить __________ (9) *(aht-krih'-tahk)* **открыток.** (postcards)
we want to buy

Мы хотим купить __________ (10) *(aht-krih'-tahk)* **открыток.** (postcards)
we want

Мы хотим купить __________ (6) .
we

(yah) (hah-choo')
Я хочу купить __________ (1) *(beel-yet')* **билет.** (ticket)
I

Мы хотим купить __________ (4) *(beel-yeh'-tih)* **билеты.** (tickets)
we

Мы хотим купить __________ (11) .

(yah) (hah-choo')
Я хочу купить __________ (3) *(chahsh'-kee) (chah'-yah)* **чашки чая.** (cups of tea)

(hah-teem')
Мы хотим купить __________ (4) *(chahsh'-kee)(kohf'-yeh)* **чашки кофе.** (cups of coffee)
to buy

(skohl'-kah) **Сколько?** (how many) __________ (2)

(skohl'-kah) **Сколько?** (how many) __________ (1)

(skohl'-kah) **Сколько?** (how many) __________ (7)

(skohl'-kah) **Сколько?** __________ (8)

(skohl'-kah) **Сколько?** __________ (5)

(skohl'-kah) **Сколько?** __________ (9)

(skohl'-kah) **Сколько?** __________ (10)

(skohl'-kah) **Сколько?** шесть (6)

(skohl'-kah) **Сколько?** __________ (1)

(skohl'-kah) **Сколько?** __________ (4)

Сколько? __________ (11)

Сколько? __________ (3)

Сколько? __________ (4)

а

- ☐ **анекдот** *(ah-nyek-doht')*.................... anecdote, joke __________
- ☐ **антенна** *(ahn-tyen'-nah)*.................... antenna __________
- ☐ **антибиотики** *(ahn-tee-bee-oh'-tee-kee)*........ antibiotics __________
- ☐ **аппетит** *(ahp-peh-teet')*.................... appetite __________
- ☐ **апрель** *(ahp-ryel')*.......................... April __________

Now see if you can translate the following thoughts **на** *(nah)* [into] **русский.** *(roos'-skee)* [Russian] **Ответы** *(aht-vyeh'-tih)* [answers] are at the bottom of the page.

1. I want to buy seven postcards.

____

2. I want to buy nine stamps. ____

3. We want to buy four cups of tea.

Мы хотим купить четыре чашки чая.

4. We want to buy three tickets.

____

Review **числа** *(chee'-slah)* [numbers] 1 through 20 **и** *(ee)* [and] answer the following **вопросы** *(vah-proh'-sih)* [questions] aloud, **и** *(ee)* then write the answers in the blank spaces.

Сколько *(skohl'-kah)* [how many] **здесь** *(zdyes)* [here] **столов?** *(stah-lohv')* [tables]

три

Сколько *(skohl'-kah)* **здесь** *(zdyes)* [here] **ламп?** *(lahmp)* [lamps]

____

Сколько *(skohl'-kah)* **здесь** *(zdyes)* **стульев?** *(stool'-yev)* [chairs]

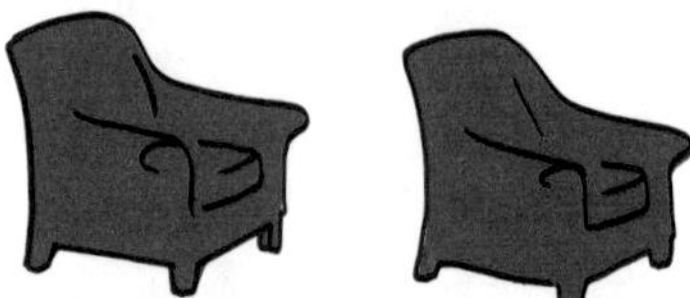

____

ОТВЕТЫ

1. Я хочу купить семь открыток.
2. Я хочу купить девять марок.
3. Мы хотим купить четыре чашки чая.
4. Мы хотим купить три билета.

(skohl´-kah) *(zdyes)* *(chah-sohv´)*
Сколько здесь часов?
how many here clocks

____

(skohl´-kah) *(zdyes)* *(oh´-kahn)*
Сколько здесь окон?
windows

____

(skohl´-kah) *(zdyes)* *(dyet-yay´)*
Сколько здесь детей?
children

____

(skohl´-kah) *(zdyes)* *(kneeg)*
Сколько здесь книг?
books

____

(skohl´-kah) *(zdyes)* *(lood-yay´)*
Сколько здесь людей?
people

____

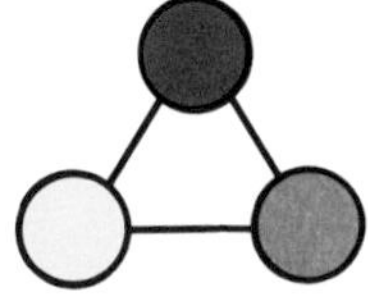

Step 5

Let's learn the basic **цвета** *(tsveh-tah´)* (colors). Colors and other adjectives have different endings, depending on the gender of the noun they modify. Once you have read through the list on the next **странице** *(strah-nee´-tseh)* (page), cover the Russian words with your hand **и** *(ee)* practice writing out the **русское** *(roos´-skah-yeh)* (Russian) next to the English. Once you've learned **цвета** *(tsveh-tah´)* (colors), quiz yourself. What color are your shoes? Your eyes? Your hair?

а

- ☐ **арена** *(ar-yeh´-nah)* . . . . arena ______________
- ☐ **арест** *(ar-yest´)* . . . . arrest ______________
- ☐ **армия** *(ar´-mee-yah)* . . . . army ______________
- ☐ **аспирин** *(ah-spee-reen´)* . . . . aspirin ______________
- ☐ **астронавт** *(ah-strah-nahvt´)* . . . . astronaut ______________

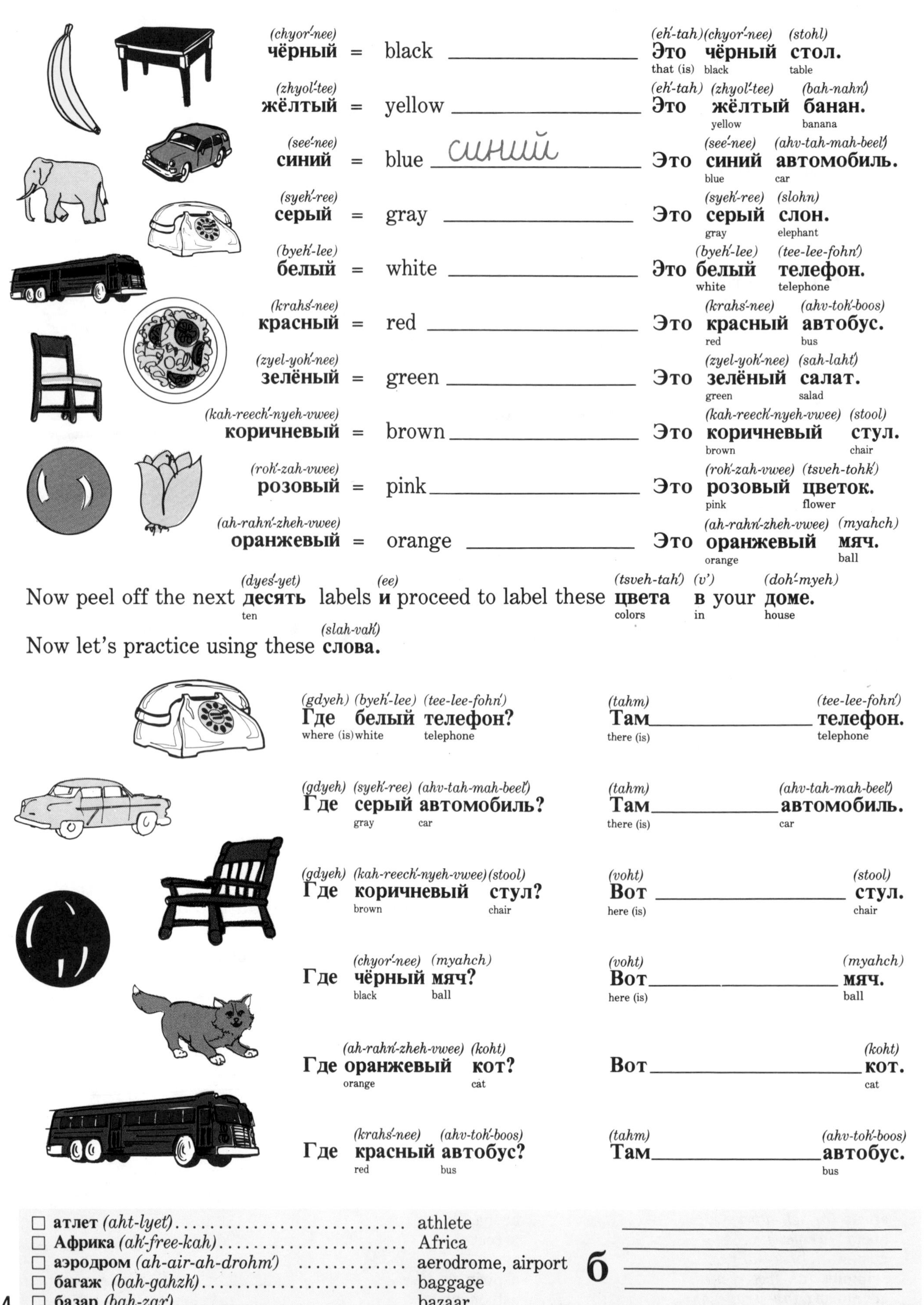

(chyor'-nee) **чёрный** = black	______________	*(eh'-tah)* **Это** that (is) *(chyor'-nee)* **чёрный** black *(stohl)* **стол.** table
(zhyol'-tee) **жёлтый** = yellow	______________	*(eh'-tah)* **Это** *(zhyol'-tee)* **жёлтый** yellow *(bah-nahn')* **банан.** banana
(see'-nee) **синий** = blue	синий	**Это** *(see'-nee)* **синий** blue *(ahv-tah-mah-beel')* **автомобиль.** car
(syeh'-ree) **серый** = gray	______________	**Это** *(syeh'-ree)* **серый** gray *(slohn)* **слон.** elephant
(byeh'-lee) **белый** = white	______________	**Это** *(byeh'-lee)* **белый** white *(tee-lee-fohn')* **телефон.** telephone
(krahs'-nee) **красный** = red	______________	**Это** *(krahs'-nee)* **красный** red *(ahv-toh'-boos)* **автобус.** bus
(zyel-yoh'-nee) **зелёный** = green	______________	**Это** *(zyel-yoh'-nee)* **зелёный** green *(sah-laht')* **салат.** salad
(kah-reech'-nyeh-vwee) **коричневый** = brown	______________	**Это** *(kah-reech'-nyeh-vwee)* **коричневый** brown *(stool)* **стул.** chair
(roh'-zah-vwee) **розовый** = pink	______________	**Это** *(roh'-zah-vwee)* **розовый** pink *(tsveh-tohk')* **цветок.** flower
(ah-rahn'-zheh-vwee) **оранжевый** = orange	______________	**Это** *(ah-rahn'-zheh-vwee)* **оранжевый** orange *(myahch)* **мяч.** ball

Now peel off the next *(dyes'-yet)* **десять** (ten) labels *(ee)* **и** proceed to label these *(tsveh-tah')* **цвета** (colors) *(v')* **в** (in) your *(doh'-myeh)* **доме.** (house)

Now let's practice using these *(slah-vah')* **слова.**

(gdyeh) **Где** where (is) *(byeh'-lee)* **белый** white *(tee-lee-fohn')* **телефон?** telephone — *(tahm)* **Там** there (is) ______________ *(tee-lee-fohn')* **телефон.** telephone

(gdyeh) **Где** *(syeh'-ree)* **серый** gray *(ahv-tah-mah-beel')* **автомобиль?** car — *(tahm)* **Там** there (is) ______________ *(ahv-tah-mah-beel')* **автомобиль.** car

(gdyeh) **Где** *(kah-reech'-nyeh-vwee)* **коричневый** brown *(stool)* **стул?** chair — *(voht)* **Вот** here (is) ______________ *(stool)* **стул.** chair

Где *(chyor'-nee)* **чёрный** black *(myahch)* **мяч?** ball — *(voht)* **Вот** here (is) ______________ *(myahch)* **мяч.** ball

Где *(ah-rahn'-zheh-vwee)* **оранжевый** orange *(koht)* **кот?** cat — **Вот** ______________ *(koht)* **кот.** cat

Где *(krahs'-nee)* **красный** red *(ahv-toh'-boos)* **автобус?** bus — *(tahm)* **Там** ______________ *(ahv-toh'-boos)* **автобус.** bus

- ☐ **атлет** *(aht-lyet')* .... athlete ______________
- ☐ **Африка** *(ah'-free-kah)* .... Africa ______________
- ☐ **аэродром** *(ah-air-ah-drohm')* .... aerodrome, airport ______________
- ☐ **багаж** *(bah-gahzh')* .... baggage ______________
- ☐ **базар** *(bah-zar')* .... bazaar ______________

б

(gdyeh) (zyel-yoh'-nee) (beel-yet') (voht) (beel-yet')
Где зелёный билет? Вот _______________ билет.
green ticket

(roh'-zah-vwee) (dohm) (tahm) (dohm)
Где розовый дом? Там _______________ дом.
pink house

(zhyol'-tee) (bah-nahn') (voht) (bah-nahn')
Где жёлтый банан? Вот _______________ банан.
yellow

Note: (pah-roos'-skee) **По-русски,** "I have" and "we have" are written as follows.

(oo) (men-yah') (yest) **у меня есть** = I have _______________ (oo)(nahs) (yest) **у нас есть** = we have _______________

Let's review (yah)(hah-choo')(koo-peet') **„я хочу купить"** (I want to buy) and (mwee)(hah-teem')(koo-peet') **„мы хотим купить,"** (we want to buy) and learn (oo) (men-yah') (yest) **„у меня есть"** (I have) and (oo) (nahs)(yest) **„у нас есть."** (we have) Repeat each sentence out loud over and over.

(yah)(hah-choo')(koo-peet') (pee'-vah)
Я хочу купить пиво.
I want to buy a beer

(oo) (men-yah') (yest) (pee'-vah)
У меня есть пиво.
I have a beer

(mwee) (hah-teem') (koo-peet') (dvah)(stah-kah'-nah)(vee-nah')
Мы хотим купить два стакана вина.
we want two glasses of wine

(oo) (nahs) (yest) (dvah)(stah-kah'-nah)(vee-nah')
У нас есть два стакана вина.
we have glasses of

(yah) (hah-choo') (sah-laht')
Я хочу купить салат.
a salad

(dohm)
У нас есть дом.
a house

(mwee) (mah'-rahk)
Мы хотим купить семь марок.
stamps

(men-yah') (yest) (dohm) (v') (ah-myeh'-ree-kyeh)
У меня есть дом в Америке.
I have a house in America

Now fill in the following blanks with (oo)(men-yah') (yest) **„у меня есть,"** (oo)(nahs) (yest) **„у нас есть,"** (yah)(hah-choo') (koo-peet') **„я хочу купить"** or (mwee) (hah-teem') (koo-peet') **„мы хотим купить."**

_______________ (dyes'-yet) (mah'-rahk) **десять марок.** stamps
(we have)

_______________ (dvah) (beel-yeh'-tah) **два билета.** tickets
(we want to buy)

_______________ (sah-laht') **салат.** salad
(I have)

_______________ (syem) (aht-krih'-tahk) **семь открыток.** postcards
(I want to buy)

☐ **бал** *(bahl)*.............................. ball (dance) _______________
☐ **балалайка** *(bah-lah-lie'-kah)*............... balalaika _______________
☐ **балерина** *(bah-leh-ree'-nah)*................ ballerina _______________
☐ **балет** *(bahl-yet')*.......................... ballet _______________
☐ **балкон** *(bahl-kohn')*........................ balcony _______________

б

(tyep-yair) **Теперь** [now] a quick review of *(tsveh-tohv)* **цветов** [colors]. Draw lines between the *(roos-skee-mee)* **русскими** [Russian] *(slah-vah-mee)* **словами** [words] *(ee)* **и** the correct *(tsveh-tah-mee)* **цветами** [colors]. On your mark, get set, *GO!*

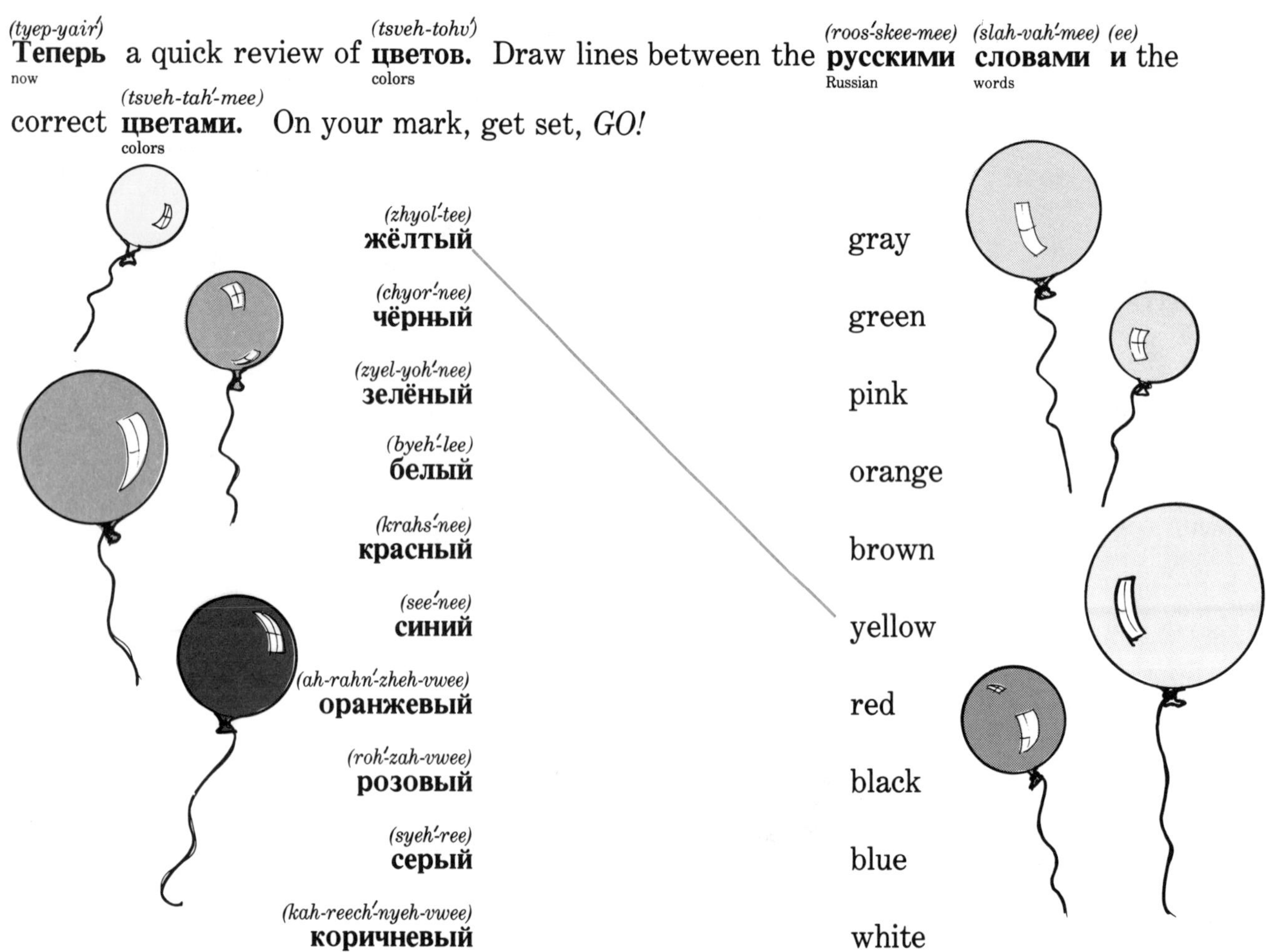

(pah-roos-skee) **По-русски** [in Russian], the letter **е** is often pronounced *"yeh"* (as in the English word "yes"). When consonants (except for **ж, ш** and **ц**) precede the *"yeh"* sound, they combine to make one sound. For example, the *(roos-skah-yeh)* **русское** [Russian] *(sloh-vah)* **слово** [word] for "no" is **„нет"** pronounced like the *(ahn-glee-skah-yeh)* **английское** [English] *(sloh-vah)* **слово** [word] "net" with a "y": *"nyet."* As you practice each of the following words, combine the sound of *"yeh"* with the letter that precedes it, making one, smooth sound.

(gdyeh) **где** where	*(syem)* **семь** seven	*(kah-bee-nyet)* **кабинет** study
(zdyes) **здесь** here	*(dyev-yet)* **девять** nine	*(byeh-lee)* **белый** white
(dyeh-tee) **дети** children	*(dyes-yet)* **десять** ten	*(syeh-ree)* **серый** blue

☐ **банан** *(bah-nahn)*........................ banana
☐ **бандит** *(bahn-deet)*........................ bandit, robber
☐ **бар** *(bar)*........................ bar (restaurant)
☐ **баржа** *(bar-zhah)*........................ barge
☐ **барьер** *(bar-yair)*........................ barrier

б

Step 6

Before starting this step, go back and review Step 4. Make sure you can count to **двадцать** *(dvahd'-tset)* [twenty] without looking **в** *(f')* [at] **книгу.** *(knee'-goo)* [the book] Let's learn the larger **числа** *(chee'-slah)* [numbers] now, so if something costs more than 20 **рублей,** *(roo-blyay')* [rubles] you will know exactly **сколько** *(skohl'-kah)* it costs. After practicing aloud **русские** *(roos'-skee-yeh)* [Russian] numbers 10 through 1000 below, write these **числа** *(chee'-slah)* [numbers] in the blanks provided. Again, notice the similarities (underlined) between **числами** *(chee'-slah-mee)* [numbers] such as **три** *(tree)* (3), **тринадцать** *(tree-nod'-tset)* (13) and **тридцать** *(treed'-tset)* (30).

10	**десять** *(dyes'-yet)*		10	десять
20	**двадцать** *(dvahd'-tset)*	(**два** = 2)	20	______
30	**тридцать** *(treed'-tset)*	(**три** = 3)	30	______
40	**сорок** *(soh'-rahk)*	(**четыре** *(cheh-tih'-ree)* = 4)	40	______
50	**пятьдесят** *(peed-dyes-yaht')*	(**пять** *(pyaht)* = 5)	50	______
60	**шестьдесят** *(shest-dyes-yaht')*	(**шесть** = 6)	60	______
70	**семьдесят** *(syem'-dyes-yet)*	(**семь** = 7)	70	______
80	**восемьдесят** *(voh'-syem-dyes-yet)*	(**восемь** = 8)	80	______
90	**девяносто** *(dyev-yah-noh'-stah)*	(**девять** *(dyev'-yet)* = 9)	90	______
100	**сто** *(stoh)*		100	______
500	**пятьсот** *(pyet-soht')*		500	______
1000	**тысяча** *(tih'-seh-chah)*		1000	______

Now take a logical guess. **Как** *(kahk)* [how] would you write **и** *(ee)* [and] say the following? **Ответы** *(aht-vyeh'-tih)* [answers] are at the bottom of **страницы.** *(strah-nee'-tsih)* [page]

140 ______________________ 52 ______________________

610 ______________________ 1100 ______________________

ОТВЕТЫ

140 = **сто сорок**	52 = **пятьдесят два**
610 = **шестьсот десять**	1100 = **тысяча сто**

The unit of currency **в** *(in)* **России** *(rahs-sih'-ih)* Russia is the **рубль,** *(roo'-bil)* abbreviated **руб.** or **р.** Bills are called **рубли** *(roo-blee')* **и** *(ee)* and coins are called **копейки,** *(kah-pay'-kee)* kopecks, abbreviated **коп.** Just as **американский** *(ah-myeh-ree-kahn'-skee)* American **или** *(ee'-lee)* **канадский** *(kah-nahd'-skee)* Canadian **доллар** *(dohl'-lar)* dollar can be broken down into 100 pennies, a **рубль** *(roo'-bil)* can be broken down into 100 **копеек.** *(kah-pyeh'-eek)* Let's learn the various kinds of **рублей** *(roo-blyay')* **и** *(ee)* **копеек.** *(kah-pyeh'-eek)* Always be sure to practice each **слово** *(sloh'-vah)* out loud. You will not be able to exchange money before your arrival, so take a few minutes now to familiarize yourself with Russian currency.

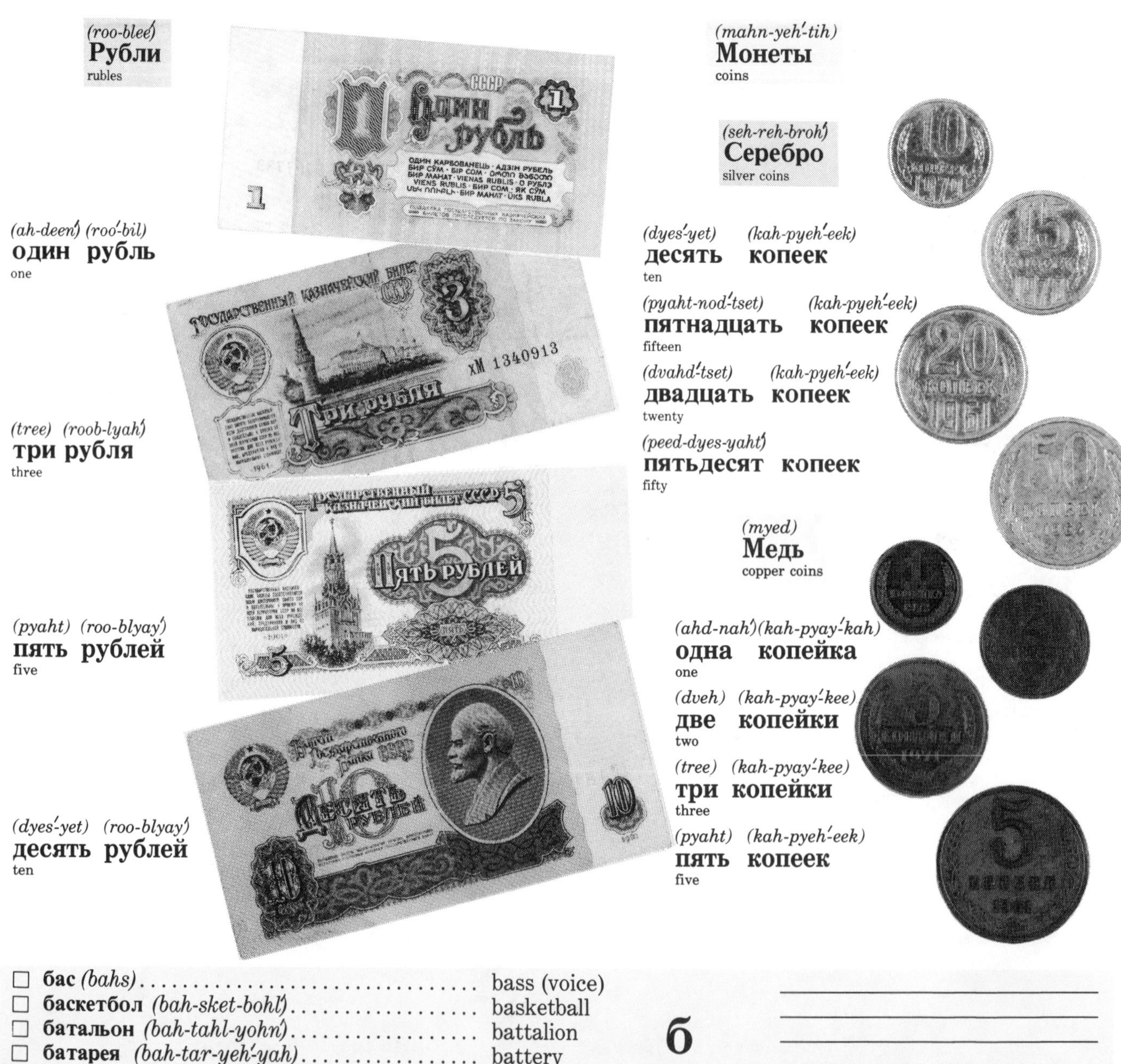

(roo-blee') **Рубли** — rubles

(ah-deen') (roo'-bil) **один рубль** — one

(tree) (roob-lyah') **три рубля** — three

(pyaht) (roo-blyay') **пять рублей** — five

(dyes'-yet) (roo-blyay') **десять рублей** — ten

(mahn-yeh'-tih) **Монеты** — coins

(seh-reh-broh') **Серебро** — silver coins

(dyes'-yet) (kah-pyeh'-eek) **десять копеек** — ten

(pyaht-nod'-tset) (kah-pyeh'-eek) **пятнадцать копеек** — fifteen

(dvahd'-tset) (kah-pyeh'-eek) **двадцать копеек** — twenty

(peed-dyes-yaht') (kah-pyeh'-eek) **пятьдесят копеек** — fifty

(myed) **Медь** — copper coins

(ahd-nah') (kah-pyay'-kah) **одна копейка** — one

(dveh) (kah-pyay'-kee) **две копейки** — two

(tree) (kah-pyay'-kee) **три копейки** — three

(pyaht) (kah-pyeh'-eek) **пять копеек** — five

☐ **бас** *(bahs)* .... bass (voice)
☐ **баскетбол** *(bah-sket-bohl')* .... basketball
☐ **батальон** *(bah-tahl-yohn')* .... battalion
☐ **батарея** *(bah-tar-yeh'-yah)* .... battery
☐ **Бельгия** *(byel'-gee-yah)* .... Belgium

б

Review **числа** *(chee'-slah)* (the numbers) **десять** *(dyes'-yet)* (ten) through **тысяча** *(tih'-seh-chah)* (one thousand) again. **Теперь,** *(tyep-yair')* (now) **как** *(kahk)* (how) do you say "twenty-two" **или** *(ee'-lee)* (or) "fifty-three" **по-русски?** *(pah-roos'-skee)* You basically put the numbers together in a logical sequence. For example, 78 (70 + 8) = **семьдесят** *(syem'-dyes-yet)* (seventy) **восемь.** *(voh'-syem)* (eight) See if you can say **и** *(ee)* (and) write out **числа** *(chee'-slah)* (numbers) on this **странице.** *(strah-nee'-tseh)* (page) **Ответы** *(aht-vyeh'-tih)* (answers) are at the bottom of **страницы.** *(strah-nee'-tsih)*

a. 25 = ______________ (20 + 5)

b. 47 = ______________ (40 + 7)

c. 84 = ______________ (80 + 4)

d. 51 = ______________ (50 + 1)

e. 36 = тридцать шесть (30 + 6)

f. 93 = ______________ (90 + 3)

g. 68 = ______________ (60 + 8)

h. 72 = ______________ (70 + 2)

To ask how much something costs **по-русски,** *(pah-roos'-skee)* one asks **„Сколько это стоит?"** *(skohl'-kah) (eh'-tah) (stoy'-eet)* **Теперь** *(tyep-yair')* (now) answer the following questions based on **числа** *(chee'-slah)* (numbers) in parentheses.

1. **Сколько** *(skohl'-kah)* (how much) **это** *(eh'-tah)* (this) **стоит?** *(stoy'-eet)* (costs) — **Это** *(eh'-tah)* (this) **стоит** *(stoy'-eet)* (costs) ______________ (10) **рублей.** *(roo-blyay')* (rubles)

2. **Сколько это стоит?** — **Это стоит** ______________ (5) **рублей.** *(roo-blyay')*

3. **Сколько стоит** *(stoy'-eet)* (costs) **книга?** *(knee'-gah)* (book) — **Книга** *(knee'-gah)* **стоит** ______________ (17) **рублей.** *(roo-blyay')*

4. **Сколько стоит карта?** *(kar'-tah)* (map) — **Карта стоит** ______________ (6) **рублей.**

5. **Сколько стоит картина?** *(kar-tee'-nah)* (picture) — **Картина стоит** ______________ (110) **рублей.**

6. **Сколько стоит банан?** *(bah-nahn')* (banana) — **Банан стоит** ______________ (20) **копеек.** *(kah-pyeh'-eek)* (kopecks)

7. **Сколько стоит открытка?** *(aht-krit'-kah)* (postcard) — **Открытка стоит** ______________ (12) **копеек.** *(kah-pyeh'-eek)*

ОТВЕТЫ

a. двадцать пять
b. сорок семь
c. восемьдесят четыре
d. пятьдесят один
e. тридцать шесть
f. девяносто три
g. шестьдесят восемь
h. семьдесят два
1. десять
2. пять
3. семнадцать
4. шесть
5. сто десять
6. двадцать
7. двенадцать

Step 7

Сегодня (see-vohd'-nyah) today, Завтра (zahv'-trah) tomorrow и (ee) and Вчера (vchee-rah') yesterday

Календарь (kah-lyen-dar') calendar

Семь дней в неделе. (syem) (dnay) (nee-dyel'-yeh) seven days in week

понедельник (pah-nee-dyel'-neek) Monday	вторник (vtor'-neek) Tuesday	среда (sree-dah') Wednesday	четверг (chet-vyairg') Thursday	пятница (pyaht'-nee-tsah) Friday	суббота (soo-boh'-tah) Saturday	воскресенье (voh-skree-syen'-yah) Sunday
1	2	3	4	5	6	7

Очень (oh'-chen) very **важно** (vahzh'-nah) important to know the days of the week **и** (ee) the various parts of the day. Let's learn them. Be sure to say them aloud before filling in the blanks below. **Русские** (roos'-skee-yeh) Russians begin counting their week on Monday with „**понедельник**." (pah-nee-dyel'-neek)

понедельник (pah-nee-dyel'-neek) Monday ______________________
вторник (vtor'-neek) Tuesday ______________________
среда (sree-dah') Wednesday ______________________
четверг (chet-vyairg') Thursday ______________________
пятница (pyaht'-nee-tsah) Friday ______________________
суббота (soo-boh'-tah) Saturday ______________________
воскресенье (voh-skree-syen'-yah) Sunday ______________________

If **сегодня** (see-vohd'-nyah) today **среда,** (sree-dah') Wednesday then **завтра** (zahv'-trah) tomorrow **будет** (boo'-dyet) will be **четверг** (chet-vyairg') Thursday and **вчера** (vchee-rah') yesterday **было** (bil'-lah) was **вторник.** (vtor'-neek) Tuesday **Теперь** (tyep-yair') now you supply the correct answers. If **сегодня** (see-vohd'-nyah) today **понедельник,** (pah-nee-dyel'-neek) Monday then **завтра** (zahv'-trah) tomorrow **будет** (boo'-dyet) ______________ and **вчера** (vchee-rah') yesterday **было** (bil'-lah) was ______________. Or, if **сегодня** (see-vohd'-nyah) today **понедельник**, (pah-nee-dyel'-neek) Monday then ___завтра___ **будет** (boo'-dyet) will be **вторник** (vtor'-neek) Tuesday and ______________ **было** (bil'-lah) **воскресенье.** (voh-skree-syen'-yah) **Что** (shtoh) what is **сегодня?** (see-vohd'-nyah) today **Сегодня** ______________.

Теперь, (tyep-yair') now peel off the next **семь** (syem) labels **и** put them on **календарь** (kah-lyen-dar') calendar you use every day. From now on, Monday is **понедельник.** (pah-nee-dyel'-neek) Notice that Friday—**пятница** (pyaht'-nee-tsah)—is the fifth day of the week **и** contains the **слово** for five—**пять.** (pyaht)

- ☐ **Библия** *(bee'-blee-yah)*.................... Bible
- ☐ **бинокль** *(bee-noh'-kil)*.................... binoculars
- ☐ **бланк** *(blahnk)*.................... blank (form)
- ☐ **бокс** *(bohks)*.................... boxing
- ☐ **Болгария** *(bahl-gah'-ree-yah)*.................... Bulgaria

б

There are (cheh-tih'-ree) **четыре** (four) parts to each (dyen) **день.** (day)

morning	=	(oo'-trah) **утро**	__________
afternoon/daytime	=	(dyen) **день**	__________
evening	=	(vyeh'-cher) **вечер**	__________
night	=	(nohch) **ночь**	__________

Notice that **„в"** means "on." For example, **„в** (voh-skree-syen'-yah) **воскресенье** (oo'-trahm) **утром"** means "on Sunday morning." (tyep-yair) **Теперь,** (now) fill in the following blanks **и** then check your answers at the bottom of (strah-nee'-tsih) **страницы.** (page) Don't be surprised that the words change slightly.

a.	on Sunday morning	=	в воскресенье утром
b.	on Friday morning	=	__________
c.	on Friday evening	=	__________
d.	on Saturday evening	=	__________
e.	on Saturday morning	=	__________
f.	on Wednesday morning	=	в среду утром
g.	on Wednesday afternoon	=	__________
h.	on Thursday afternoon	=	__________
i.	on Thursday evening	=	__________
j.	yesterday evening	=	__________
k.	yesterday afternoon	=	__________
l.	yesterday morning	=	__________
m.	tomorrow morning	=	__________
n.	tomorrow afternoon	=	__________

ОТВЕТЫ

a. **в воскресенье утром**
b. **в пятницу утром**
c. **в пятницу вечером**
d. **в субботу вечером**
e. **в субботу утром**
f. **в среду утром**
g. **в среду днём**
h. **в четверг днём**
i. **в четверг вечером**
j. **вчера вечером**
k. **вчера днём**
l. **вчера утром**
m. **завтра утром**
n. **завтра днём**

So, with merely eleven *(slah-vah-mee)* **словами,** (words) you can specify any *(dyen)* **день** (day) of *(nee-dyeh-lee)* **недели** (week) **и** any time of *(dnyah)* **дня.** (day) *(see-vohd-nyah)* **Сегодня,** (today) *(zahv-trah)* **завтра** (tomorrow) **и** *(vchee-rah)* **вчера** (yesterday) will be *(oh-chen)* **очень** (very) *(vahzh-nih-yeh)* **важные** (important) **слова** for you in making reservations **и** appointments, in getting *(beel-yeh-tih)* **билеты** (tickets) for *(tee-ah-ter)* **театр** (theater) **и** for many other things you will want to do. Knowing the parts of *(dnyah)* **дня** (day) will help you to learn **и** (and) understand the various *(roos-skee-yeh)* **русские** (Russian) greetings below. Practice these every day until your trip.

good morning	=	*(doh-brah-yeh)(oo-trah)* **доброе утро**	______________________
good day / good afternoon	=	*(doh-brih) (dyen)* **добрый день**	______________________
good evening	=	*(doh-brih) (vyeh-cher)* **добрый вечер**	______________________
good night	=	*(spah-koy-noy) (noh-chee)* **спокойной ночи**	______________________
How are you? / How are things going?	=	*(kahk) (dee-lah)* **Как дела?**	______________________

Notice that "good afternoon" and "good day" are the same **по-русски:** *(doh-brih) (dyen)* **„добрый день"**

Take the next *(pyaht)* **пять** (five) labels **и** stick them on the appropriate things in your *(doh-mee)* **доме.** (house) How about the bathroom mirror for *(doh-brah-yeh)(oo-trah)* **„доброе утро"?** *(ee-lee)* **Или** the front door for *(doh-brih) (dyen)* **„добрый день"?** *(ee-lee)* **Или** (or) your alarm clock for *(spah-koy-noy) (noh-chee)* **„спокойной ночи"?** **Или** your kitchen cabinet for *(kahk) (dee-lah)* **„Как дела"?** You are about one-fourth of your way through *(eh-too)* **эту** (this) *(knee-goo)* **книгу,** (book) **и** it is a good time to quickly review **слова** you have learned before doing the crossword puzzle on the next *(strah-nee-tseh)* **странице.** (page) *(oo-dah-chee)* **Удачи!** **Или,** as we say *(pah-ahn-glee-skee)* **по-английски,** (in English) "Good luck!"

ОТВЕТЫ TO THE CROSSWORD PUZZLE

ACROSS

1. банк
4. купить
6. гостиница
9. страница
10. нет
12. кухня
13. стена
14. зелёный
15. два
21. оранжевый
23. где
25. стоит
26. копейки
27. открытка
28. почему
32. кофе
33. лампа
35. доллар
36. четырнадцать
38. утро
40. картина
42. стол
43. это

DOWN

2. когда
3. такси
4. коричневый
5. туалет
7. телефон
8. банан
11. американский
12. кто
16. пятьдесят
17. синий
18. занавес
19. дверь
20. автомобиль
22. сколько
24. как
29. один
30. почта
31. или
32. красный
34. пять
37. цвет
39. окно
41. ночь

CROSSWORD PUZZLE

ACROSS

1. bank
4. to buy
6. hotel/inn
9. page
10. no
12. kitchen
13. wall
14. green
15. two
21. orange
23. where
25. costs
26. kopecks
27. postcard
28. why
32. coffee
33. lamp
35. dollar
36. fourteen
38. morning
40. picture
42. table
43. this

DOWN

2. when
3. taxi
4. brown
5. toilet
7. telephone
8. banana
11. American
12. who
16. fifty
17. blue
18. curtain
19. door
20. automobile
22. how much
24. how
29. one
30. mail
31. or
32. red
34. five
37. color
39. window
41. zero

Step 8

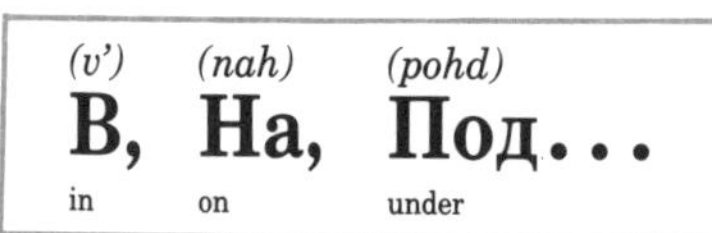

(roos'-skee-yeh) **Русские** (Russian) prepositions (words like "in," "on," "through" and "next to") are easy to learn (ee) **и** they allow you to be precise (s') **с** (with) a minimum of effort. Instead of having to point (shest) **шесть** (six) times at a piece of yummy pastry you would like, you can explain precisely which one you want by saying it is behind, in front of, next to (ee'-lee) **или** under the piece of pastry that the salesperson is starting to pick up. Let's learn some of these (mah'-lyen-kee-eh) **маленькие** (little) **слова** (words) by studying (pree-myair'-ih) **примеры** (examples) below.

(eez) **из** = out of/from	(ryah'-dahm) (s') **рядом с** = next to	(pohd) **под** = under
(v') **в** = into/in		(nahd) **над** = over

(moozh-chee'-nah) **Мужчина** (man) (vih'-shel) **вышел** (comes) (eez) **из** (out of) (gah-stee'-nee-tsih) **гостиницы.**

(zhen'-shchee-nah) **Женщина** (woman) (ee-dyoht') **идёт** (goes) **в** (into) (gah-stee'-nee-tsoo) **гостиницу.** (hotel)

(vrahch) **Врач** (doctor) **в** ((is) in) (gah-stee'-nee-tseh) **гостинице.** (hotel)

(kar-tee'-nah) **Картина** (picture) (nahd) **над** ((is) over) (stah-lohm') **столом.** (table)

(kar-tee'-nah) **Картина** (picture) (ryah'-dahm) **рядом с** ((is) next to) (chah-sah'-mee) **часами.** (clock)

(sah-bah'-kah) **Собака** (dog) (pohd) **под** ((is) under) (stah-lohm') **столом.**

(chah-sih') **Часы** (clock) **над** ((is) over) (stah-lohm') **столом.**

Часы (ryah'-dahm) **рядом с** ((is) next to) (kar-tee'-noy) **картиной.** (picture)

- ☐ **Боливия** *(bah-lee'-vee-yah)* .... Bolivia
- ☐ **бомба** *(bohm'-bah)* .... bomb
- ☐ **борщ** *(borshch)* .... borsch (beet soup)
- ☐ **бронза** *(brohn'-zah)* .... bronze
- ☐ **брюнет** *(broo-nyet')* .... brunette (male)

б

Fill in the blanks below **с** (with) the correct prepositions according to *(kar-teen'-kahm)* **картинкам** (pictures) on the previous *(strah-nee'-tseh)* **странице.** (page)

(moozh-chee'-nah) **Мужчина** (man) *(vih'-shel)* **вышел** (comes) ______ (out of) *(gah-stee'-nee-tsih)* **гостиницы.**

(sah-bah'-kah) **Собака** (dog) под ______ (under) *(stah-lohm')* **столом.** (table)

(chah-sih') **Часы** (clock) ______ (over) **столом.** (table)

(vrahch) **Врач** (doctor) ______ (in) *(gah-stee'-nee-tseh)* **гостинице.**

Часы ______ (next to) *(kar-tee'-noy)* **картиной.** (picture)

Картина (picture) ______ (over) **столом.**

Стол (table) ______ (under) **картиной.**

Картина ______ (next to) *(chah-sah'-mee)* **часами.** (clock)

(zhen'-shchee-nah) **Женщина** (woman) *(ee-dyoht')* **идёт** (goes) ______ (into) *(gah-stee'-nee-tsoo)* **гостиницу.**

Стол ______ (under) **часами.**

(tyep-yair') **Теперь,** (now) answer *(vah-proh'-sih)* **вопросы** (questions) based on *(kar-teen'-kahk)* **картинках** (pictures) on the previous *(strah-nee'-tseh)* **странице.** (page)

(gdyeh)(vrahch) **Где врач?** (doctor) ______

(sah-bah'-kah) **Где собака?** (dog) ______

Где стол? (table) ______

(kar-tee'-nah) **Где картина?** (picture) ______

(shtoh) **Что** (what) *(dyeh'-lah-yet)* **делает** (does) **эта** *(zhen'-shchee-nah)* **женщина?** (woman) ______

Что *(dyeh'-lah-yet)* **делает** (does) *(eh'-tut)* **этот** (this) *(moozh-chee'-nah)* **мужчина?** (man) ______

(chah-sih') **Часы** ((is) clock) *(zyel-yoh'-nih-yeh)* **зелёные?** (green) ______

Собака ((is) dog) *(syeh'-rah-yah)* **серая?** (gray) ______

- ☐ **бульвар** *(bool-var')* .... boulevard ______
- ☐ **бюрократ** *(byoo-rah-kraht')* .... bureaucrat ______
- ☐ **ваза** *(vah'-zah)* .... vase ______
- ☐ **вальс** *(vahls)* .... waltz ______
- ☐ **Ватикан** *(vah-tee-kahn')* .... the Vatican ______

В

(tyep-yair´) **Теперь** (now) for some more practice with (roos´-skee-mee) **русскими** (Russian) prepositions!

(nah) **на**	=	on
(myezh´-doo) **между**	=	between
(pyeh´-red) **перед**	=	in front of
(zah) **за**	=	behind

(stah-kahn´) (vah-dih´) (nah) (stohl-yeh´)
Стакан воды на столе.
glass of water (is) on table

Стакан воды ___на___ столе. (table)

(kar-tee´-nah) (styen-yeh´)
Картина на стене.
picture (is) on wall

Картина ______________ стене. (wall)

(lahm´-pah) (zah) (stah-lohm´)
Лампа за столом.
lamp (is) behind table

Лампа ______________ столом. (table)

(stohl) (pyeh´-red) (kroh-vaht´-yoo)
Стол перед кроватью.
table (is) in front of bed

Стол ______________ (kroh-vaht´-yoo) кроватью. (bed)

(lahm´-pah) (myezh´-doo) (kroh-vaht´-yoo)
Лампа между столом и кроватью.
lamp (is) between table and bed

Лампа ______________ столом и кроватью.

Answer the following (vah-proh´-sih) **вопросы,** (questions) based on (kar-teen´-kahk) **картинках,** (pictures) by filling in the blanks **с** the correct prepositions. Choose the prepositions from those you have just learned.

(gdyeh) (knee´-gah)
Где книга?
book

Книга ______________ (on) (stohl-yeh´) **столе.**

(ahv-toh´-boos)
Где автобус?
bus

Автобус ______________ (in front of) (gah-stee´-nee-tsay) **гостиницей.** (hotel)

В

- ☐ **веранда** *(vee-rahn´-dah)* . . . . veranda ______________
- ☐ **витамин** *(vee-tah-meen´)* . . . . vitamin ______________
- ☐ **водка** *(vohd´-kah)* . . . . vodka ______________
- ☐ **волейбол** *(voh-lay-bohl´)* . . . . volleyball ______________
- ☐ **Волга** *(vohl´-gah)* . . . . Volga River ______________

(tee-lee-fohn') *(kahv-yor')*
Где телефон? **Где ковёр?** **Где картина?**
telephone carpet picture

(syeh'-ree) *(styen-yeh')*
Серый телефон ______________________ **стене.**
gray (on) wall

(kar-tee'-noy)
Серый телефон ______________________ **картиной.**
(next to) picture

(stah-lohm')
Серый телефон ______________________ **столом.**
(over) table

(zyel-yoh'-nee) *(kahv-yor')*
Зелёный ковёр ______________________ **столом.**
green carpet (under)

Картина ______________________ **стене.**
picture (on)

(tyep-yair') *(gah-stee'-nee-tseh)*
Теперь, fill in each blank on **гостинице** below **с** the best possible preposition.
now hotel

(aht-vyeh'-tih) *(strah-nee'-tsih)*
The correct **ответы** are at the bottom of **страницы.** Have fun!
answers page

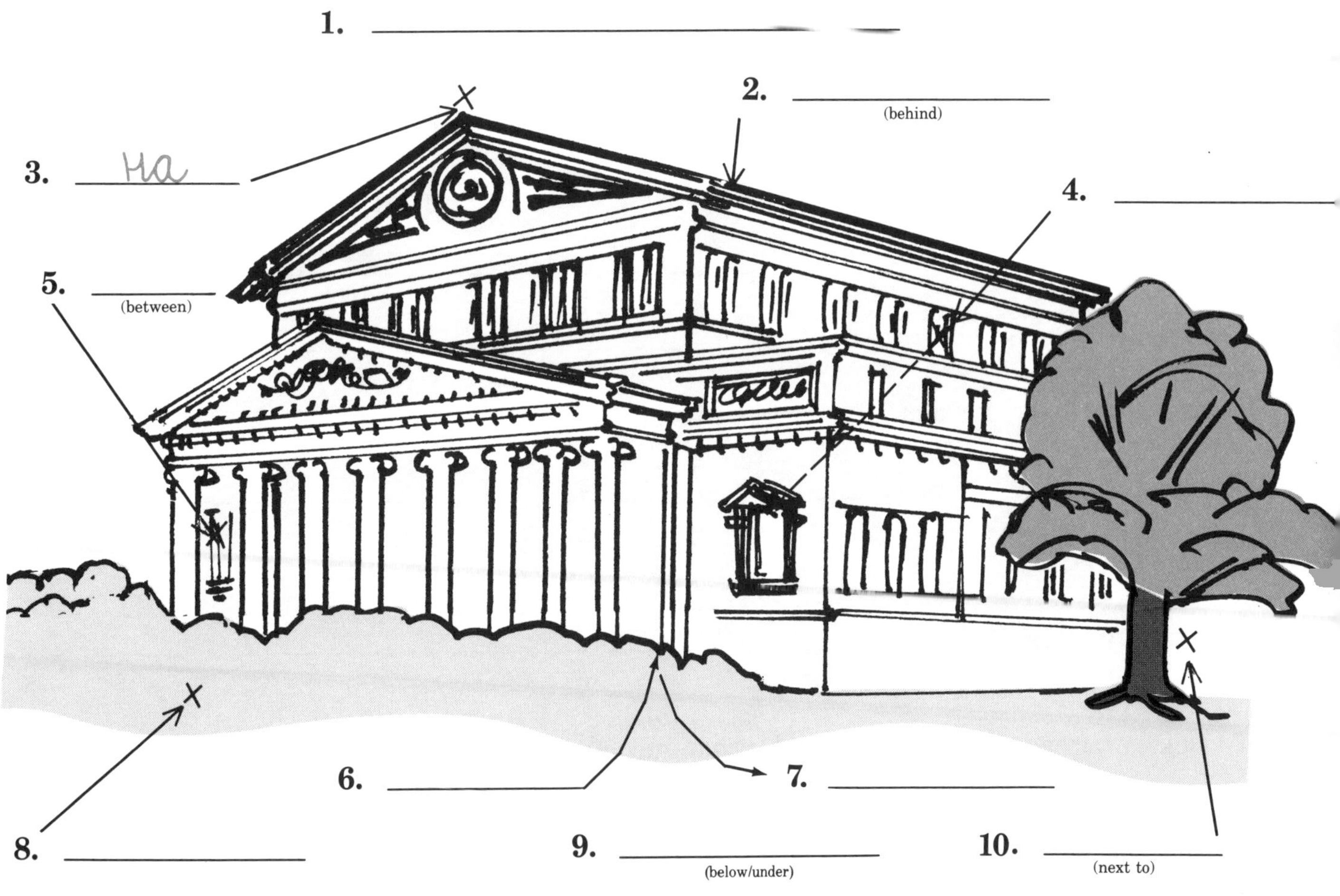

ОТВЕТЫ

1. над	3. на	5. между	7. из	9. под
2. за	4. в	6. в	8. перед	10. рядом с

Step 9

В in *(yahn-var-yeh')* **Январе,** January *(fyev-rahl-yeh')* **Феврале,** February *(mart'-yeh)* **Марте** March

(treed'-tset) **Тридцать** thirty *(dnay)* **дней** days **в** *(syen-tyah-bryeh')* **сентябре,** September *(ahp-ryel'-yeh)* **апреле,** April
(ee-yoon'-yeh) **июне,** June **и** *(nah-yah-bryeh')* **ноябре.** November

Sound familiar? You have learned *(dnee)* **дни** days of *(nee-dyeh'-lee)* **недели,** week so now it is time to learn *(myeh'-syeh-tsee)* **месяцы** months of *(go'-dah)* **года** year **и** all the different kinds of *(pah-go'-dih)* **погоды.** weather *(nah-pree-myair')* **Например,** for example you ask about the *(pah-go'-dyeh)* **погоде** weather *(pah-roos'-skee)* **по-русски** in Russian just as you would *(pah-ahn-glee'-skee)* **по-английски:** „*(kah-kah'-yah)* **Какая** how is *(see-vohd'-nyah)* **сегодня** today *(pah-go'-dah)* **погода?**" weather Practice all the possible answers to this *(vah-prohs')* **вопрос** question **и** *(tahg-dah')* **тогда** then write the answers in the blanks below.

(kah-kah'-yah) **Какая** *(see-vohd'-nyah)* **сегодня** *(pah-go'-dah)* **погода?**

(see-vohd'-nyah) **Сегодня** today *(ee-dyoht')* **идёт** it is *(dohzhd)* **дождь.** raining ____________________

Сегодня *(ee-dyoht')* **идёт** it is *(snyeg)* **снег.** snowing ____________________

Сегодня *(zhar'-kah)* **жарко.** hot Сегодня жарко.

Сегодня *(hoh'-lahd-nah)* **холодно.** cold ____________________

Сегодня *(hah-roh'-shah-yah)* **хорошая** good *(pah-go'-dah)* **погода.** weather ____________________

Сегодня *(plah-hah'-yah)* **плохая** bad *(pah-go'-dah)* **погода.** weather ____________________

Сегодня *(too-mahn')* **туман.** fog ____________________

Сегодня *(vyet'-ren-ah)* **ветрено.** windy ____________________

Сегодня *(tyep-loh')* **тепло.** warm ____________________

(tyep-yair') **Теперь,** now practice **слова** on the next *(strah-nee'-tseh)* **странице** **и** *(tahg-dah')* **тогда** then fill in the blanks *(s')* **с** the names *(myeh'-syeh-tsyev)* **месяцев** of months **и** the appropriate weather reports.

Г

- ☐ **газ** *(gahz)* .... natural gas ________
- ☐ **газета** *(gah-zyet'-ah)* .... gazette, newspaper ________
- ☐ **—газетчик** *(gah-zyet'-cheek)* .... newspaper man ________
- ☐ **галерея** *(gahl-yair-eh'-yah)* .... gallery ________
- ☐ **генерал** *(gee-nee-rahl')* .... general ________

в (in)	*(yahn-var-yeh')* **январе** (January) ____	В январе идёт снег. *(ee-dyoht') (snyeg)* (in January it snows) ____
в	*(fyev-rahl-yeh')* **феврале** (February) ____	В феврале идёт снег. (February it snows) ____
в	*(mart'-yeh)* **марте** (March) ____	В марте идёт дождь. *(dohzhd)* (it rains) ____
в	*(ahp-ryel'-yeh)* **апреле** (April) ____	В апреле идёт дождь. *(dohzhd)* ____
в	*(mah'-yeh)* **мае** (May) ____	В мае ветрено. *(vyet'-ren-ah)* (windy) ____
в	*(ee-yoon'-yeh)* **июне** (June) ____	В июне ветрено. *(vyet'-ren-ah)* (June) ____
в	*(ee-yool'-yeh)* **июле** (July) ____	В июле жарко. *(zhar'-kah)* (hot) ____
в	*(ahv'-goost-yeh)* **августе** (August) ____	В августе жарко. (hot) ____
в	*(syen-tyah-bryeh')* **сентябре** (September) ____	В сентябре хорошая погода. *(hah-roh'-shah-yah) (pah-go'-dah)* (September good weather) ____
в	*(ahk-tyah-bryeh')* **октябре** (October) ____	В октябре туман. *(too-mahn')* (fog) ____
в	*(nah-yah-bryeh')* **ноябре** (November) ____	В ноябре холодно. *(hoh'-lahd-nah)* (cold) ____
в	*(dee-kah-bryeh')* **декабре** (December) ____	В декабре плохая погода. *(plah-hah'-yah)* (bad) ____

(tyep-yair') **Теперь,** answer the following *(vah-proh'-sih)* **вопросы** (questions) based on *(kar-teen'-kahk)* **картинках** (pictures) to the right.

(kah-kah'-yah) (pah-go'-dah) **Какая погода в** *(fyev-rahl-yeh')* **феврале?** (how is … February) ____

Какая погода в *(ahp-ryel'-yeh)* **апреле?** (April) ____

Какая погода в *(mah'-yeh)* **мае?** (May) ____

Какая погода в *(ahv'-goost-yeh)* **августе?** ____

Какая погода *(see-vohd'-nyah)* **сегодня?** *(hah-roh'-shah-yah)* **Хорошая или** *(plah-hah'-yah)* **плохая?** (bad) ____

Г

- ☐ **география** *(gee-ah-grah'-fee-yah)*.......... geography ____
- ☐ **геология** *(gee-ah-loh'-gee-yah)*............ geology
- ☐ **–геолог** *(gee-oh'-lohg)*.................. geologist ____
- ☐ **геометрия** *(gee-ah-myet'-ree-yah)*.......... geometry ____
- ☐ **Гибралтар** *(gee-brahl'-tar)*.............. Gibraltar ____

Теперь for the seasons of **года...** (year)

(zee-moy') **зимой** — in winter
(vees-noy') **весной** — in spring
(lyet'-ahm) **летом** — in summer
(oh'-syen-yoo) **осенью** — in autumn

(zee-moy') (hoh'-lahd-nah) **Зимой холодно.**

(vees-noy') (ee-dyoht') **Весной идёт дождь.**

(lyet'-ahm) (zhar'-kah) **Летом жарко.**

(oh'-syen-yoo) (vyet'-ren-ah) **Осенью ветрено.** (windy)

At this point, it is *(hah-roh'-shah-yah)* **хорошая** (good) idea to familiarize yourself **с** *(roos'-skee-mee)* **русскими** *(tyem-pee-rah-too'-rah-mee)* **температурами.** (temperatures)

Read the typical weather forecasts below **и** carefully study the thermometer because *(tyem-pee-rah-too'-rih)* **температуры** (temperatures) in the former *(sah-vyet'-skahm)* **Советском** (Soviet) *(sah-yoo'-zeh)* **Союзе** (Union) are calculated on the basis of Celsius, not Fahrenheit.

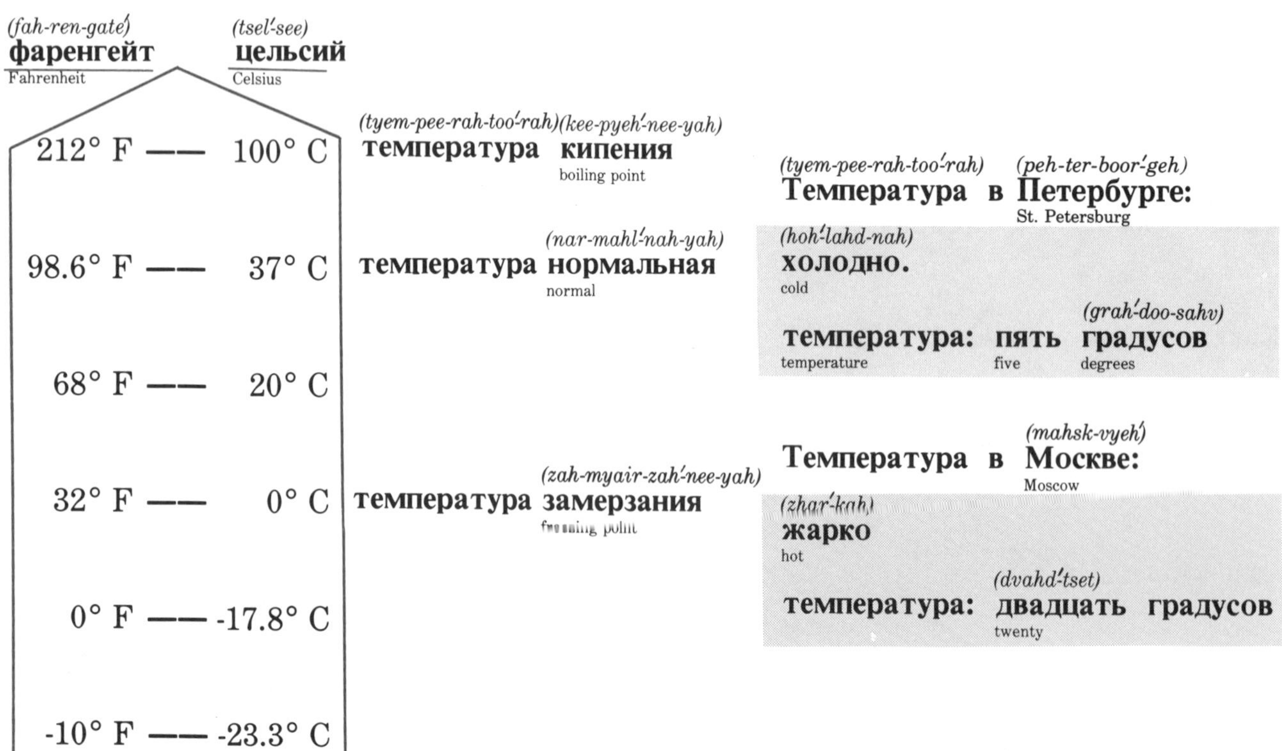

☐ **гид** *(geed)*	guide	______
☐ **гимнастика** *(geem-nah'-stee-kah)*	gymnastics	______
☐ **гитара** *(gee-tah'-rah)*	guitar	**Г** ______
☐ **грамм** *(grahm)*	gram	______
☐ **гранит** *(grah-neet')*	granite	______

Step 10

Семья: Кухня, Церковь, и Дети

(syem-yah') (koohk'-nyah) (tsair'-kahv) (dyeh'-tee)

family, kitchen, church, children

One of the charming aspects of Russian life concerns names. A father's first name becomes the middle name for both his sons **и** his daughters. Daughters add **-овна,** (ohv-nah) **-евна,** (yev-nah) or **-ична** (eech-nah) to the father's first name **и** sons add **-ович** (ah-veech) **-евич** (yev-eech) or **-ич.** (eech) Both the given first name **и** the father's name (patronymic) are constantly used **по-русски.** (pah-roos'-skee) Mastering these will help you master the language. Study **картинки** (kar-teen'-kee) pictures below **и** **тогда** (tahg-dah') then practice these new names on the next **странице.** (strah-nee'-tseh)

Семья

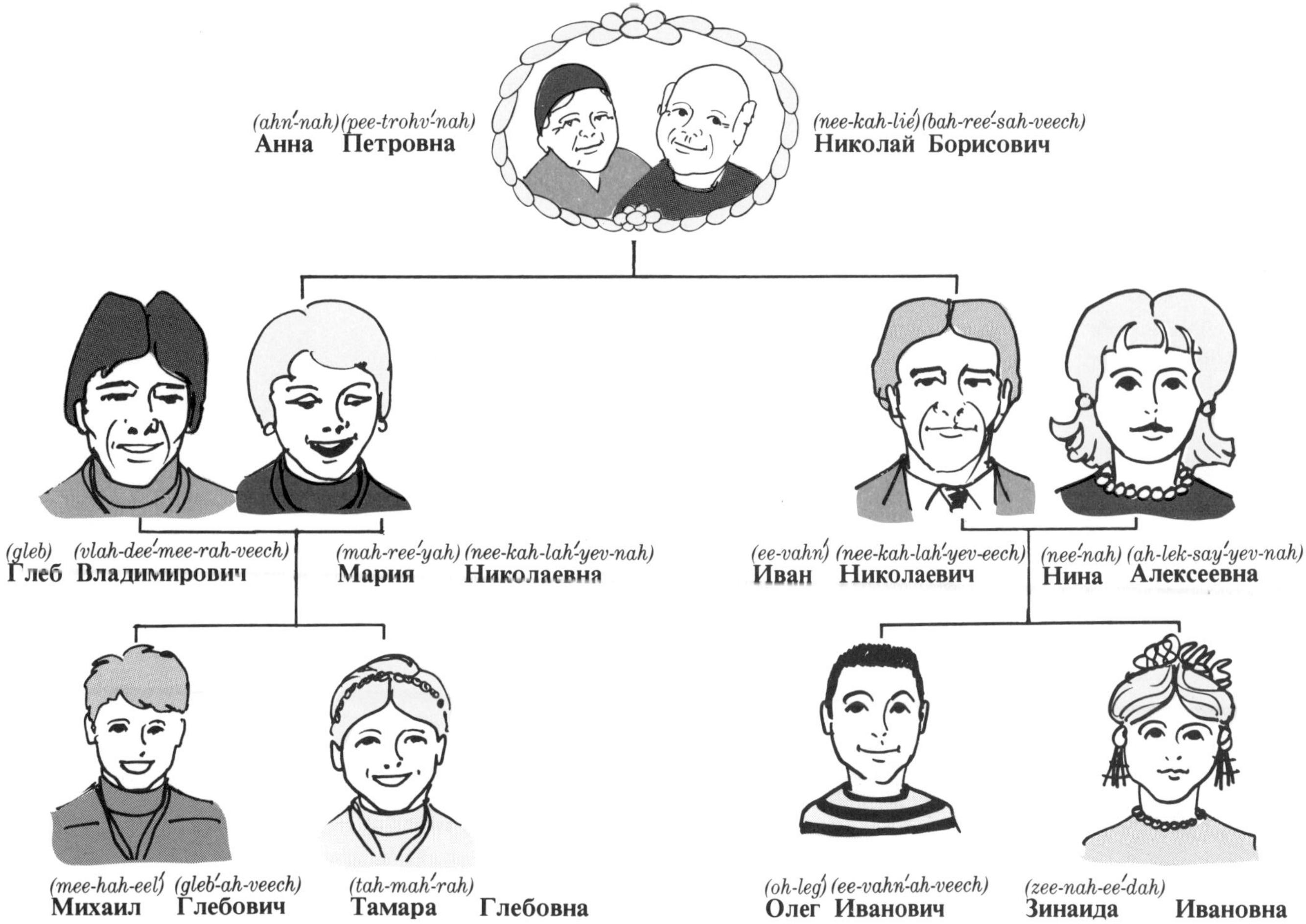

(ahn'-nah) (pee-trohv'-nah) **Анна Петровна**

(nee-kah-lie') (bah-ree'-sah-veech) **Николай Борисович**

(gleb) (vlah-dee'-mee-rah-veech) **Глеб Владимирович**

(mah-ree'-yah) (nee-kah-lah'-yev-nah) **Мария Николаевна**

(ee-vahn') (nee-kah-lah'-yev-eech) **Иван Николаевич**

(nee'-nah) (ah-lek-say'-yev-nah) **Нина Алексеевна**

(mee-hah-eel') (gleb'-ah-veech) **Михаил Глебович**

(tah-mah'-rah) **Тамара Глебовна**

(oh-leg') (ee-vahn'-ah-veech) **Олег Иванович**

(zee-nah-ee'-dah) **Зинаида Ивановна**

Г

- ☐ **Греция** *(greh'-tsee-yah)* .... Greece
  —where they speak **по-гречески** *(pah-greh'-chee-skee)*
- ☐ **группа** *(groop'-pah)* .... group
- ☐ **ГУМ** *(goom)* .... department store in Moscow
- ☐ **гусь** *(goose)* .... goose

(rohd'-stveen-nee-kee)
родственники
relatives

(rah-dee'-tee-lee)
родители
parents

(dyed)
дед ______________________________
grandfather

(bah'-boosh-kah)
бабушка ______________________________
grandmother

(aht-yets')
отец ______________________________
father

(maht)
мать ______________________________
mother

(dyeh'-tee)
дети
children

(rohd'-stveen-nee-kee)
родственники
relatives

(sin)
сын сын, сын, сын, сын
son

(dohch)
дочь ______________________________
daughter

(dyah'-dyah)
дядя ______________________________
uncle

(tyoh'-tyah)
тётя ______________________________
aunt

(sin) *(dohch)* *(braht)* *(see-strah')*
Сын и дочь = брат и сестра!
brother sister

Let's learn how to identify *(syem-yah')* **семья** family by name. Study the following examples carefully.

(kahk) *(zah-voot')* *(aht-tsah')*
Как зовут отца?
how is called father

(aht-tsah') *(zah-voot')*
Отца зовут ______________________________.
father is called

(kahk) *(zah-voot')* *(maht)*
Как зовут мать?
how is called mother

(zah-voot')
Мать зовут ______________________________.
mother is called

(kahk) *(zah-voot')* *(sih'-nah)*
Как зовут сына?
how is called son

Сына зовут ______________________________
is called

(kahk) *(zah-voot')* *(dohch)*
Как зовут дочь?
daughter

Дочь зовут ______________________________
is called

(zah-voot') *(dyeh'-dah)*
Как зовут дода?
how is called grandfather

Деда зовут ______________________________

(bah'-boosh-koo)
Как зовут бабушку?
grandmother

Бабушку зовут ______________________________

(vahs) *(zah-voot')*
Как вас зовут?
how are you called

(men-yah') *(zah-voot')*
Меня зовут ______________________________
I am called (your name)

☐ **дама** *(dah'-mah)* . . . . dame, lady, woman ______________
☐ **Дания** *(dah'-nee-yah)* . . . . Denmark ______________
—where they speak **по-датски** *(pah-daht'-skee)* ______________
☐ **дата** *(dah'-tah)* . . . . date ______________
☐ **делегат** *(dyeh-leh-gaht')* . . . . delegate ______________

Д

(koohk'-nyah) **Кухня** kitchen

Study all these *(kar-teen'-kee)* **картинки** (pictures) **и** then practice saying *(ee)* **и** writing out **слова.**

Это *(koohk'-nyah)* **кухня.** (kitchen)

(hah-lah-deel'-neek) **холодильник** refrigerator

____

(plee-tah') **плита** stove

____

(vee-noh') **вино** wine

____

(pee'-vah) **пиво** beer

____

(mah-lah-koh') **молоко** milk

____

(mah'-slah) **масло** butter

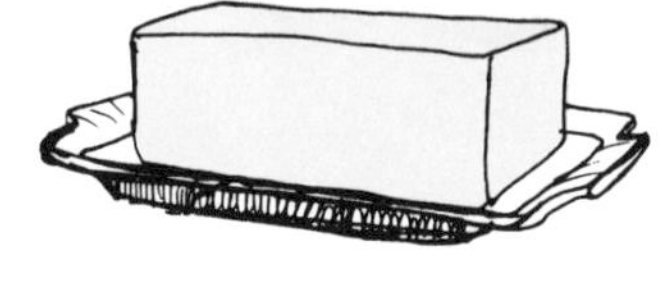

масло

Answer these *(vah-proh'-sih)* **вопросы** (questions) aloud.

(gdyeh) **Где** *(pee'-vah)* **пиво?** (beer) .... **Пиво в** *(hah-lah-deel'-neek-yeh)* **холодильнике.** (refrigerator)

Где *(mah-lah-koh')* **молоко?** (milk) **Где** *(vee-noh')* **вино?** (wine) **Где** *(bah-nahn')* **банан?**

Где *(mah'-slah)* **масло?** (butter) **Где** *(sah-laht')* **салат?** (salad) **Где** *(ah-bree-koh'-sih)* **абрикосы?** (apricots)

Д

- ☐ **демонстрация** *(dyeh-mahn-strah'-tsee-yah)*... demonstration ______________________
- ☐ **джаз** *(dzhahs)* .... jazz ______________________
- ☐ **джин** *(dzheen)* .... gin ______________________
- ☐ **диагноз** *(dee-ahg'-nas)*................. diagnosis ______________________
- ☐ **диаграмма** *(dee-ah-grahm'-mah)* .... diagram, blueprint ______________________

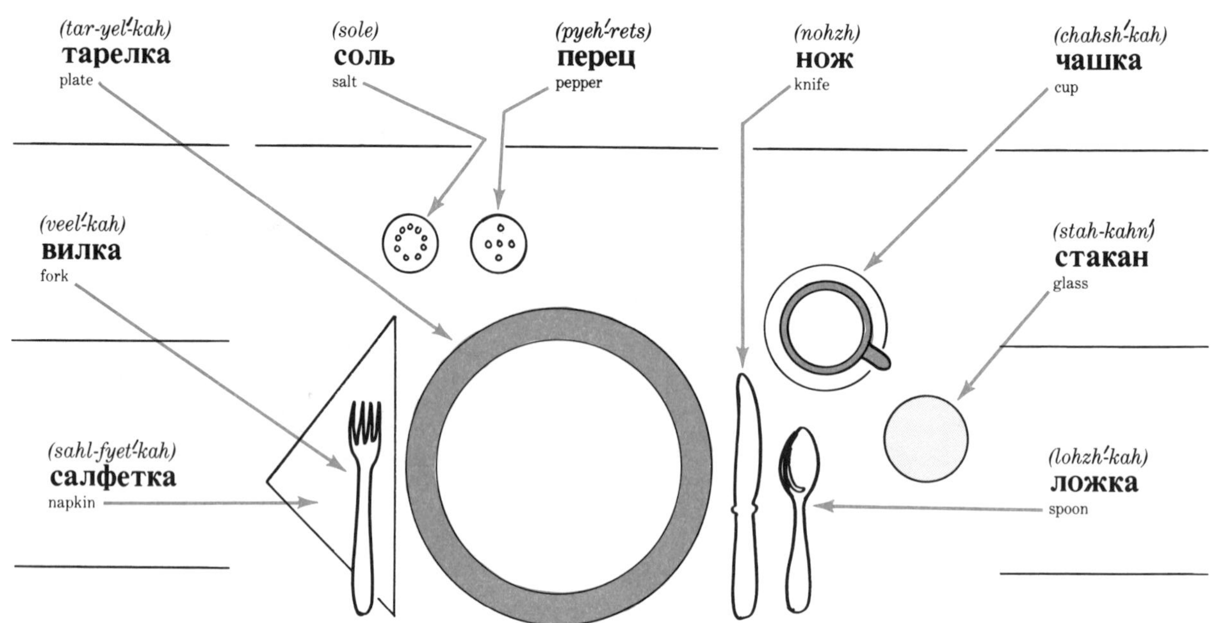

И more...

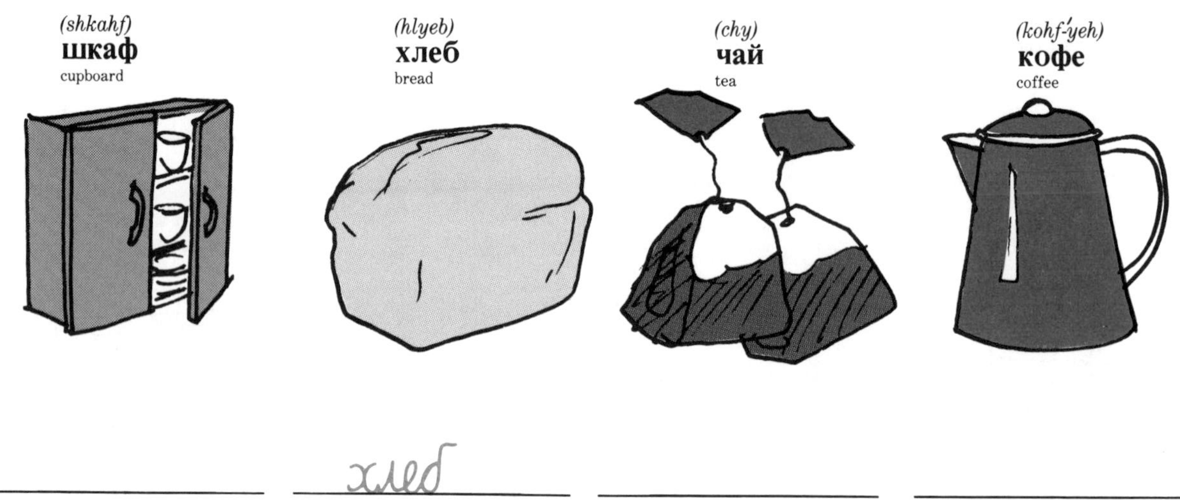

(gdyeh) **Где** *(hlyeb)* **хлеб?** (bread) **Хлеб в** (in) *(hah-lah-deel'-neek-yeh)* **холодильнике.** (refrigerator) **Где** *(chy)* **чай?** (tea) **Где** *(kohf'-yeh)* **кофе?** (coffee) **Теперь** open your *(knee'-goo)* **книгу** (book) *(nah)* **на** (to) *(strah-nee'-tseh)* **странице** *(s')* **с** the labels **и** remove the next *(div-yet-nod'-tset)* **девятнадцать** labels **и** proceed to label all these things in your *(koohk'-nyeh)* **кухне.** (kitchen) Do not forget to use every opportunity to say these **слова** out loud. **Это** *(oh'-chen)* **очень** (very) *(vahzh'-nah)* **важно.** (important)

- ☐ **диван** *(dee-vahn')* . . . . divan, couch
- ☐ **дизель** *(dee'-zyel)* . . . . diesel
- ☐ **диплом** *(dee-plohm')* . . . . diploma
- ☐ **дипломат** *(dee-plah-maht')* . . . . diplomat
- ☐ **директор** *(dee-rek'-tar)* . . . . director

Д

В **России** *(rahs-sih'-ih)* [Russia], there is a wide variety of **религий** *(ree-lee'-gee-ee)* [religions]. A person's **религия** *(ree-lee'-gee-yah)* [religion] is usually one of the following.

1. **православная** *(prah-vah-slahv'-nah-yah)* [Orthodox woman] / **православный** *(prah-vah-slahv'-nee)* [Orthodox man] ______________
2. **еврейка** *(yev-ray'-kah)* [Jewish woman] / **еврей** *(yev-ray')* [Jewish man] ______________
3. **католичка** *(kah-tah-leech'-kah)* [Catholic woman] / **католик** *(kah-toh'-leek)* [Catholic man] ______________
4. **мусульманка** *(moo-sool-mahn'-kah)* [Moslem woman] / **мусульманин** *(moo-sool-mah'-neen)* [Moslem man] ______________

Церковь *(tsair'-kahv)* [church] **в Москве.**

Это [is it] **православная** *(prah-vah-slahv'-nah-yah)* [Orthodox] **церковь?** *(tsair'-kahv)*

Это [is it] **новая** *(no'-vah-yah)* [new] **церковь? Нет,** *(nyet)* [no] **старая.** *(stah'-rah-yah)* [old]

You will see **много** *(mnoh'-gah)* [many] **красивых** *(krah-see'-vihk)* [pretty] **церквей** *(tsair-kvay')* [churches] like this during your holiday.

Теперь, let's learn how to say "I am" **по-русски:** *(pah-roos'-skee)*

I am = **я** *(yah)* ______________

Practice saying „**я**" *(yah)* **с** the following **словами.** **Теперь** write each sentence for more practice. Make sure you understand what you are saying.

Я [I am] **католичка.** *(kah-tah-leech'-kah)* ______________

Я православная. *(prah-vah-slahv'-nah-yah)* ______________

Я еврей. *(yev-ray')* ______________

Я американец. *(ah-myeh-ree-kah'-nyets)* [American] ______________

Я в Москве. ______________

Я канадец. *(kah-nahd'-yets)* [Canadian] ______________

Я австралиец. *(ahv-strah-lee'-yets)* [Australian] ______________

Я англичанка. *(ahn-glee-chahn'-kah)* [English] ______________

Д

- ☐ **дискуссия** *(dee-skoos'-see-yah)* . . . . discussion ______________
- ☐ **доктор** *(dohk'-tar)* . . . . doctor ______________
- ☐ **документ** *(dah-koo-myent')* . . . . document ______________
- ☐ **доллар** *(dohl'-lar)* . . . . dollar ______________
- ☐ **драма** *(drah'-mah)* . . . . drama ______________

(yah) (tsair'-kvee)
Я в церкви. ______________
I am in church

(yah) (koohk'-nyeh)
Я в кухне. ______________

(moo-sool-mah'-neen)
Я мусульманин. ______________

(yev-ray'-kah)
Я еврейка. ______________

(gah-stee'-nee-tseh)
Я в гостинице. ______________
hotel

(res-tah-rahn'-yeh)
Я в ресторане. ______________
restaurant

(go'-lah-dyen)
Я голоден. ______________
hungry

(hah-choo') (peet)
Я хочу пить. ______________
thirsty

Теперь identify all **людей** (lood-yay') [people] **на картинке** (kar-teen'-kyeh) below by writing **правильное** (prah'-veel-nah-yeh) [correct] **русское** (roos'-skah-yeh) **слово** for each person on the line with the corresponding number **под** (pohd) [under] **картинкой** (kar-teen'-koy) [picture].

1. ______________ 2. ______________

3. ______________ 4. ______________

5. ______________ 6. ______________

7. Михаил Глебович 8. ______________

9. ______________ 10. ______________

Are **вы** ready for a Russian rhyme?

(eh'-tah) (kohl'-yah) (shkohl'-yeh) (pyah'-tahm) (klas'-seh)
Это Коля с братом Васей. Коля в школе в пятом классе.
Kolya (his) brother Vasya school fifth class

- ☐ **жакет** *(zhah-kyet')* .... jacket (woman's) ______________
- ☐ **жасмин** *(zhahs-meen')* .... jasmine ______________
- ☐ **желе** *(zhyel-yeh')* .... jelly ______________ **Ж**
- ☐ **журнал** *(zhoor-nahl')* .... journal, magazine ______________
- ☐ **—журналист** *(zhoor-nah-leest')* .... journalist ______________

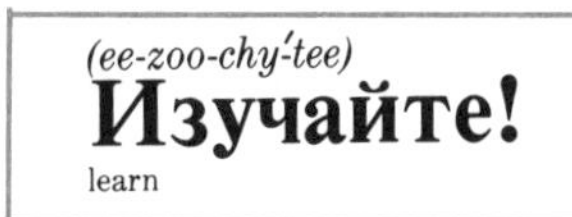

Step 11

You have already used the verbs **у меня** (oo)(men-yah') [I have] **есть,** (yest) **я** (yah) [I] **хочу** (hah-choo') [want] and **идёт.** (ee-dyoht') [goes] Although you might be able to get by with these verbs, let's assume you want to do better. First a quick review.

How do you say **"I"** **по-русски?** (pah-roos'-skee) ________ How do you say **"we"** **по-русски?** ________

Study these **два** (dvah) [two] charts **очень** (oh'-chen) [very] carefully **и** learn these **шесть** (shest) [six] **слов** (slohv) on the right.

I	=	**я** (yah)
he	=	**он** (ohn)
she	=	**она** (ah-nah')

we	=	**мы** (mwee)
you	=	**вы** (vwee)
they	=	**они** (ah-nee')

Not too hard, is it? **Теперь** draw lines between the matching English **и русские** (roos'-skee-yeh) **слова** (slah-vah') below to see if you can keep these **слова** straight in your mind.

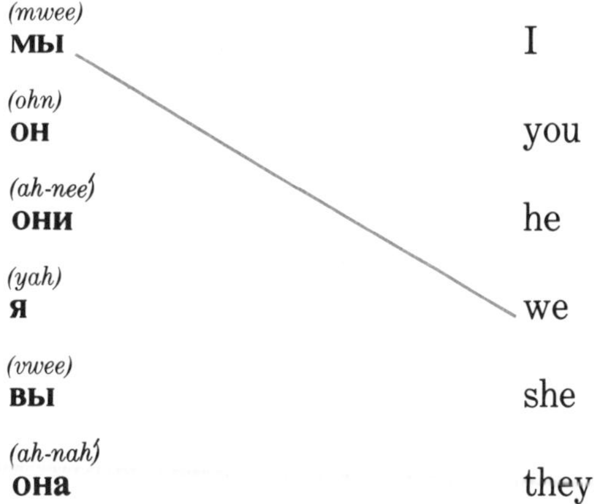

Теперь (tyep-yair') close **книгу** (knee'-goo) **и** (ee) write out both columns of the above practice on **бумаге.** (boo-mahg'-yeh) [paper] How did **вы** (vwee) [you] do? **Хорошо** (hah-rah-shoh') [well] **или** [or] **плохо?** (ploh'-hah) [badly] **Хорошо** (hah-rah-shoh') [well] **или нет?** (nyet) [not] **Теперь** that **вы** (vwee) [you] know these **слова**, **вы** (vwee) [you] can say almost anything **по-русски** with one basic formula: the "plug-in" formula. With this formula, **вы** (vwee) [you] can correctly use any **слова вы** wish.

☐ **зона** *(zoh'-nah)*	zone	________
☐ **зоопарк** *(zah-ah-park')*	zoo	________
☐ **импортный** *(eem'-part-nee)*	imported	________
☐ **Индия** *(een'-dee-yah)*	India	________
☐ **индустриальный** *(een-doo-stree-ahl'-nee)*	industrial	________

З

To demonstrate, let's take (*shest*) **шесть** (six) basic **и** practical verbs **и** see how the "plug-in" formula works. Write the verbs in the blanks below after **вы** have practiced saying them out loud many times.

(*zah-kah'-zih-vaht*) **заказывать**	=	to order/ reserve	(*pah-koo-paht'*) **покупать**	=	to buy	(*ee-zoo-chaht'*) **изучать**	=	to learn
____________			____________			____________		
(*pahv-tar-yaht'*) **повторять**	=	to repeat	(*pah-nee-maht'*) **понимать**	=	to understand	(*gah-vah-reet'*) **говорить**	=	to speak
____________			____________			____________		

Study the following patterns carefully.

(*yah*) **я**	(*zah-kah'-zih-vah-yoo*) **заказываю**	=	I *order*
	(*pah-koo-pah'-yoo*) **покупаю**	=	I *buy*
	(*ee-zoo-chah'-yoo*) **изучаю**	=	I *learn*
	(*pahv-tar-yah'-yoo*) **повторяю**	=	I *repeat*
	(*pah-nee-mah'-yoo*) **понимаю**	=	I *understand*
	(*gah-vah-ryoo'*) **говорю**	=	I *speak*

(*ohn*) **он** / (*ah-nah'*) **она**	(*zah-kah'-zih-vah-yet*) **заказывает**	=	he/she *orders*
	(*pah-koo-pah'-yet*) **покупает**	=	he/she *buys*
	(*ee-zoo-chah'-yet*) **изучает**	=	he/she *learns*
	(*pahv-tar-yah'-yet*) **повторяет**	=	he/she *repeats*
	(*pah-nee-mah'-yet*) **понимает**	=	he/she *understands*
	(*gah-vah-reet'*) **говорит**	=	he/she *speaks*

Note:
- With all these verbs, the first thing you do is drop the final „**ть**" from the basic verb form.
- With **я,** you add (*yoo*) **ю** or (*oo*) **у** to the basic verb form. This is basically the sound "*oo.*"
- With **он** or **она,** you add the sound "*yet*" (**ет**) to the basic verb form or the sound "*eet*" (**ит**).

Some verbs just will not conform to the pattern! But don't worry. Speak slowly **и** clearly, **и** you will be perfectly understood whether you say (*ee-zoo-chah'-yoo*) **изучаю** or (*ee-zoo-chah'-yet*) **изучает. Русские** (Russians) will be delighted that you have taken the time to learn their language.

- ☐ **инженер** (*een-zhyen-yair'*) .... engineer ____________
- ☐ **инспектор** (*een-spyek'-tar*) .... inspector ____________
- ☐ **институт** (*een-stee-toot'*) .... institute ____________
- ☐ **инструктор** (*een-strook'-tar*) .... instructor ____________
- ☐ **инструмент** (*een-stroo-myent'*) .... instrument ____________

И

Here's your pattern for **мы** *(mwee)* we. Add the sound *"yem"* **(ем)** or *"eem"* **(им)**.

мы	*(zah-kah'-zih-vah-yem)* **заказываем** = we *order*	*(pah-koo-pah'-yem)* **покупаем** = we *buy*	*(ee-zoo-chah'-yem)* **изучаем** = we *learn*	**мы**	*(pahv-tar-yah'-yem)* **повторяем** = we *repeat*	*(pah-nee-mah'-yem)* **понимаем** = we *understand*
					(gah-vah-reem') **говорим** = we *speak*	

Here's your pattern for **вы** *(vwee)*. Add the sound *"yet-yeh"* **(ете)** or *"eet-yeh"* **(ите)**.

вы	*(zah-kah'-zih-vah-yet-yeh)* **заказываете** = you *order*	**вы**	*(pahv-tar-yah'-yet-yeh)* **повторяете** = you *repeat*
	(pah-koo-pah'-yet-yeh) **покупаете** = you *buy*		*(pah-nee-mah'-yet-yeh)* **понимаете** = you *understand*
	(ee-zoo-chah'-yet-yeh) **изучаете** = you *learn*		*(gah-vah-reet'-yeh)* **говорите** = you *speak*

Finally, here's your pattern for **они** *(ah-nee')* they, which calls for the sound *"yoot"* **(ют)** or sometimes *"yaht"* **(ят)**.

они	*(zah-kah'-zih-vah-yoot)* **заказывают** = they *order*	**они**	*(pahv-tar-yah'-yoot)* **повторяют** = they *repeat*
	(pah-koo-pah'-yoot) **покупают** = they *buy*		*(pah-nee-mah'-yoot)* **понимают** = they *understand*
	(ee-zoo-chah'-yoot) **изучают** = they *learn*		*(gah-var-yaht')* **говорят** = they *speak*

Теперь it is your turn to practice **что** *(shtoh)* what **вы** *(vwee)* have learned. Fill in the following blanks **с** the correct form of the verb. Each time **вы** write out the sentence, be sure to say it aloud.

(zah-kah'-zih-vaht) **заказывать** to order/reserve

(yah) **Я** __________ **стакан** *(stah-kahn')* glass **воды** *(vah-dih')* water.

Он / Она __________ **стакан вина** *(vee-nah')*.

(mwee) **Мы** __________ **стакан молока** *(mah-lah-kah')*.

(vwee) **Вы** заказываете **чашку** *(chahsh'-koo)* cup **чая** *(chah'-yah)* tea.

(ah-nee') **Они** __________ **чашку кофе** *(kohf'-yeh)*.

(pah-koo-paht') **покупать** to buy

Я __________ **книгу** *(knee'-goo)* book.

Он / Она покупает **салат**.

Мы __________ **лампу** *(lahm'-poo)*.

Вы __________ **часы** *(chah-sih')* clock.

Они __________ **билет** *(beel-yet')* ticket.

И

- ☐ **интеллигент** *(een-tyel-lee-gyent')* .... intellectual __________
- ☐ **интервью** *(een-tyair-view')* .... interview __________
- ☐ **интерес** *(een-tyair-yes')* .... interest __________
- ☐ **интернациональный** *(een-tyair-nah-tsee-ah-nahl'-nee)* international __________
- ☐ **информация** *(een-far-mah'-tsee-yah)* .... information __________

(ee-zoo-chaht')
изучать
to learn

Я ______________ (roos'-skee) **русский.** Russian

Он / Она ______________ **русский.**

Мы ______________ (ahn-glee'-skee) **английский.** English

Вы изучаете **английский.**

Они ______________ (nee-myeh'-tskee) **немецкий.** German

(pahv-tar-yaht')
повторять
to repeat

(yah) Я ______________ (sloh'-vah) **слово.**

Он / Она ______________ (aht-vyeh'-tih) **ответы.** answers

Мы повторяем **ответы.**

Вы ______________ (chee'-sloh) **число.** number

Они ______________ (vah-proh'-sih) **вопросы.** questions

(pah-nee-maht')
понимать
to understand

Я понимаю (pah-ahn-glee'-skee) **по-английски.**

Он / Она ______________ **по-русски.**

Мы ______________ (pah-nee-myeh'-tskee) **по-немецки.** German

Вы ______________ (pah-frahn-tsoo'-skee) **по-французски.** French

Они ______________ (pah-ee-spahn'-skee) **по-испански.** Spanish

(gah-vah-reet')
говорить
to speak/say

Я ______________ (pah-roos'-skee) **по-русски.** Russian

Он / Она ______________ **по-английски.**

Мы ______________ (pah-ee-tahl-yahn'-skee) **по-итальянски.** Italian

Вы ______________ **по-русски.**

Они говорят **по-английски.**

(voht) (shest)
Вот шесть more verbs.
here are six

(yek'-haht) **ехать** = to go (by vehicle)

(pree-yez-zhaht') **приезжать** = to arrive

(vee'-dyet) **видеть** = to see

______________ ______________ ______________

(zheet) **жить** = to live/reside

(zhdaht) **ждать** = to wait for

(ees-kaht') **искать** = to look for

______________ ______________ ______________

At the back of (knee'-gee) **книги,** **вы** will find (syem) **семь** (strah-neets') **страниц** (pages) of flash cards to help you learn these (noh'-vih-yeh) **новые** (new) **слова.** Cut them out; carry them in your briefcase, purse, pocket **или** knapsack; **и** review them whenever (vwee) **вы** have a free moment.

- ☐ **Исландия** (ees-lahn'-dee-yah)............... Iceland
- ☐ **история** (ees-toh'-ree-yah)................... history
- ☐ **Италия** (ee-tah'-lee-yah)...................... Italy
- ☐ —where they speak **по-итальянски** (pah-ee-tahl-yahn'-skee)
- ☐ **кабина** (kah-bee'-nah)......................... cabin, booth

К

Теперь fill in the following blanks with the correct form of each verb. Be sure to say each sentence out loud until **вы** (you) have it down pat!

(yek'-haht) **ехать** — to go

- Я _еду_ в *(v')* Смоленск *(smahl-yensk')*. — to Smolensk
- Он / Она _едет_ в Москву *(mahsk-voo')*.
- Мы _едем_ в Новгород *(nohv'-gah-rahd)*. — Novgorod
- Вы _едете_ в гостиницу *(gah-stee'-nee-tsoo)*. — hotel
- Они _едут_ в Горький *(gor'-kee)*. — Gorki

(pree-yez-zhaht') **приезжать** — to arrive

- Я _приезжаю_ из *(eez)* Москвы *(mahsk-vih')*. — from
- Он / Она _приезжает_ из *(eez)* Канады *(kah-nah'-dih)*. — Canada
- Мы _приезжаем_ из *(leez)* Новгорода *(nohv'-gah-rah-dah)*. — Novgorod
- Вы _приезжаете_ из Смоленска *(smahl-yen'-skah)*. — Smolensk
- Они _приезжают_ из Австралии *(ahv-strah'-lee-ee)*. — Australia

(vee'-dyet) **видеть** — to see

- Я _вижу_ гостиницу *(gah-stee'-nee-tsoo)*. — hotel
- Он / Она _видит_ такси *(tahk-see')*. — taxi
- Мы _видим_ ресторан *(res-tah-rahn')*. — restaurant
- Вы _видите_ банк *(bahnk)*. — bank
- Они _видят_ Москву *(mahsk-voo')*.

(zheet) **жить** — to live/reside

- Я _живу_ в *(v')* Москву *(mahsk-voo')*.
- Он / Она _живёт_ в Америке *(ah-myeh'-reek-yeh)*. — America
- Мы _живём_ в Канаде *(kah-nahd'-yeh)*. — Canada
- Вы _живёте_ в Англии *(ahn'-glee-ee)*. — England
- Они _живут_ в Австралии *(ahv-strah'-lee-ee)*. — Australia

(zhdaht) **ждать** — to wait for

- Я _жду_ такси *(tahk-see')*.
- Он / Она _ждёт_ автобуса *(ahv-toh'-boo-sah)*. — bus
- Мы _ждём_ Ивана *(ee-vah'-nah)*. — Ivan
- Вы _ждёте_ Анну *(ahn'-noo)*. — Anna
- Они _ждут_ меню *(myen-yoo')*. — menu

(ees-kaht') **искать** — to look for

- Я _ищу_ марку *(mar'-koo)*. — stamp
- Он / Она _ищет_ цветы *(tsveh-tih')*. — flowers
- Мы _ищем_ туалет *(too-ahl-yet')*.
- Вы _ищете_ дом *(dohm)*. — house
- Они _ищут_ книгу *(knee'-goo)*. — book

- ☐ **камера** *(kah'-myair-ah)* . . . . camera
- ☐ **Канада** *(kah-nah'-dah)* . . . . Canada
- ☐ **канал** *(kah-nahl')* . . . . canal
- ☐ **канарейка** *(kah-nah-ray'-kah)* . . . . canary
- ☐ **кандидат** *(kahn-dee-daht')* . . . . candidate

К

Теперь take a deep breath. See if *(vwee)* **вы** can fill in the blanks below. The correct **ответы** are at the bottom of **этои** (this) **страницы.**

1. I speak Russian. ______________________________
2. He arrives from America. ______________________________
3. We learn Russian. ______________________________
4. They repeat the number. ______________________________
5. She understands English. ______________________________
6. We go to the bank. ______________________________
7. I see the hotel. ______________________________
8. I live in Canada. ______________________________
9. You buy a book. ______________________________
10. He orders a glass of water. ______________________________

(dah) **Да,** (yes) it is hard to get used to all those *(noh'-vim)* **новым** (new) **словам.** But just keep practicing *(ee)* **и,** before *(vwee)* **вы** know it, **вы** will be using them naturally.

In the following steps, *(vwee)* **вы** will be introduced to more **и** more verbs, **и вы** should drill them in exactly the same way as *(vwee)* **вы** did in this section. Look up *(noh'-vih-yeh)* **новые слова** (new) in your *(slah-var-yeh')* **словаре** (dictionary) **и** make up your own sentences using the same type of pattern. Try out your *(noh'-vih-yeh)* **новые слова,** (new) for that's how you make them yours to use on your holiday. Remember, the more *(vwee)* **вы** practice *(tyep-yair')* **теперь,** the more enjoyable your trip will be. *(oo-dah'-chee)* **Удачи!** (good luck)

Теперь is a perfect time to turn to the back of this *(knee'-gee)* **книги,** clip out your verb flash cards **и** start flashing. Also, don't skip over your free **слова.** Be sure to check them off in the box provided as **вы** *(ee-zoo-chah'-yet-yeh)* **изучаете** (learn) each one.

ОТВЕТЫ

1. **Я говорю по-русски.**
2. **Он приезжает из Америки.**
3. **Мы изучаем русский.**
4. **Они повторяют число.**
5. **Она понимает по-английски.**
6. **Мы едем в банк.**
7. **Я вижу гостиницу.**
8. **Я живу в Канаде.**
9. **Вы покупаете книгу.**
10. **Он заказывает стакан воды.**

(skohl'-kah) (vreh'-mee-nee)
Сколько Времени?
what time is it

Step 12

(vwee) *(kahk)* *(dnee)* *(nee-dyeh'-lee)* *(myeh'-syeh-tsih)* *(go'-dah)*
Вы know **как** to tell **дни недели и месяцы года,** so now let's learn to tell time.
days of week months of year

(rez-yair-vah'-tsee-yoo)
As a traveler, **вы** need to be able to tell time in order to make **резервацию и** to catch
reservations

(poh-yez-dah') *(voht)*
поезда и автобусы. Вот the "basics."
trains buses here are

o'clock/hour	=	*(chahs)* **час** ________
minutes	=	*(mee-noot')* **минут** ________
half	=	*(pah-lah-vee'-nah)* **половина** ________
minus	=	*(byez)* **без** ________

What time is it?	=	*(vreh'-mee-nee)* **Сколько времени?**
		(kah-toh'-ree) (chahs) **Который час?**
special endings	=	*(oh-vah/ah-vah)* **-ого**
		(yeh-vah) **-его**

(pree-myair'-ih) *(vnee-zoo')*
Теперь, как are these **слова** used? Study **примеры внизу.** When **вы** think it through, it
examples below

(nyeh)
really is **не** too difficult. Just notice that the pattern changes after the halfway mark.
not

(chah-sohv')
Пять часов.
o'clock

(dyes'-yet) (mee-noot') (shes-toh'-vah)
Десять минут шестого. = 5:10
ten minutes (toward) sixth hour

(dvahd'-tset) (mee-noot') (shes-toh'-vah)
Двадцать минут шестого. = 5:20
twenty minutes (toward) sixth hour

(pah-lah-vee'-nah)
Половина шестого. = 5:30
half (of) sixth hour

(byez) (dvahd-tseh-tee') (shest)
Без двадцати шесть. = 5:40
minus twenty (from) six

(dyes-yeh-tee')
Без десяти шесть. = 5:50
ten (from)

(chah-sohv')
Шесть часов.

(syem) (chah-sohv')
Семь часов.

(dvahd'-tset) (vahs-moh'-vah)
Двадцать минут восьмого.
twenty minutes (toward) eighth hour

(pah-lah-vee'-nah) (vahs-moh'-vah)
Половина восьмого.
half (of) eighth hour

(dvahd-tseh-tee') (voh'-syem)
Без двадцати восемь.
twenty (from) eight

(chah-sohv')
Восемь часов.

(vrem'-yah) *(chah-sahk)* *(kah-toh'-ree)* *(chahs)*
Теперь fill in the blanks according to **время** indicated on **часах. Который час?**
time clocks

1. ____________________

2. Семь часов

3. ____________________

4. ____________________

ОТВЕТЫ

1. Восемь часов.
2. Семь часов.
3. Половина восьмого.
4. Четыре часа.

Вот more time-telling **слова** to add to your vocabulary.

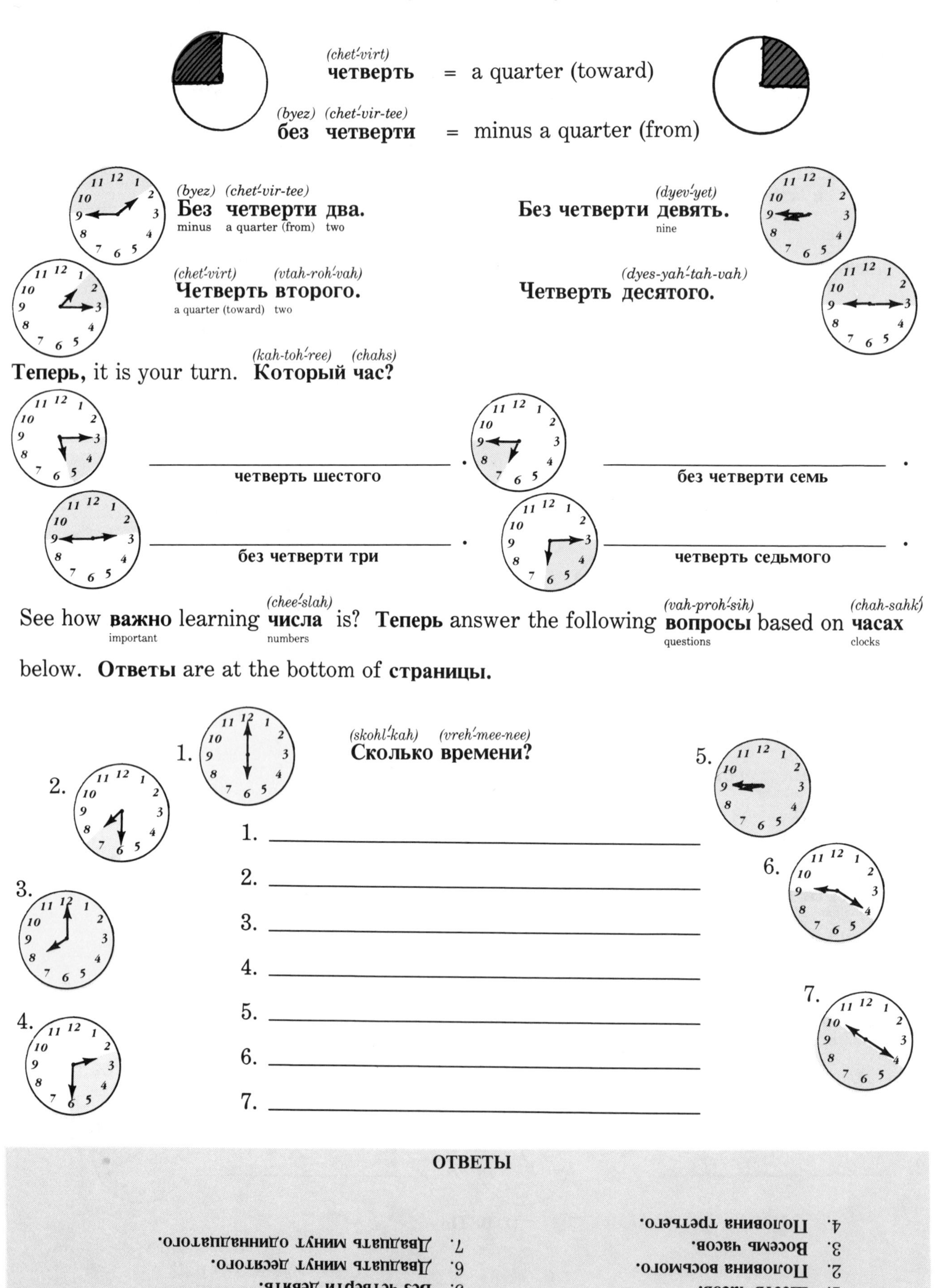

(chet'-virt)
четверть = a quarter (toward)

(byez) (chet'-vir-tee)
без четверти = minus a quarter (from)

(byez) (chet'-vir-tee)
Без четверти два.
minus a quarter (from) two

(dyev'-yet)
Без четверти девять.
nine

(chet'-virt) (vtah-roh'-vah)
Четверть второго.
a quarter (toward) two

(dyes-yah'-tah-vah)
Четверть десятого.

Теперь, it is your turn. *(kah-toh'-ree) (chahs)* **Который час?**

__________________________ .
четверть шестого

__________________________ .
без четверти семь

__________________________ .
без четверти три

__________________________ .
четверть седьмого

See how **важно** (important) learning *(chee'-slah)* **числа** (numbers) is? **Теперь** answer the following *(vah-proh'-sih)* **вопросы** (questions) based on *(chah-sahk')* **часах** (clocks) below. **Ответы** are at the bottom of **страницы.**

(skohl'-kah) (vreh'-mee-nee)
Сколько времени?

1. ______________________________
2. ______________________________
3. ______________________________
4. ______________________________
5. ______________________________
6. ______________________________
7. ______________________________

ОТВЕТЫ

1. Шесть часов.
2. Половина восьмого.
3. Восемь часов.
4. Половина третьего.
5. Без четверти девять.
6. Двадцать минут десятого.
7. Двадцать минут одиннадцатого.

When (vwee) **вы** answer a (kahg-dah) **„когда“** (when) question, say (v') **„в“** (at) before (vwee) **вы** give the time.

поезд 43 | 6:00

Когда (pree-dyoht) **придёт** (comes) (poh-yezd) **поезд?** (train) в шесть часов.

Теперь answer the following (vah-proh-sih) **вопросы** (questions) based on (chah-sahk) **часах** (clocks) (vnee-zoo) **внизу.** (below) Be sure to practice saying each (vah-prohs) **вопрос** (question) out loud several times.

(kahg-dah) **Когда** (nah-chee-nah-yet-syah) **начинается** (begins) (kohn-tsairt) **концерт?** (concert) ____________________

Когда (nah-chee-nah-yet-syah) **начинается** (begins) (feelm) **фильм?** (film) в семь часов

(kahg-dah) **Когда** (pree-dyoht) **придёт** (comes) (ahv-toh-boos) **автобус?** (bus) ____________________

Когда (pree-dyoht) **придёт** (comes) (tahk-see) **такси?** ____________________

Когда (aht-krih-vah-yet-syah) **открывается** (opens) (res-tah-rahn) **ресторан?** (restaurant) ____________________

Когда (zah-krih-vah-yet-syah) **закрывается** (closes) **ресторан?** ____________________

В (at) (voh-syem) **восемь часов** (oo-trah) **утра,** (in morning) **мы** (gah-vah-reem) **говорим** (say) (doh-brah-yeh) **„Доброе** (good) (oo-trah) **утро,** (morning) **Мария** (nee-kah-lah-yev-nah) **Николаевна.“**

В восемь (chah-sohv) **часов** (vyeh-cheh-rah) **вечера,** (in evening) **мы говорим** (doh-brih) **„Добрый** (vyeh-cher) **вечер,** **Анна** (pee-trohv-nah) **Петровна.“**

В (chahs) **час** (one) (dnyah) **дня,** (in afternoon) (mwee) **мы говорим** **„Добрый** (dyen) **день,** **Иван** (nee-kah-lah-yev-eech) **Николаевич.“**

В (dyes-yet) **десять** (ten) **часов вечера,** (in evening) **мы говорим** (spah-koy-noy) **„Спокойной** (good) (noh-chee) **ночи,** (night) **Зина Ивановна.“**

- ☐ **капитал** *(kah-pee-tahl)* . . . . capital (money) ____________
- ☐ **—капиталист** *(kah-pee-tah-leest)* . . . . capitalist ____________
- ☐ **карамель** *(kah-rah-myel)* . . . . caramel ____________
- ☐ **класс** *(klahs)* . . . . class ____________
- ☐ **классик** *(klahs-seek)* . . . . classic ____________

К

Remember:

What time is it?	=	*(kah-toh'-ree)* **Который час?** *(vreh'-mee-nee)* **Сколько времени?**

When	=	**Когда**

Can *(vwee)* **вы** pronounce **и** understand the following paragraph?

(poh'-yezd) **Поезд** (train) *(eez)* **из** (from) **Москвы** *(pree-dyoht')* **придёт в** *(chet'-virt)* **четверть** *(shes-toh'-vah)* **шестого.** **Теперь** *(dvahd'-tset)* **двадцать минут шестого.** **Поезд** *(ah-pahz-dahl')* **опоздал** (late). *(see-vohd'-nyah)* **Сегодня** (today) **поезд** *(pree-dyoht')* **придёт в четверть** *(vahs-moh'-vah)* **восьмого.** *(zahv'-trah)* **Завтра** (tomorrow) **поезд** *(pree-dyoht')* **придёт в четверть шестого.**

(voht) **Вот** some more practice exercises. Answer *(vah-proh'-sih)* **вопросы** based on the times given below.

(kah-toh'-ree) **Который** *(chahs)* **час?**

1. (10:30) ____________________
2. (6:30) ____________________
3. (6:15) ____________________
4. (10:45) ____________________
5. (5:45) ____________________
6. (7:20) ____________________
7. (3:10) ____________________
8. (4:05) ____________________
9. (8:30) ____________________
10. (4:00) ____________________

☐ **клоун** *(kloh'-oon)*.......................... clown
☐ **коллекция** *(kahl-yek'-tsee-yah)* .... collection
☐ **командир** *(kah-mahn-deer')*................. commander
☐ **комедия** *(kah-myeh'-dee-yah)*.............. comedy
☐ **комиссар** *(kah-mees-sar')*.................. commissar

К

(voht) **Вот** a quick quiz. Fill in the blanks **с** the correct **числами** (chee-slah'-mee) numbers. **Ответы** (aht-vyeh'-tih) **внизу** (vnee-zoo').

1. **В минуте** (mee-noot'-yeh) minute (there are) ________________ **секунд** (see-koond') seconds.
2. **В часе** (chahs'-yeh) hour ________________ **минут** minutes.
3. **В неделе** (nee-dyel'-yeh) week ________________ **дней** (dnyay) days.
4. **В месяце** (myeh'-syeh-tseh) ________________ **дней** days.
5. **В году** (gah-doo') ________________ **месяцев** (myeh'-syeh-tsyev) months.
6. **В году** ________________ **недели** (nee-dyeh'-lee) weeks.
7. **В году триста** (tree'-stah) 300 ________________ **дней.**
8. **В феврале** ________________ **дней.**

If **вы** are traveling between large cities, **вы** will more than likely take **поезд** (poh'-yezd) train. **Вы** may want to do as the **русские** (roos'-skee-yeh) Russians do **и** carry your luggage on the train, rather than check it on board.

(voht) **Вот** a sample **страница из** (eez) **русского** (roos'-skah-vah) **расписания** (rah-spee-sah'-nee-yah) schedule **поездов** (pah-yez-dohv') of trains.

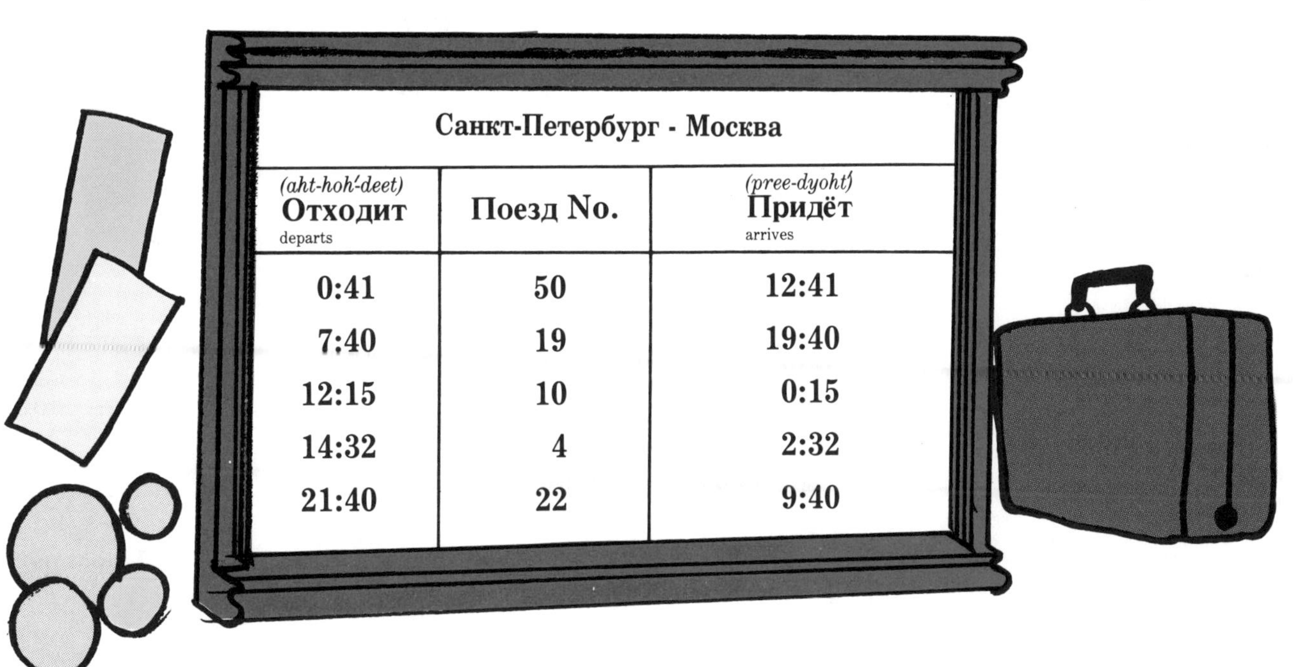

Санкт-Петербург - Москва		
(aht-hoh'-deet) **Отходит** departs	**Поезд No.**	(pree-dyoht') **Придёт** arrives
0:41	50	12:41
7:40	19	19:40
12:15	10	0:15
14:32	4	2:32
21:40	22	9:40

ОТВЕТЫ

1. шестьдесят
2. шестьдесят
3. семь
4. тридцать
5. двенадцать
6. пятьдесят две
7. шестьдесят пять
8. двадцать восемь

Вот **новые** *(noh'-vih-yeh)* new verbs for Step 12.

(gah-vah-reet') **говорить** = to say/speak	*(yest)* **есть** = to eat	*(peet)* **пить** = to drink

(gah-vah-reet') **говорить** to say

Я ________ **„доброе** *(doh'-brah-yeh)* **утро."**

Он / Она ________ **„добрый** *(doh'-brih)* **день."** *(dyen)*

Мы говорим **„нет."** *(nyet)* no

Вы ________ **„да."** *(dah)* yes

(ah-nee) **Они** ________ **„Спасибо."** *(spah-see'-bah)*

(yest) **есть** to eat

(yah) **Я** ем/ **суп.** *(soop)*

Он / Она ест/ **борщ.** *(borshch)*

Мы едим/ **много.** *(mnoh'-gah)* a lot

Вы едите/ **хлеб.** *(hlyeb)* bread

Они едят/ **рыбу.** *(rih'-boo)* fish

(peet) **пить** to drink

Я пью/ **молоко.** milk

Он / Она пьёт/ **белое** *(byeh'-lah-yeh)* white **вино.** *(vee-noh')*

(mwee) **Мы** пьём/ **пиво.** *(pee'-vah)*

Вы пьёте/ **стакан** *(stah-kahn')* **воды.** *(vah-dih')*

Они пьют/ **чай.** *(chy)* tea

As **вы** have probably noticed, the sound of the Russian letter **„й"** varies greatly. Here are some examples.

(kar-teen'-koy) **картинкой** picture	*(yev-ray'-kah)* **еврейка** Jewish woman	*(moo-zyay')* **музей** museum	*(chy)* **чай** tea	*(syeh'-ree)* **серый** blue

- ☐ **коммунист** *(kahm-moo-neest')* .... communist
- ☐ **компас** *(kohm'-pahs)* .... compass
- ☐ **композитор** *(kahm-pah-zee'-tar)* .... composer
- ☐ **конференция** *(kahn-fyair-yen'-tsee-yah)* .... conference
- ☐ **концерт** *(kohn-tsairt')* .... concert

К

(kar-tee′-nah)
картина

(pah-tah-lohk′)
потолок

(oog′-ahl)
угол

(ahk-noh′)
окно

(lahm′-pah)
лампа

(dee-vahn′)
диван

(stool)
стул

(kahv-yor′)
ковёр

(stohl)
стол

(dvyair)
дверь

(chah-sih′)
часы

(zah′-nahv-yes)
занавес

(styen-ah′)
стена

(tee-lee-fohn′)
телефон

(dohm)
дом

(kah-bee-nyet′)
кабинет

(vahn′-nah-yah)
ванная

(koohk′-nyah)
кухня

(spahl′-nyah)
спальня

(stah-loh′-vah-yah)
столовая

(gah-stee′-nah-yah)
гостиная

(gah-rahzh′)
гараж

(pahd-vahl′)
подвал

(ahv-tah-mah-beel′)
автомобиль

(mah-tah-tsee′-kul)
мотоцикл

(sah-bah′-kah)
собака

(koht)
кот

(sahd)
сад

(poach′-tah)
почта

(pahch-toh′-vee) (yahsh′-chik)
почтовый ящик

(tsveh-tih′)
цветы

(zvah-nohk′)
звонок

(ah-deen′)
1 один

(dvah)
2 два

(tree)
3 три

(cheh-tih′-ree)
4 четыре

(pyaht)
5 пять

(shest)
6 шесть

(syem)
7 семь

(voh′-syem)
8 восемь

(dyev′-yet)
9 девять

(dyes′-yet)
10 десять

(chyor′-nee)
чёрный

(zhyol′-tee)
жёлтый

(see′-nee)
синий

(syeh′-ree)
серый

(byeh′-lee)
белый

(krahs′-nee)
красный

(zyel-yoh′-nee)
зелёный

(kah-reech′-nyeh-vwee)
коричневый

(roh′-zah-vwee)
розовый

(ah-rahn′-zheh-vwee)
оранжевый

(pah-nee-dyel′-neek)
понедельник

(vtor′-neek)
вторник

(sree-dah′)
среда

(chet-vyairg′)
четверг

(pyaht′-nee-tsah)
пятница

(soo-boh′-tah)
суббота

(voh-skree-syen′-yah)
воскресенье

(doh′-brah-yeh) (oo′-trah)
доброе утро

(doh′-brih) (dyen)
добрый день

(doh′-brih) (vyeh′-cher)
добрый вечер

(spah-koy′-noy) (noh′-chee)
спокойной ночи

(kahk) (dee-lah′)
Как дела?

(hah-lah-deel′-neek)
холодильник

(plee-tah′)
плита

(vee-noh′)
вино

(pee′-vah)
пиво

(mah-lah-koh′)
молоко

(mah′-slah)
масло

(tar-yel′-kah)
тарелка

(sole)
соль

(pyeh′-rets)
перец

(nohzh)
нож

(chahsh′-kah)
чашка

(veel′-kah)
вилка

(stah-kahn′)
стакан

(sahl-fyet′-kah)
салфетка

(lohzh′-kah)
ложка

(shkahf)
шкаф

STICKY LABELS

This book has over 150 special sticky labels for you to use as you learn new words. When you are introduced to a word, remove the corresponding label from these pages. Be sure to use each of these unique labels by adhering them to a picture, window, lamp or whatever object they refer to. The sticky labels make learning to speak Russian much more fun and a lot easier than you ever expected.

For example, when you look in the mirror and see the label, say

(zyair'-kah-lah)
„зеркало.“

Don't just say it once, say it again and again.

And once you label the refrigerator, you should never again open that door without saying

(hah-lah-deel'-neek)
„холодильник.“

By using the sticky labels, you not only learn new words but friends and family also learn along with you!

(hlyeb)
хлеб

(chy)
чай

(kohf-yeh)
кофе

(krah-vaht)
кровать

(ah-dee-yah-lah)
одеяло

(pah-doosh-kah)
подушка

(boo-deel-neek)
будильник

(shkahf)
шкаф

(oo-mih-vahl-neek)
умывальник

(doosh)
душ

(too-ahl-yet)
туалет

(zyair-kah-lah)
зеркало

(pah-lah-tyen-tsah)
полотенца

(kah-rahn-dahsh)
карандаш

(rooch-kah)
ручка

(boo-mah-gah)
бумага

(pees-moh)
письмо

(aht-krit-kah)
открытка

(mar-kah)
марка

(knee-gah)
книга

(zhoor-nahl)
журнал

(gah-zyeh-tah)
газета

(ahch-kee)
очки

(tee-lee-vee-zar)
телевизор

(kar-zee-nah)
корзина

(pahs-port)
паспорт

(beel-yet)
билет

(cheh-mah-dahn)
чемодан

(soom-kah)
сумка

(boo-mahzh-neek)
бумажник

(dyen-gee)
деньги

(foh-toh-ahp-pah-raht)
фотоаппарат

(foh-toh-plyohn-kah)
фотоплёнка

(koo-pahl-nee) (kohst-yoom)
купальный костюм

(sahn-dah-lee-ee)
сандалии

(mwee-lah)
мыло

(zoob-nah-yah) (shchoht-kah)
зубная щётка

(zoob-nah-yah) (pahs-tah)
зубная паста

(breet-vah)
бритва

(dyeh-zah-doh-rahnt)
дезодорант

(gryeb-yen)
гребень

(pahl-toh)
пальто

(plahshch)
плащ

(zohn-teek)
зонтик

(pyair-chaht-kee)
перчатки

(shlah-pah)
шляпа

(sah-pah-gee)
сапоги

(too-flee)
туфли

(nah-skee)
носки

(chool-kee)
чулки

(pee-zhah-mah)
пижама

(nohch-nah-yah) (roo-bahsh-kah)
ночная рубашка

(koo-pahl-nee) (hah-laht)
купальный халат

(bahsh-mah-kee)
башмаки

(kahst-yoom)
костюм

(gahl-stook)
галстук

(plah-tohk)
платок

(roo-bahsh-kah)
рубашка

(peed-zhahk)
пиджак

(bryoo-kee)
брюки

(plaht-yeh)
платье

(blooz-kah)
блузка

(yoob-kah)
юбка

(sveet-yair)
свитер

(leef-cheek)
лифчик

(kohm-bee-nah-tsee-yah)
комбинация

(troo-sih)
трусы

(my-kah)
майка

(zahn-yah-tah)
занято

(eez-vee-neet-yeh)
извините

(aht-krih-tah)
открыто

(pree-yaht-nah-vah) (ahp-pyeh-tee-tah)
приятного аппетита

(zah-krih-tah)
закрыто

(voh-dah)
вода

(yah) (ah-myeh-ree-kah-nyets)
Я американец.

(yah) (hah-choo) (ee-zoo-chaht) (roos-skee)
Я хочу изучать русский.

(men-yah) (zah-voot)
Меня зовут ________.

PLUS . . .

Your book includes a number of other innovative features. At the back of the book, you'll find seven pages of flash cards. Cut them out and flip through them at least once a day.

On pages 112 and 113, you'll find a beverage guide and a menu guide. Don't wait until your trip to use them. Clip out the menu guide and use it tonight at the dinner table. And use the beverage guide to practice ordering your favorite drinks.

By using the special features in this book, you will be speaking Russian before you know it.

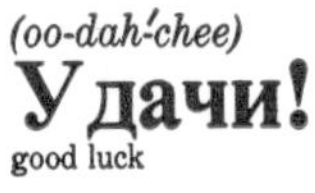

Север (syev'-yair) north - Юг (yoog) south, Восток (vah-stohk') east - Запад (zah'-pahd) west

Step 13

If **вы** (vwee) are looking at **карту** (kar'-too) map **и вы** see the following **слова,** it should **не** (nyeh) not be too difficult to figure out **что** (shtoh) what **они** (ah-nee') they mean. Take an educated guess. **Ответы внизу** (vnee-zoo') below**.**

Северная (syev'-yair-nah-yah) **Дакота** (dah-koh'-tah)	**Южная** (yoozh'-nah-yah) **Дакота**
Северная Америка (ah-myeh'-ree-kah)	**Южная Америка**
Северная Каролина (kah-roh-lee'-nah)	**Южная Каролина**
Северная Корея (kah-reh'-yah)	**Южная Африка** (ah'-free-kah)

Do **вы** recognize **русское слово** (sloh'-vah) for east in **„Владивосток“** (vlah-dee-vah-stohk')? It means "eastern domain."

Владивосток (vlah-dee-vah-stohk') is the easternmost seaport **в России.** It is also the terminus of the Trans-Siberian Railroad, 5700 miles east of **Москвы** (mahsk-vih') Moscow**.**

север (syev'-yair)	=	the north	________
юг (yoog)	=	the south	________
восток (vah-stohk')	=	the east	________
запад (zah'-pahd)	=	the west	________

северный (syev'-yair-nee)	=	northern	________
южный (yoozh'-nee)	=	southern	________
восточный (vah-stohch'-nee)	=	eastern	________
западный (zah'-pahd-nee)	=	western	________

But what about more basic **указания** (oo-kah-zah'-nee-yah) directions such as "left," "right," **и** "straight ahead"?

Let's learn these **слова.**

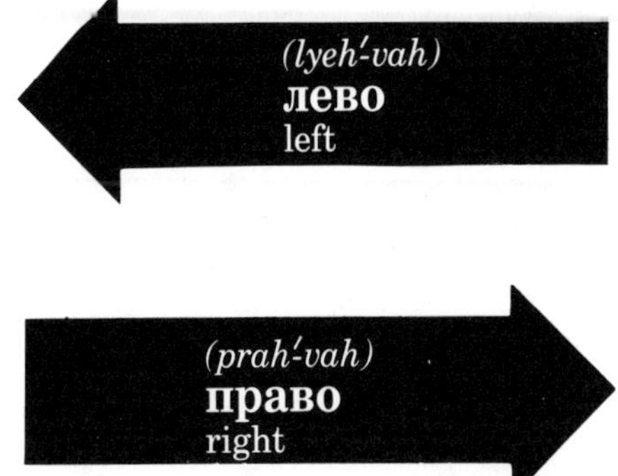

to the left	=	**налево** (nah lyeh'-vah)
to the right	=	**направо** (nah-prah'-vah)
straight ahead	=	**прямо** (pryah'-mah)
on the corner	=	**на углу** (nah) (oo-gloo')

ОТВЕТЫ

North Dakota	South Dakota
North America	South America
North Carolina	South Carolina
North Korea	South Africa

Just as **по-английски** (in English), these **слова** go a long way.

(spah-see'-bah) **спасибо**	=	thank you ______
(eez-vee-neet'-yeh) **извините**	=	excuse me ______
(pah-zhah'-loo-stah) **пожалуйста**	=	you're welcome/please ______

(voht) **Вот** *(dvah)* **два** (two) typical *(dee-ah-loh'-gah)* **диалога** (dialogues/conversations) *(dlyah)* **для** (for) someone who is trying to find something.

(bah-rees') **Борис:** *(eez-vee-neet'-yeh)* **Извините** (excuse me). **Где** *(gah-stee'-nee-tsah)* **гостиница** (hotel) **Москва?**

(lyeh'-nah) **Лена:** *(prahee-dyoht'-yeh)* **Пройдёте** (go) *(doh)* **до** (to) *(oo'-lee-tsih)* **улицы** (street) *(gair'-tseh-nah)* **Герцена и там** (there) *(nah-prah'-vah)* **направо** (to the right). *(gah-stee'-nee-tsah)* **Гостиница Москва** *(nah)* **на** (on) *(oo-gloo')* **углу** (corner).

(ahl-yeg') **Олег:** *(eez-vee-neet'-yeh)* **Извините** (excuse me). **Где** *(moo-zyay')* **Музей** (museum) *(tahl-stoh'-vah)* **Толстого** (Tolstoy)?

(ohl'-gah) **Ольга:** *(prahee-dyoht'-yeh)* **Пройдёте** (go) *(nah-prah'-vah)* **направо** (to the right); *(pah-tohm')* **потом** (then) *(pryah'-mah)* **прямо** (straight ahead) *(doh)* **до** (to) *(oo'-lee-tsih)* **улицы** (street) *(tahl-stoh'-vah)* **Толстого** (Tolstoy). **Там** *(nah-lyeh'-vah)* **налево** (to the left), **и** *(moo-zyay')* **музей** *(nah)* **на** *(oo-gloo')* **углу.**

Are **вы** lost? There is no need to be lost if *(vwee)* **вы** have learned the basic direction **слова.** Do not try to memorize these *(dee-ah-loh'-gee)* **диалоги** (dialogues/conversations) because **вы** will never be looking for precisely these places. One day, **вы** might need to ask *(oo-kah-zah'-nee-yeh)* **указание** (directions) to the *(bahl-shoy')* **Большой** (Bolshoi) *(tee-ah'-ter)* **Театр** (Theater), *(goom)* **ГУМ** (GUM Department Store) or *(kreml)* **Кремль** (Kremlin). Learn the key direction **слова и** be sure **вы** can find your destination. **Вы** may want to buy a guidebook to start planning what places **вы** would like to visit. Practice asking *(oo-kah-zah'-nee-yah)* **указания** (directions) to these special places. What if the person responding to your *(vah-prohs')* **вопрос** answers too quickly for **вы** to understand the entire reply? Look at the reply on the next **странице.** Practice saying…

К

- ☐ **коньяк** *(kohn-yahk')* .... cognac ______
- ☐ **корт** *(kort)* .... court (tennis) ______
- ☐ **кот** *(koht)* .... cat ______
- ☐ **краб** *(krahb)* .... crab ______
- ☐ **Куба** *(koo'-bah)* .... Cuba ______

(yah)(nyeh) (pah-nee-mah'-yoo) (pah-zhah'-loo-stah) (pahv-tah-reet'-yeh) (spah-see'-bah)
Извините. Я не понимаю. Пожалуйста повторите. Спасибо.
excuse me I (do) not understand please repeat

Теперь say it again **и** again.

Извините. Я не понимаю. Пожалуйста повторите. Спасибо.

(dah) **Да,** (yes) it is difficult at first but don't give up! *(kahg-dah)* **Когда** (when) *(oo-kah-zah'-nee-yah)* **указания** (directions) are repeated, **вы** will be able to understand if **вы** have learned the key **слова** for *(oo-kah-zah'-nee-yah)* **указания.** Quiz yourself by filling in the blanks below **с** the correct *(roos'-skee-mee)* **русскими** *(slah-vah'-mee)* **словами** (words).

(ee-vahn) Иван: *(eez-vee-neet'-yeh)* **Извините. Где** *(res-tah-rahn)* **ресторан** (restaurant) *(sahd-koh)* **Садко?**

Таня: **Пройдёте** (go) ______________ (straight ahead) **и** *(oo)* **у** (at) *(moo-zyoh'-yah)* **музея, пройдёте** ______________ (to the right). *(oo)* **У** (by) *(gah-stee'-nee-tsih)* **гостиницы** (hotel) *(kohs'-mahs)* **Космос пройдёте** ______________ (to the left). **Ресторан** *(sahd-koh)* **Садко** ______________ (on the corner). *(oo-dah'-chee)* **Удачи!** (good luck)

Вот *(cheh-tih'-ree)* **четыре** *(noh'-vihk)* **новых** (new) verbs. *(ah-nee)* **Они** (they) are different from the patterns **вы** have learned, so pay close attention. **Вы** will probably use these verbs more than any others.

(yah)(hah-choo) **я хочу** = I want ______________

(mnyeh) (noozh'-nah) **мне нужно** = I need ______________

(men-yah) (zah-voot) **меня зовут** = my name is... ______________

(oo) (men-yah) (yest) **у меня есть** = I have ______________

Л

- ☐ **лаборатория** *(lah-bah-rah-toh'-ree-yah)*...... laboratory ______________
- ☐ **лимон** *(lee-mohn)*........................ lemon ______________
- ☐ **—лимонад** *(lee-mah-nahd)*................ lemonade ______________
- ☐ **линия** *(lee'-nee-yah)*..................... line ______________
- ☐ **литература** *(lee-tyair-ah-too'-rah)*........... literature ______________

As always, say each sentence out loud. Say each **и** every **слово** carefully, pronouncing each **русский** sound as well as **вы** can.

(yah) (hah-choo')
я хочу
I want

(stah-kahn') (vee-nah')
Я ____________ **стакан вина.**
glass of

(mah-lah-kah')
Он ____________ **стакан молока.**
Она

(mwee) *(vah-dih')*
Мы ____________ **стакан воды.**

(chahsh'-koo) (kohf'-yeh)
Вы ____________ **чашку кофе.**
cup of

(chah'-yah)
Они ____________ **чашку чая.**
they

(men-yah') (zah-voot')
меня зовут...
my name is

(men-yah') *(nah-tahl'-yah)*
Меня ____________ **Наталья.**

(yee-voh')
Его ____________ **Олег/Ольга.**
(ee-yoh')
Её

(bah-rees') (lyeh'-nah)
Нас ____________ **Борис и Лена.**
our name is

(vahs) *(ahn-tohn')*
Вас ____________ **Антон.**
your name is

(eehk) *(ahn'-nah) (pyoh'-ter)*
Их ____________ **Анна и Пётр.**
their name is

(mnyeh) (noozh'-nah)
мне нужно
I need

(mnyeh) *(stah-kahn') (lee-mah-nah'-dah)*
Мне ____________ **стакан лимонада.**

(ee-moo')
Ему ____________ **стакан молока.**
(yay)
Ей

(chahsh'-koo)
Нам ____________ **чашку кофе.**

(vahm) *(chah'-yah)*
Вам ____________ **чашку чая.**

(eem) *(kah-kah'-oh)*
Им ____________ **чашку какао.**
cocoa

(oo) (men-yah') (yest)
у меня есть
I have

(oo) (men-yah') *(pyaht) (kah-pyeh'-eek)*
У меня ____________ **пять копеек.**

(nyeh-voh') *(shest) (roo-blyay')*
У него ____________ **шесть рублей.**
(nyeh-yoh')
У неё

(dyes'-yet)
У нас ____________ **десять рублей.**

(vahs) *(dveh) (kah-pyay'-kee)*
У вас ____________ **две копейки.**

(neehk) *(tree) (roob-lyah')*
У них ____________ **три рубля.**

(tyep-yair') *(aht-vyeh'-tih) (vnee-zoo')*
Теперь see if **вы** can translate the following thoughts **на русский.** **Ответы внизу.**
below

1. My name is .... ____________
2. We would like a cup of coffee. ____________
3. I have six rubles. ____________
4. We need to buy a glass of lemonade. ____________
5. I need a cup of tea. ____________
6. We have five rubles. ____________

ОТВЕТЫ

1. Меня зовут...
2. Мы хотим чашку кофе.
3. У меня есть шесть рублей.
4. Нам нужно купить стакан лимонада.
5. Мне нужно чашку чая.
6. У нас есть пять рублей.

(nah-vyair-hoo') Наверху - (vnee-zoo') Внизу
upstairs — downstairs/below

Before **вы** begin Step 14, review Step 8. (tyep-yair') **Теперь** let's learn (bohl'-shee) **больше** (more) **слов.**

(tyep-yair') **Теперь** go to your (spahl'-nyoo) **спальню** (bedroom) **и** look around the (kohm'-nah-too) **комнату** (room). Let's learn the names of the things **в** (spahl'-nyeh) **спальне** (bedroom), just like **мы** learned the various parts of (doh'-mah) **дома.** Be sure to practice saying all **слова** as **вы** write them in the spaces (vnee-zoo') **внизу** (below). Also say out loud the example sentences (pohd) **под** (under) (kar-teen'-kah-mee) **картинками** (pictures).

(krah-vaht') **кровать** — bed

(ah-dee-yah'-lah) **одеяло** — blanket

(pah-doosh'-kah) **подушка** — pillow

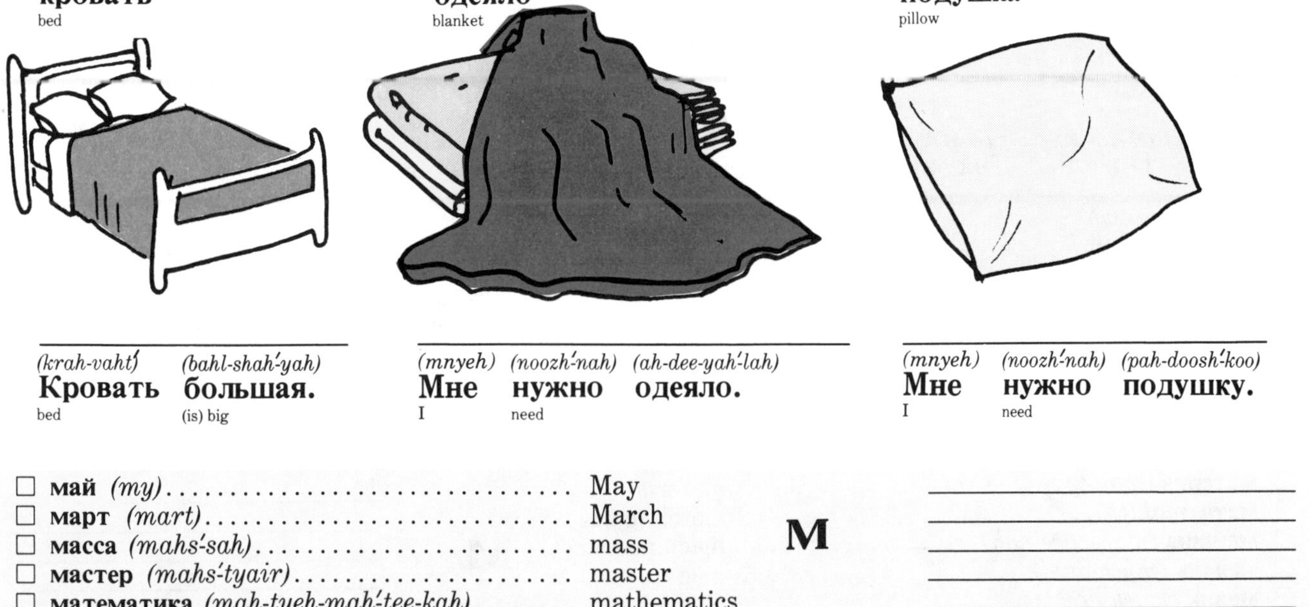

(krah-vaht') **Кровать** (bed) (bahl-shah'-yah) **большая** (is big).

(mnyeh) **Мне** (I) (noozh'-nah) **нужно** (need) (ah-dee-yah'-lah) **одеяло.**

(mnyeh) **Мне** (I) (noozh'-nah) **нужно** (need) (pah-doosh'-koo) **подушку.**

М

- ☐ **май** *(my)* .... May
- ☐ **март** *(mart)* .... March
- ☐ **масса** *(mahs'-sah)* .... mass
- ☐ **мастер** *(mahs'-tyair)* .... master
- ☐ **математика** *(mah-tyeh-mah'-tee-kah)* .... mathematics

(boo-deel′-neek)
будильник
alarm clock

(shkahf)
шкаф
wardrobe

(oo) (men-yah′) (yest)
У меня есть
I have
(boo-deel′-neek)
будильник.

(spahl′-nyeh)
Шкаф в спальне.
bedroom

Теперь, remove the next **пять** *(pyaht)* stickers **и** label these things **в** *(vuh)* your **спальне.** *(spahl′-nyeh)*

(spahl′-nyah) *(gah-stee′-nee-tseh)*
Спальня в гостинице
hotel

(spaht)
спать = to sleep, so a sleeping room.

Study the following **вопросы** *(vah-proh′-sih)* (questions) **и** their **ответы** *(aht-vyeh′-tih)* based **на** *(nah)* (on) **картинке** *(kar-teen′-kyeh)* (picture) to the left.

1. **Где** *(gdyeh)* **будильник?** *(boo-deel′-neek)* (alarm clock)
   Будильник *(boo-deel′-neek)* **на** *(nah)* (on) **столе.** *(stohl-yeh′)* (table)
2. **Где одеяло?** *(ah-dee-yah′-lah)* (blanket)
   Одеяло *(ah-dee-yah′-lah)* **на** *(nah)* **кровати.** *(krah-vah′-tee)* (bed)
3. **Где шкаф?** *(shkahf)*
   Шкаф в *(shkahf)* **спальне.** *(spahl′-nyeh)* (bedroom)
4. **Где подушка?** *(pah-doosh′-kah)* (pillow)
   Подушка *(pah-doosh′-kah)* **на** *(nah)* **кровати.** *(krah-vah′-tee)*
5. **Где кровать?** *(krah-vaht′)* (bed)
   Кровать *(krah-vaht′)* **в спальне.** *(spahl′-nyeh)*
6. **Кровать** *(krah-vaht′)* (bed) **большая** *(bahl-shah′-yah)* (big) **или** *(ee′-lee)* **маленькая?** *(mah′-lyen-kah-yah)* (small)
   Кровать *(krah-vaht′)* **не** *(nyeh)* (not) **большая.** *(bahl-shah′-yah)* (big)
   Кровать маленькая. *(mah′-lyen-kah-yah)* (small)

M

- ☐ **материя** *(mah-tyair′-ee-yah)* .... material ________
- ☐ **матч** *(mahtch)* .... match (game) ________
- ☐ **машина** *(mah-shee′-nah)* .... machine (car) ________
- ☐ **медаль** *(myeh-dahl′)* .... medal ________
- ☐ **медик** *(myeh′-deek)* .... medic ________

Теперь answer **вопросы** *(vah-proh'-sih)* questions based on **картинке** *(kar-teen'-kyeh)* picture on **странице** 54.

Где будильник? *(boo-deel'-neek)*

Где кровать? *(krah-vaht')*

______________________________ ______________________________

Let's move **в** into **ванную** *(vahn'-noo-yoo)* bathroom **и** do the same thing.

умывальник *(oo-mih-vahl'-neek)* washstand

душ *(doosh)* shower

туалет *(too-ahl-yet')* toilet

Зелёный *(zyel-yoh'-nee)* green **умывальник** *(oo-mih-vahl'-neek)* **в номере.** *(nohm'-yair-yeh)* hotel room

Серый *(syeh'-ree)* gray **душ** *(doosh)* **тоже** *(toh'-zheh)* also **в номере.** *(nohm'-yair-yeh)* hotel room

Белый *(byeh'-lee)* white **и зелёный** *(zyel-yoh'-nee)* green **туалет тоже в номере.** *(nohm'-yair-yeh)*

зеркало *(zyair'-kah-lah)* mirror ______________________________

полотенца *(pah-lah-tyen'-tsah)* towels ______________________________

красное *(krahs'-nah-yeh)* **полотенце** ______________________________

коричневое *(kah-reech'-nyeh-vah-yeh)* **полотенце** ______________________________

оранжевое *(ah-rahn'-zheh-vah-yeh)* **полотенце** ______________________________

Не *(nee)* not forget to remove the next **пять** *(pyaht)* stickers **и** label these things in your **ванной.** *(vahn'-noy)* bathroom

- ☐ **медицина** *(myeh-dee-tsee'-nah)* .... medicine
- ☐ **мелодия** *(myeh-loh'-dee-yah)* .... melody
- ☐ **металл** *(myeh-tahl')* .... metal
- ☐ **метод** *(myeh'-tohd)* .... method
- ☐ **метро** *(myeh-troh')* .... metro

М

(vahn'-nah-yah)
Ванная в номере.
bathroom

Study **картинку** и answer **вопросы внизу.**

Где душ?

(doosh) *(ryah'-dahm)*
Душ рядом с ______________________.
next to

(too-ahl-yet') *(myezh'-doo)*
Где туалет? Туалет между ______________________ **и** ______________________.
between

(oo-mih-vahl'-neek) *(ryah'-dahm)*
Где умывальник? Умывальник рядом с ______________________.
washstand

(zyair'-kah-lah) *(nahd)*
Где зеркало? Зеркало над ______________________.
mirror over

(see'-nee-yeh) *(pah-lah-tyen'-tsah)*
Где синие полотенца?
towels

(pah-lah-tyen'-tsah)(nahd) *(nah)*
Полотенца над ______________________. **Полотенца на** ______________________.
over on

Remember, **ванная** *(vah'-nah-yah)* means a **комната** (room) to bathe in. If **вы в ресторане и вам нужно** *(vwee)* (you need) to use the lavatory, **вы** want to ask for **туалет** not for **ванная.**

Restrooms are marked **с** the letters **Д** и **М**. This should be easy to remember as **М** stands for men's, just as it does in English.

(zhen'-skee)
Ж = женский
ladies'
(dahm'-skee)
Д = дамский
ladies'

и **М = мужской.** *(moozh-skoy')*
men's

- ☐ **механик** *(myeh-hah'-neek)*.................. mechanic
- ☐ **микрофон** *(mee-krah-fohn')*................. microphone
- ☐ **миллион** *(meel-lee-ohn')*.................... million
- ☐ **миниатюра** *(mee-nee-ah-tyoo'-rah)*.......... miniature
- ☐ **миссия** *(mees'-see-yah)*.................... mission

М

____
____
____
____
____

Next stop — **кабинет** (kah-bee-nyet) study, specifically **стол** (stohl) desk/table **в кабинете** (kah-bee-nyet-yeh) study. **Что** (shtoh) what **на столе?**

Let's identify things that one normally finds **на столе** or strewn about **дома.**

(kah-rahn-dahsh)
карандаш
pencil

(rooch-kah)
ручка
pen

(boo-mah-gah)
бумага
paper

(pees-moh)
письмо
letter

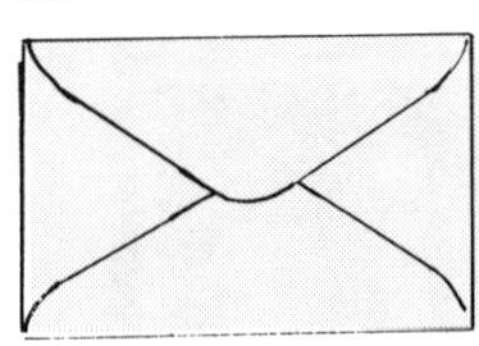

(aht-krit-kah)
открытка
postcard

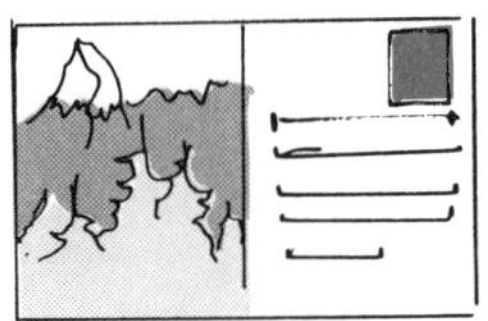

(mar-kah)
марка
stamp

(knee-gah)
книга
book

(zhoor-nahl)
журнал
magazine

(gah-zyeh-tah)
газета
newspaper

(ahch-kee)
очки
eyeglasses

(tee-lee-vee-zar)
телевизор
television

(kar-zee-nah)
корзина
basket

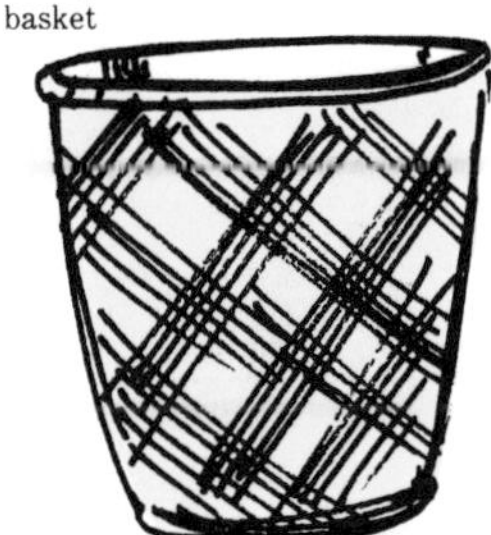

☐ **митинг** *(mee-teeng)* .... meeting
☐ **модель** *(mah-dyel)* .... model
☐ **момент** *(mah-myent)* .... moment
☐ **мотор** *(mah-tor)* .... motor
☐ **муза** *(moo-zah)* .... muse

М

Теперь label these things **в** (kah-bee-nyet'-yeh) **кабинете** with your stickers. Do not forget to say these **слова** out loud whenever **вы** write them, **вы** see them **или вы** apply the stickers. **Теперь** identify the things **на картинке** (vnee-zoo') **внизу** by filling in each blank with the correct **русскими словами.**

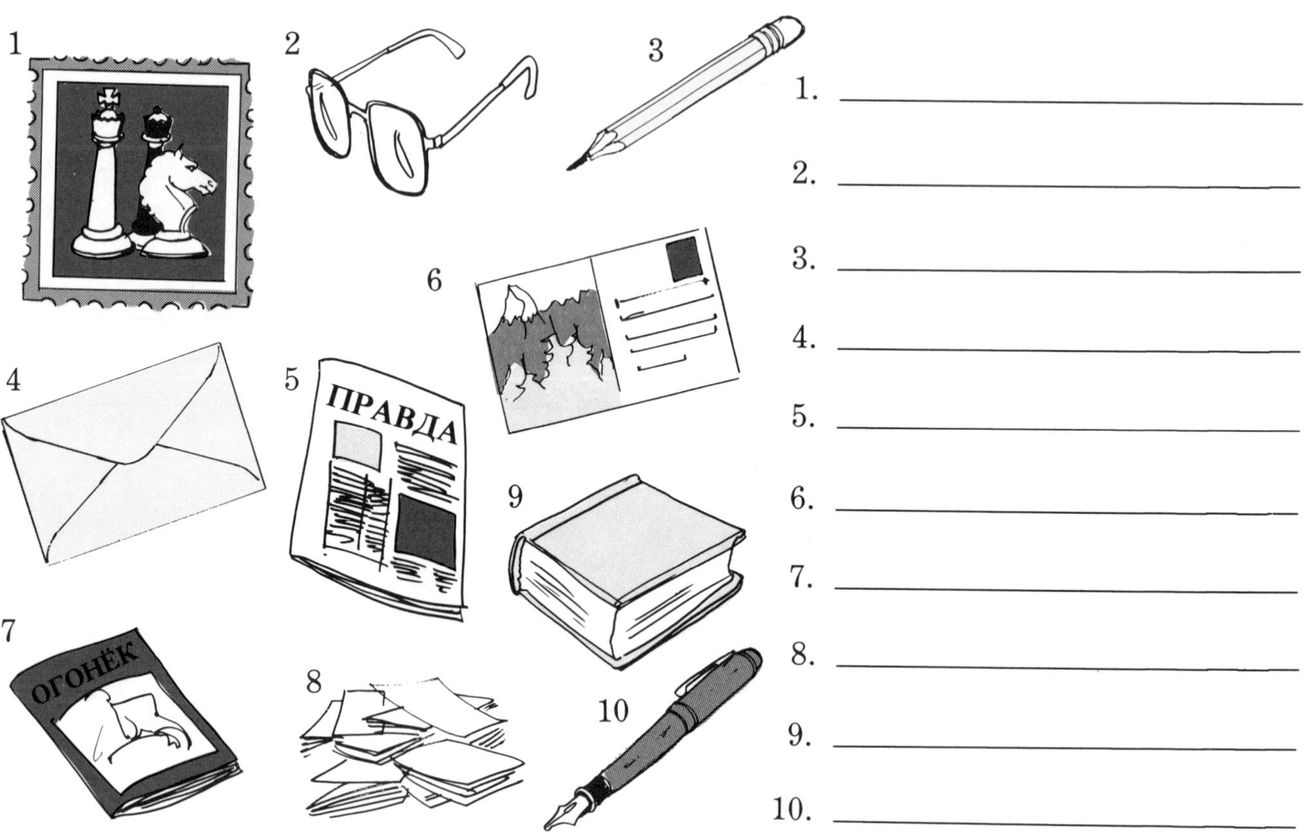

1. ______________________
2. ______________________
3. ______________________
4. ______________________
5. ______________________
6. ______________________
7. ______________________
8. ______________________
9. ______________________
10. ______________________

Вот четыре verbs.

(prah-dah-vaht') **продавать** = to sell (pah-sih-laht') **посылать** = to send (spaht) **спать** = to sleep (zvah-neet') **звонить** = to phone

______________ ______________ ______________ ______________

Теперь fill in the blanks on the next **странице** with the correct form of these verbs. Practice saying the sentences out loud many times. Don't get discouraged! Just look at how much **вы** have already learned **и** think ahead to (eek-rah') **икра,** (caviar) (bahl-yet') **балет и** adventure.

☐ **музей** *(moo-zyay')* .... museum
☐ **музыка** *(moo'-zih-kah)*.................... music
☐ **нация** *(nah'-tsee-yah)* .... nation
☐ **не** *(nee)* .... not, no
☐ **–несерьёзный** *(nee-syair-ohz'-nee)*........ not serious

М

(prah-dah-vaht)
продавать
to sell

Я ~~продаю/~~ *(tsveh-tih)* **цветы.** flowers

Он / Она ~~продаёт/~~ *(frook-tih)* **фрукты.** fruit

Мы ~~продаём/~~ *(beel-yeh-tih)* **билеты.**

Вы ~~продаёте/~~ *(mnoh-gah)* *(beel-yeh-tahv)* **много билетов.** many

Они ~~продают/~~ *(aht-krit-kee)* **открытки.**

(pah-sih-laht)
посылать
to send

Я ~~посылаю/~~ *(pees-moh)* **письмо.** letter

Он / Она ~~посылает/~~ *(aht-krit-koo)* **открытку.**

Мы ~~посылаем/~~ *(knee-goo)* **книгу.**

Вы ~~посылаете/~~ *(cheh-tih-ree)(aht-krit-kee)* **четыре открытки.**

Они ~~посылают/~~ **три** *(pees-mah)* **письма.**

(spaht)
спать
to sleep

Я ~~сплю/~~ **в** *(spahl-nyeh)* **спальне.** bedroom

Он / Она ~~спит/~~ *(krah-vah-tee)* **на кровати.**

Мы ~~спим/~~ **в гостинице.**

Вы ~~спите/~~ **в доме.**

Они ~~спят/~~ *(ah-dee-yah-lahm)* **под одеялом.** under blanket

(zvah-neet)
звонить
to phone

Я ~~звоню/~~ **в России.**

Он / Она ~~звонит/~~ **в** *(shah)* **США.** U.S.A.

Мы ~~звоним/~~ **в Канаду.**

Вы ~~звоните/~~ **в Англию.** England

Они ~~звонят/~~ **во Владивосток.**

The word *(nyeh)* **не** (not) is extremely useful **по-русски.** Add **не** before a verb **и вы** negate the sentence.

я посылаю письмо.	=	I send a letter.
я не посылаю письмо.	=	I do not send a letter.

Simple, isn't it? **Теперь, вы** negate the following sentences.

Я хочу стакан воды. ________________________

Мы звоним в Канаду. ________________________

Я понимаю по-русски. ________________________

Н

- ☐ **нейлон** *(nay-lohn)*........................ nylon ____________
- ☐ **нет!** *(nyet)*............................... no! ____________
- ☐ **никель** *(neek-yehl)*...................... nickel ____________
- ☐ **норма** *(nor-mah)*......................... norm, standard ____________
- ☐ **нос** *(nohs)*............................... nose ____________

Step 15

Теперь (vwee) **вы** know (kahk) **как** to count, **как** to ask (vah-proh'-sih) **вопросы, как** to use verbs **с** the "plug-in" formula, **как** to make statements, **и как** to describe something, be it the location of **гостиница или** (tsvet) **цвет** (color) **дома** (of house). Let's now take the basics that **вы** have learned **и** expand them in special areas that will be most helpful in your travels. What does everyone do on a holiday? Send (aht-krit'-kee) **открытки,** of course! Let's learn exactly **как русское** (poach-toh'-vah-yeh) **почтовое** (post) (aht-dyel-yeh'-nee-yeh) **отделение,** (office) commonly called (poach'-tah) **„почта,"** works.

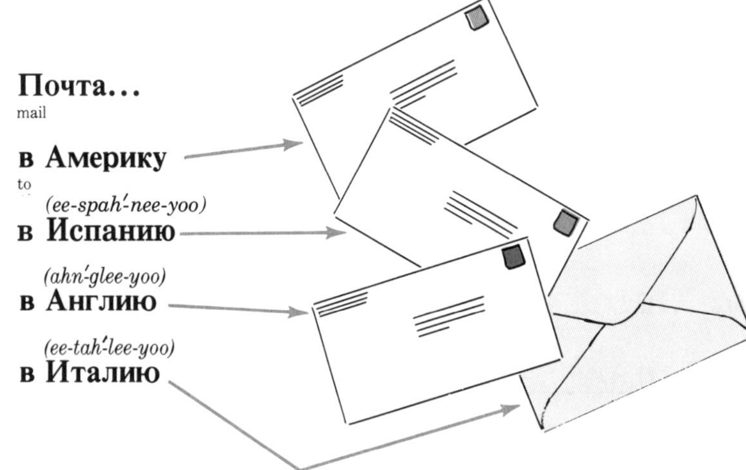

Почта is where **вы** need to go to buy (mar'-kee) **марки и** (kahn-vyair'-tih) **конверты,** (envelopes) mail a package, send a telegram or use **телефон.** (voht) **Вот** (here are) some necessary **слова** (dlyah) **для** (for) (poach'-tih) **почты** (post office). Be sure to practice them out loud **и** (tahg-dah') **тогда** write **слова** (pohd) **под** (under) (kar-teen'-koy) **картинкой.**

(kahn-vyairt') **конверт** — envelope

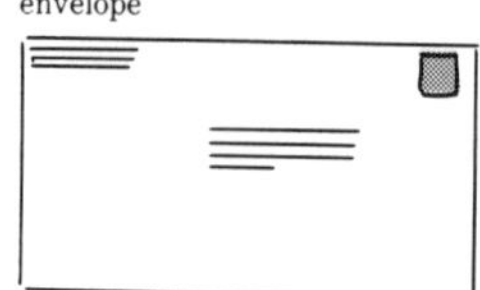

____

(aht-krit'-kah) **открытка** — postcard

____

(mar'-kah) **марка** — stamp

____

(tee-lee-grahm'-mah) **телеграмма**

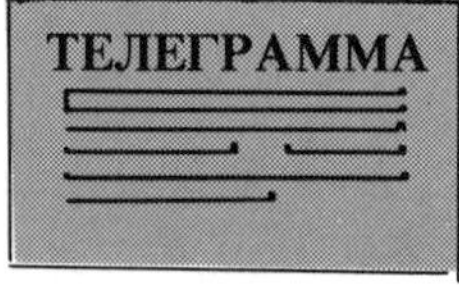

____

- ☐ **Норвегия** *(nar-vyeh'-gee-yah)* .... Norway
- ☐ —where they speak **по-норвежски** *(pah-nar-vyezh'-skee)*
- ☐ **ноябрь** *(nah-yah'-bair)* .... November
- ☐ **октябрь** *(ahk-tyah'-bair)* .... October
- ☐ **олимпиада** *(ah-leem-pee-ah'-dah)* .... Olympics

O

(pah-sil'-kah)
посылка
package

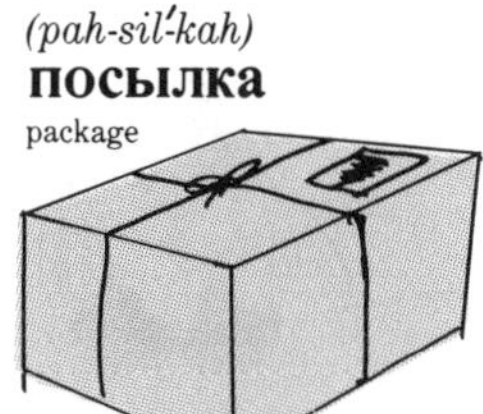

(pahch-toh'-vee) (yahsh'-chik)
почтовый ящик
mailbox

(ah-vee-ah-poach'-toy)
авиапочтой
by airmail

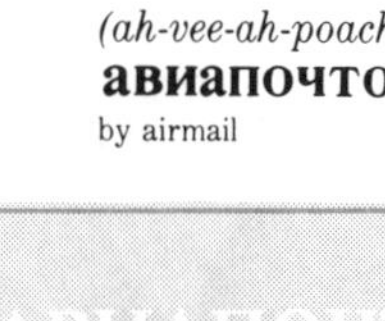

(ahk-noh')
окно
window

(tee-lee-fohn'-ahv-tah-maht')
телефон-автомат
public telephone

(tee-lee-fohn')
телефон
telephone

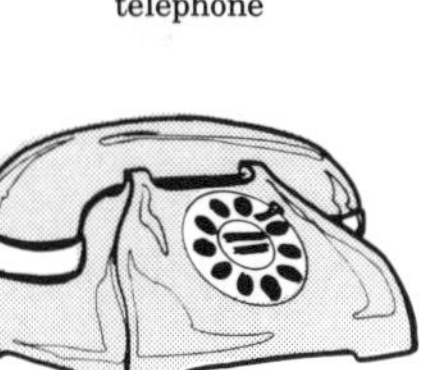

(poach'-tah)
почта
post office

Почта has everything. **Вы** send **посылки** *(pah-sil'-kee)* packages, **письма** *(pees'-mah)* letters **и открытки** *(aht-krit'-kee)* postcards **с** from **почты** *(poach'-tih)*. **Вы** buy **марки на** *(nah)* at **почте.** **Вы** can send **телеграмму** *(tee-lee-grahm'-moo)* telegram **с почты. Почта** is generally **открыта** *(aht-krih'-tah)* open **с** from **9-ти** *(tee)* **часов** *(chah-sohv')* o'clock **утра** *(oo-trah')* morning **до** *(doh)* until **20-ти** *(tee)* **часов вечера** *(vyeh'-cheh-rah)* evening. **По** *(pah)* on **субботам** *(soo-boh'-tahm)* Saturdays **и воскресеньям** *(voh-skree-syen'-yahm)* Sundays, **почта закрыта** *(zah-krih'-tah)* closed. If **вам** *(vahm)* you **нужно** *(noozh'-nah)* need to send **телеграмму** telegram **в США** *(shah)* U.S.A. **или Канаду** *(kah-nah'-doo)*, this can be done **на** at **почте.** Let's go to **почту** *(poach'-too)*. Okay. First step—enter **почту.**

The following is **хороший** *(hah-roh'-shee)* good sample **диалога** *(dee-ah-loh'-gah)* dialogue. Familiarize yourself **с** these **словами** *(slah-vah'-mee)*. Don't wait until your holiday.

☐ **опера** *(oh'-pyair-ih)* .... opera ________________
☐ **органист** *(ar-gah-neest')* .... organist ________________
☐ **оркестр** *(ar-kyes'-ter)* .... orchestra ________________
☐ **офицер** *(ah-fee-tsyair')* .... officer ________________
☐ **официальный** *(ah-fee-tsee-ahl'-nih)* .... official ________________

О

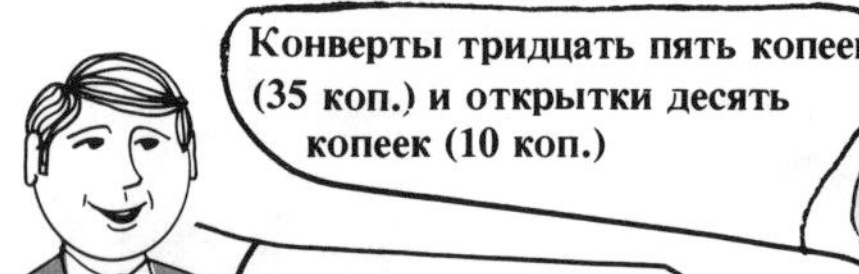

Next step—**вы** ask **вопросы** like those **внизу,** depending on what **вы** *(hah-teet'-yeh)* **хотите** (want).

Где я *(mah-goo')* **могу** *(koo-peet')* **купить** *(mar'-kee)* **марки?** (I can buy)

(mah-goo') *(pah-slaht')* *(tee-lee-grahm'-moo)* **Где я могу послать телеграмму?** (send)

(aht-krit'-koo) **Где я могу купить открытку?**

(pah-sil'-koo) **Где я могу послать посылку?** (package)

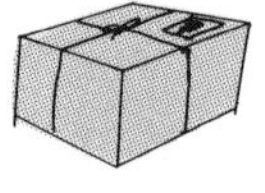

Где телефон?

(zvah-neet') *(shah)* **Где я могу звонить в США?** (phone, U.S.A.)

(pahch-toh'-vee) *(yahsh'-chik)* **Где почтовый ящик?** (mailbox)

(stoy'-eet) **Сколько это стоит?** (costs)

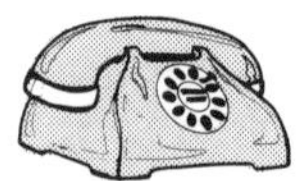

Где телефон-автомат? (public telephone)

(zvah-neet') *(yahl'-too)* **Где я могу звонить в Ялту?** (Yalta)

(pahv-tah-ryaheet'-yeh) **Повторяйте** (repeat) the above sentences many times.

Теперь, quiz yourself. See if **вы** can translate the following thoughts **на русский.**

Ответы are at the bottom of the next **страницы.**

1. Where is a public telephone? ______________________________
2. Where can I phone? ______________________________
3. Where can I phone to the U.S.A.? ______________________________
4. Where can I phone to Moscow? ______________________________
5. Where is the post office? ______________________________

П

- ☐ **павильон** *(pah-veel-yohn')* . . . . pavilion ______________
- ☐ **пакет** *(pah-kyet')* . . . . small package ______________
- ☐ **Пакистан** *(pah-kee-stahn')* . . . . Pakistan ______________
- ☐ **парад** *(pah-rahd')* . . . . parade ______________
- ☐ **парк** *(park)* . . . . park ______________

6. Where can I buy stamps? ____________________

7. Airmail envelopes? ____________________

8. Where can I send a package? ____________________

9. Where can I send a telegram? ____________________

10. Where is window eight? ____________________

(voht)
Вот are more verbs.

(die'-tee) **дайте** = give (me) *(pee-saht')* **писать** = to write *(pah-kah'-zih-vaht)* **показывать** = to show *(plah-teet')* *(zah)* **платить за** = to pay for

__________ __________ __________ __________

(die'-tee)
дайте
give (me)

Дайте мне ______ **пожалуйста,** *(shyoht)* **счёт.** bill

______ **пожалуйста,** *(ah'-dres)* **адрес.** address

______ **пожалуйста,** *(sdah'-choo)* **сдачу.** change

Дайте мне ______ **пожалуйста, меню.**

______ **пожалуйста, билет.**

(pee-saht')
писать
to write

Я пишу/ ______ **письмо.**

Он / Она пишет/ ______ *(mnoh'-gah)* **много.** a lot

Мы пишем/ ______ **телеграмму.**

Вы пишете/ ______ *(ah'-dres)* **адрес.**

Они пишут/ ______ **открытку.**

(pah-kah'-zih-vaht)
показывать
to show

Я показываю/ ______ *(vahm)* **вам** (to you) **книгу.**

Он / Она показывает/ ______ *(mnyeh)* **мне** (to me) **Кремль.**

Мы показываем/ ______ *(vahm)(moo-zyay')* **вам** (to you) **музей.**

Вы показываете/ ______ **мне** (to me) **письмо** (letter).

Они показывают/ ______ **мне почту.**

(plah-teet') *(zah)*
платить за
to pay for

Я плачу за/ ______ *(shyoht)* **счёт** (bill) **в** *(res-tah-rahn'-yeh)* **ресторане** (restaurant).

Он / Она платит за/ ______ **счёт в** *(gah-stee'-nee-tseh)* **гостинице.**

Мы платим за/ ______ *(beel-yeh'-tih)* **билеты** (tickets) **в** *(tee-ah'-ter)* **театр** (theater).

Вы платите за/ ______ **билеты на** *(bahl-yet')* **балет.**

Они платят за/ ______ **билеты на** *(kahn-tsairt')* **концерт** (concert).

ОТВЕТЫ

1. Где телефон-автомат?
2. Где я могу позвонить?
3. Где я могу позвонить в США?
4. Где я могу позвонить в Москву?
5. Где почта?
6. Где я могу купить марки?
7. Конверты авиапочты?
8. Где я могу послать посылку?
9. Где я могу послать телеграмму?
10. Где окно восемь?

Step 16

Как Платить
(kahk) (plah-teet') how to pay

Да, there are also **счета** *(shyee-tah')* [bills] to pay. **Вы** have just finished your delicious dinner **и вы хотите** *(hah-teet'-yeh)* [would like] **счёт** *(shyoht)* [bill]. **Как вы можете** *(moh'-zhet-yeh)* [can] **платить** *(plah-teet')* [pay]? **Вы** call for **официанта** *(ah-fee-tsee-ahn'-tah)* [waiter]: **„Официант!"**

Официант *(ah-fee-tsee-ahnt')* [waiter] will normally reel off what **вы** have eaten, while writing rapidly. **Он** will then place **счёт** *(shyoht)* [bill] **на стол** *(stohl)* that looks something like the one **на картинке,** while saying something like

„Вот [here is] **счёт. Восемь рублей** *(roo-blyay')*, **пожалуйста."**

Вы will pay **официанту** *(ah-fee-tsee-ahn'-too)* **или** perhaps **вы** will pay **кассиру** *(kahs-see'-roo)* [cashier].
Being a seasoned traveler, **вы** know that tipping as **мы** *(mwee)* know it **в США и Канаде нет** *(nyet)* [is not] a custom **в России.** Generally the service is included **в счёте** *(shyoht'-yeh)*.

If **вы** are planning to dine out, **вы** should definitely make reservations. It can be very difficult to get into a popular **ресторан** *(res-tah-rahn')*. Nevertheless, the experience is well worth the trouble **вы** will go to obtain a reservation. **И** remember, **вы** know enough **русский** to make a reservation.

☐ **парламент** *(par-lah'-myent)*............... parliament ________
☐ **партия** *(par'-tee-yah)*..................... party ________
☐ **паспорт** *(pahs'-port)*..................... passport ________
☐ **пассажир** *(pahs-sah-zheer')*............... passenger ________
☐ **позиция** *(pah-zee'-tsee-yah)*............... position ________

П

Remember these key **слова** when dining out.

(myen-yoo') **меню** menu

(shyoht) **счёт** bill

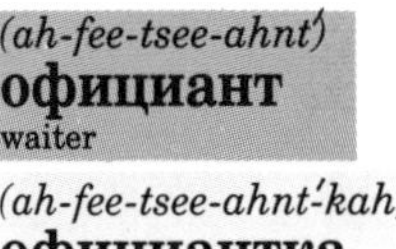

(ah-fee-tsee-ahnt') **официант** waiter

(kvee-tahn'-tsee-yah) **квитанция** receipt

(sdah'-chah) **сдача** change

(ah-fee-tsee-ahnt'-kah) **официантка** waitress

Politeness is **очень** *(oh'-chen)* **важна** *(vahzh'-nah)*. **Вы** will feel more **как** (like) **русский** ((a) Russian) if **вы** practice **и** use these expressions.

(eez-vee-neet'-yeh) **извините** excuse me

(pah-zhah'-loo-stah) **пожалуйста** please/you're welcome

(spah-see'-bah) **спасибо** thank you

Вот a sample conversation involving paying **счёт** *(shyoht)* **когда** leaving **гостиницу.**

(zee'-nah) Зина:	**Извините. Я хочу оплатить** *(ah-plah-teet')* (to pay) **счёт.**
(ahd-mee-nee-strah'-tor) Администратор:	**Номер** *(nohm'-yair)* (number), **пожалуйста** *(pah-zhah'-loo-stah)*?
Зина:	**Номер** *(nohm'-yair)* (number) **триста** *(tree'-stah)* **десять** *(dyes'-yet)*.
Администратор:	**Спасибо. Одну** *(ahd-noo')* **минуту, пожалуйста.**
Администратор:	**Вот счёт. Сорок** *(so'-rahk)* **пять рублей** *(roo-blyay')*, **пожалуйста.**
Зина:	**Спасибо. (И Зина** hands him **пятьдесят рублей. Администратор** returns shortly **и говорит** *(gah-vah-reet')*...)
Администратор:	**Вот ваша** *(vah'-shah)* (your) **квитанция** *(kvee-tahn'-tsee-yah)* (receipt) **и ваша** *(vah'-shah)* (your) **сдача** *(sdah'-chah)* (change). **Спасибо и до** *(doh)* **свидания** *(svee-dah'-nee-yah)* (goodbye).

Simple, right? If **вы** have any problems **с числами** *(chee'-slah-mee)* (numbers), just ask someone to write out **числа** *(chee'-slah)*, so that **вы** can be sure you understand everything correctly.

Пожалуйста напишите *(nah-pee-sheet'-yeh)* (write out) **числа. Спасибо.**

Let's take a break from **денег** *(dyen'-yeg)* **и,** starting on the next **странице,** learn some **новые** *(noh'-vih-yeh)* fun **слова.**

- ☐ **полиция** *(pah-lee'-tsee-yah)*............... police
- ☐ **Польша** *(pohl'-shah)*..................... Poland
- ☐ **порт** *(port)*.............................. port
- ☐ **портрет** *(part-ryet')*...................... portrait
- ☐ **программа** *(prah-grahm'-mah)*........... program

П ______________

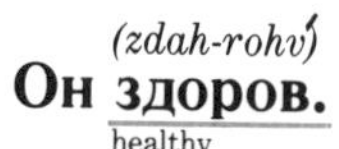

(zdah-rohv)
Он **здоров.**
healthy

(bohl'-yen)
Он **болен.**
sick

(hah-rah-shoh)
Это **хорошо.**
good

(nee)
Это **не хорошо.**
not good

(ploh'-hah)
Это **плохо.**
bad

(vah-dah) (gar-yah'-chah-yah)
Вода горячая -
water hot

(grah'-doo-sahv)
тридцать пять **градусов.**
degrees

(hah-lohd'-nah-yah)
Вода **холодная** -
cold

пять градусов.

(gah-vah-reet'-yeh) (grohm'-kah)
Вы **говорите громко.**
speak loudly

(gah-vah-reet) (tee'-hah)
Он говорит **тихо.**
speaks softly

(lee'-nee-yah) (kah-roht'-kah-yah)
Красная линия **короткая.**
line short

(dleen'-nah-yah)
Синяя линия **длинная.**
long

(zhen'-shchee-nah) (vwee-soh'-kah-yah)
Женщина высокая.
woman tall

(ryeb-yoh'-nahk) (mah'-lyen-kee)
Ребёнок маленький.
child small/short

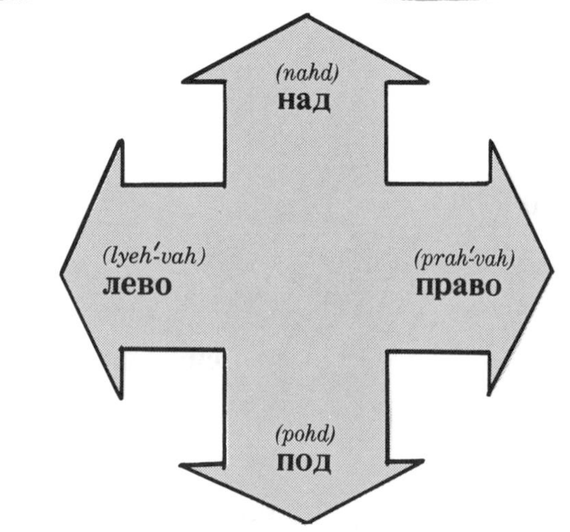

(tohl'-stah-yah)
Красная книга **толстая.**
thick

(tohn'-kah-yah)
Зелёная книга **тонкая.**
green thin

(kee-lah-myeh'-trahv) (f') (chahs)
20 километров в час

(myed'-lyen-nah)
медленно
slow

200 километров в час

(bis'-trah)
быстро
fast

- ☐ **прогресс** *(prahg-ryes)* . . . . progress
- ☐ **продукт** *(prah-dookt)* . . . . product
- ☐ **проект** *(prah-yekt)* . . . . project
- ☐ **профессия** *(prah-fyes'-see-yah)* . . . . profession
- ☐ **профессор** *(prah-fyes'-sar)* . . . . professor

П

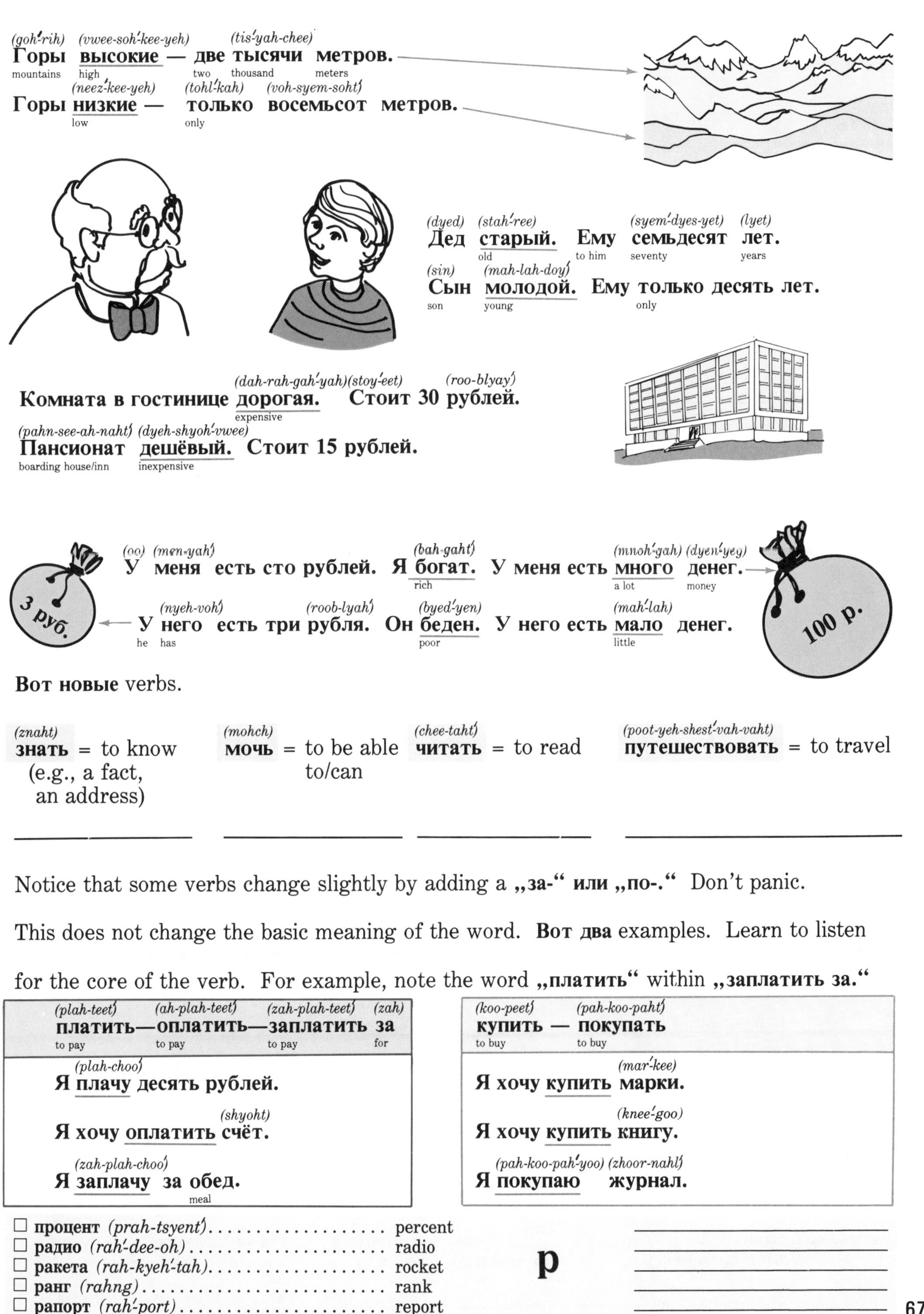

(goh'-rih) *(vwee-soh'-kee-yeh)* *(tis'-yah-chee)*
Горы высокие — две тысячи метров.
mountains high two thousand meters

(neez'-kee-yeh) *(tohl'-kah)* *(voh-syem-soht)*
Горы низкие — только восемьсот метров.
low only

(dyed) *(stah'-ree)* *(syem'-dyes-yet)* *(lyet)*
Дед старый. Ему семьдесят лет.
old to him seventy years

(sin) *(mah-lah-doy)*
Сын молодой. Ему только десять лет.
son young only

(dah-rah-gah'-yah) *(stoy'-eet)* *(roo-blyay)*
Комната в гостинице дорогая. Стоит 30 рублей.
expensive

(pahn-see-ah-naht) *(dyeh-shyoh'-vwee)*
Пансионат дешёвый. Стоит 15 рублей.
boarding house/inn inexpensive

(oo) *(men-yah)* *(bah-gaht)* *(mnoh'-gah)* *(dyen'-yeg)*
У меня есть сто рублей. Я богат. У меня есть много денег.
rich a lot money

(nyeh-voh) *(roob-lyah)* *(byed'-yen)* *(mah'-lah)*
У него есть три рубля. Он беден. У него есть мало денег.
he has poor little

Вот новые verbs.

(znaht) **знать** = to know (e.g., a fact, an address)	*(mohch)* **мочь** = to be able to/can	*(chee-taht)* **читать** = to read	*(poot-yeh-shest'-vah-vaht)* **путешествовать** = to travel
______	______	______	______

Notice that some verbs change slightly by adding a **„за-" или „по-."** Don't panic. This does not change the basic meaning of the word. **Вот два** examples. Learn to listen for the core of the verb. For example, note the word **„платить"** within **„заплатить за."**

(plah-teet) *(ah-plah-teet)* *(zah-plah-teet)* *(zah)*
платить—оплатить—заплатить за
to pay to pay to pay for

(plah-choo)
Я плачу десять рублей.

(shyoht)
Я хочу оплатить счёт.

(zah-plah-choo)
Я заплачу за обед.
meal

(koo-peet) *(pah-koo-paht)*
купить — покупать
to buy to buy

(mar'-kee)
Я хочу купить марки.

(knee'-goo)
Я хочу купить книгу.

(pah-koo-pah'-yoo) *(zhoor-nahl)*
Я покупаю журнал.

р

- ☐ **процент** *(prah-tsyent)* . . . . percent ______
- ☐ **радио** *(rah'-dee-oh)* . . . . radio ______
- ☐ **ракета** *(rah-kyeh'-tah)* . . . . rocket ______
- ☐ **ранг** *(rahng)* . . . . rank ______
- ☐ **рапорт** *(rah'-port)* . . . . report ______

Study the patterns **внизу** closely, as **вы** will use these verbs a lot.

(znaht)
знать
to know

Я знаю/ **всё.** *(vsyoh)* everything

Он / Она знает/ **адрес.** *(ah-dres)* address

Мы знаем/ **как** (how) **говорить** *(gah-vah-reet)* (to speak) **по-русски.**

Вы знаете/ **название** *(nahz-vah-nee-yeh)* (name) **гостиницы.**

Они знают/ **название ресторана.** *(res-tah-rah-nah)*

(mohch)
мочь
to be able to/can

Я могу/ **говорить** *(gah-vah-reet)* (speak) **по-русски.**

Он / Она может/ **понимать** *(pah-nee-maht)* (understand) **по-английски.**

Мы можем/ **понимать по-русски.**

Вы можете/ **говорить по-английски.**

Они могут/ **говорить по-русски тоже.** *(toh-zheh)* also

(chee-taht)
читать
to read

Я читаю/ **книгу.**

Он / Она читает/ **журнал.** magazine

Мы читаем/ **меню.**

Вы читаете/ **много.** a lot

Они читают/ **газету.** newspaper

(poot-yeh-shest-vah-vaht)
путешествовать
to travel

Я путешествую/ **в январе.** *(yahn-var-yeh)* January

Он / Она путешествует/ **зимой.** *(zee-moy)* in winter

Мы путешествуем/ **в июле.** *(ee-yool-yeh)* July

Вы путешествуете/ **летом.** *(lyet-ahm)* in summer

Они путешествуют/ **весной.** *(vees-noy)* in spring

Вы можете *(mohzh-yet-yeh)* (can) translate the sentences **внизу на** (into) **русский? Ответы внизу.**

1. I can speak Russian. ______________________
2. They can pay the bill. ______________________
3. He needs to pay the bill. ______________________
4. We know the address. ______________________
5. She knows a lot. ______________________
6. We can read Russian. ______________________

ОТВЕТЫ

1. Я могу говорить по-русски.
2. Они могут оплатить счёт.
3. Ему нужно оплатить счёт.
4. Мы знаем адрес.
5. Она знает много.
6. Мы можем читать по-русски.

Теперь, draw **линию** *(lee'-nee-yoo)* (lines) **между** *(myezh'-doo)* (between) the opposites **внизу.** **Не** forget to say them out loud. Use **эти** *(eh'-tee)* **слова** every day to describe **вещи** *(vesh'-chee)* **в доме** (home), **в школе** *(shkohl'-yeh)* (school), at work, etc.

(vwee-soh'-kah-yah) **высокая**
(lyeh'-vah) **лево**
(mah-lah-doy') **молодой**
(byed'-yen) **беден**
(zdah-rohv') **здоров**
(dleen'-nah-yah) **длинная**
(mnoh'-gah) **много**
(hah-rah-shoh') **хорошо**
(tohl'-stah-yah) **толстая**
(vwee-soh'-kee-yeh) **высокие**
(gar-yah'-chah-yah) **горячая**
(pohd) **под**
(myed'-lyen-nah) **медленно**
(dah-rah-gah'-yah) **дорогая**
(tee'-hah) **тихо**

(nahd) **над**
(neez'-kee-yeh) **низкие**
(kah-roht'-kah-yah) **короткая**
(grohm'-kah) **громко**
(tohn'-kah-yah) **тонкая**
(dyeh-shyoh'-vwee) **дешёвый**
(mah'-lah) **мало**
(bohl'-yen) **болен**
(stah'-ree) **старый**
(bis'-trah) **быстро**
(prah'-vah) **право**
(hah-lohd'-nah-yah) **холодная**
(bah-gaht') **богат**
(ploh'-hah) **плохо**
(mah'-lyen-kee) **маленький**

Теперь вы знаете что (that) **„большой“** means "large" **по-русски.** Haven't **вы** heard of the world famous **„Большой Театр“?** In addition to being one of the world's foremost ballet companies, it is also **старейший** *(star-yeh'-shee)* (oldest) **московский театр.** It is a must to see **когда вы** are **в Москве.** If **вы** travel **в Петербург** (Petersburg), **тогда** (then) visit **театр оперы** *(oh'-pyair-ih)* ((of) opera) **и балета**, formerly called **Кировский театр,** now known by its prerevolutionary name, **Мариинский** *(mah-ree'-een-skee)* **театр.**

- ☐ **револьвер** *(ryeh-vahl-vyair')* .... revolver
- ☐ **революция** *(ryeh-vahl-yoo'-tsee-yah)* .... revolution
- ☐ **регистрация** *(ryeh-geest-rah'-tsee-yah)* ...... registration
- ☐ **рекорд** *(ryeh-kord')* .... record
- ☐ **религия** *(ree-lee'-gee-yah)* .... religion

р

____
____
____
____
____

Step 17

(poot-yeh-shest'-vah-vaht)
Путешествовать
to travel

(vchee-rah') *(peh-ter-boor'-geh)*
Вчера в Петербурге!
yesterday

(see-vohd'-nyah) *(nohv'-gah-rahd-yeh)*
Сегодня в Новгороде!
today

(zahv'-trah) *(smahl-yensk'-yeh)*
Завтра в Смоленске!

If you know a few key **слова,** traveling can be easy, clean **и** **очень** *(oh'-chen)* (very) efficient. **Россия** *(rahs-sih'-yah)* (Russia) is 6,000 miles wide, which is equivalent to the distance **между** *(myezh'-doo)* (between) California **и** France, **и** it has **одиннадцать** *(ah-deen'-nud-tset)* time zones. This can make traveling a major undertaking.

Иван едет *(yed'-yet)* **на машине.**
Ivan goes

Борис летит *(lee-teet')* **на самолёте** *(sah-mahl-yoht'-yeh)*.
flies, airplane

Ирина *(ee-ree-nah)* **едет на мотоцикле** *(mah-tah-tseek'-lyeh)*.
motorcycle

Нина едет на поезде *(poh'-yezd-yeh)*.
train

Зина едет на метро *(myeh-troh')*.
subway

Виктор *(veek'-tor)* **едет на автобусе.**

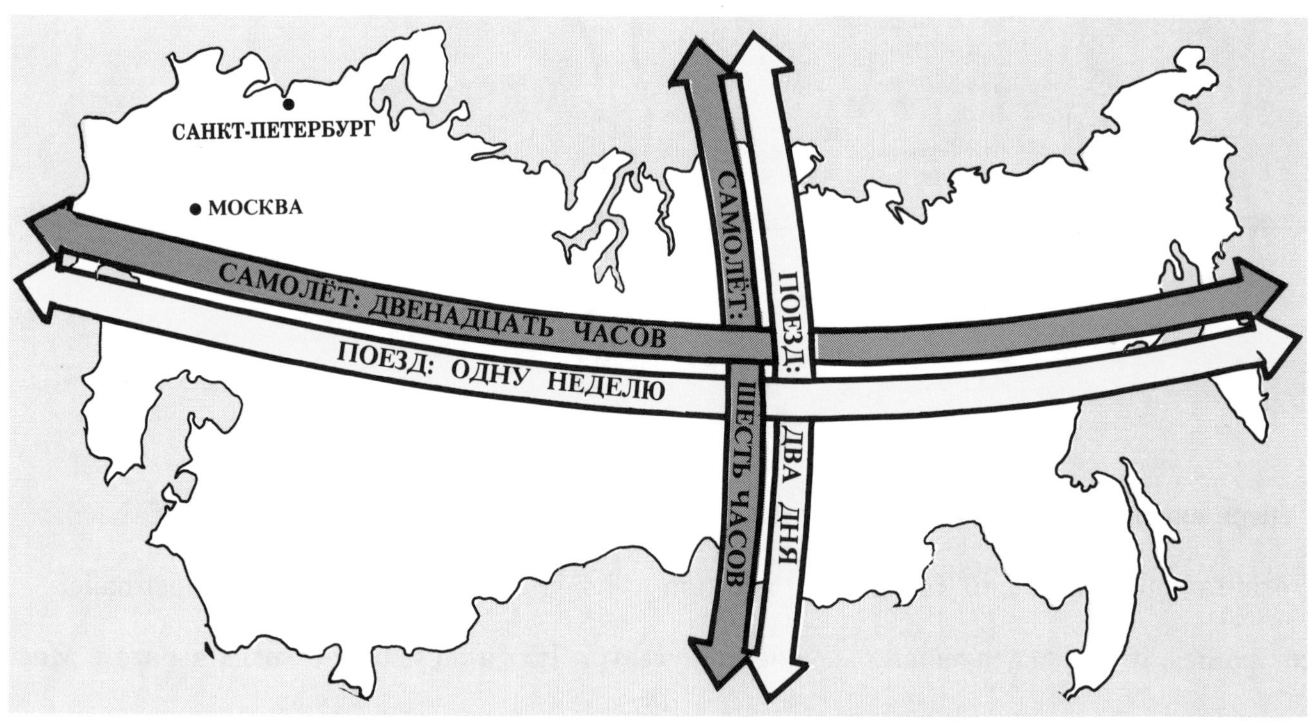

Вы (do you) **видите** *(vee'-deet-yeh)* (see) **карту** (map) **наверху?** *(nah-vyair-hoo')* **Ехать** *(yek'-haht)* (to go) **с** (from) **севера** *(syev'-yair-ah)* (north) **на** (to) **юг,** *(yoog)* (south) **занимает** *(zah-nee-mah'-yet)* (it takes) **шесть часов на самолёте, и два дня** *(dnyah)* (days) **на поезде. Это не плохо** (bad).

☐ **салат** *(sah-laht')* .... salad
☐ **самовар** *(sah-mah-var')* .... samovar
☐ **сезон** *(syeh-zone')* .... season
☐ **секунда** *(syek-oon'-dah)* .... second
☐ **семинар** *(syem-ee-nar')* .... seminar

с

Русские *(loob'yaht)* **любят** [love] *(poot-yeh-shest'-vah-vaht)* **путешествовать,** so **это не** surprise to find **много слов** revolving around the concept of travel, which is exactly what **вы** *(hah-teet'-yeh)* **хотите** [want] to do. Practice saying the following **слова** many times. **Вы** will see them *(chah'-stah)* **часто.** [often]

(pah-yezd'-kah) **поездка** — journey, trip

(poot-yeh-shest'-vah-vaht) **путешествовать** — to travel

(poot-yeh-shest'-vyen-neek) **путешественник** — traveler

(lee-tyet') **лететь на самолёте** — to fly

ехать на машине — to go

ехать на поезде

ехать на автобусе — bus

ехать на мотоцикле

ехать на *(myeh-troh')* **метро** — subway

(eed-tee') **идти** — to walk

(byoo-roh') **бюро** *(poot-yeh-shest'-vee-ee)* **путешествий** — travel agency

(schahst-lee'-vah-vah) **Счастливого** *(poo-tee')* **пути!** — have a good trip

(vnee-zoo') **Внизу** some basic signs which *(vahm)* **вам** *(noozh'-nah)* **нужно** *(znaht)* **знать** [to know]. Most of these **слов** come from the verbs, *(vhah-deet')* **входить** = to enter **и** *(vwee-hah-deet')* **выходить** = to go out/to exit.

(vhohd) **вход** — entrance ______________________

(glahv'-nee) **главный вход** — main entrance ______________________

(vhoh'-dah) **входа нет** — do not enter ______________________

(vwee'-hahd) **выход** — exit ______________________

(zah-pahs-noy') **запасной выход** — emergency exit ______________________

(oht) (syeb-yah') **от себя** — push (doors) ______________________

(k') (syeb-yeh') **к себе** — pull (doors) ______________________

ВХОД

ВЫХОД

ОТ СЕБЯ

К СЕБЕ

с

- ☐ **сигара** *(see-gah'-rah)*........................ cigar ______________
- ☐ **сигарета** *(see-gah-ryet'-ah)*................. cigarette ______________
- ☐ **симфония** *(seem-foh'-nee-yah)*............... symphony ______________
- ☐ **советский** *(sah-vyet'-skee)*.................. Soviet ______________
- ☐ **стадион** *(stah-dee-ohn')*..................... stadium ______________

(yek´-haht) „Ехать" is очень (vahzh´-nee) важный verb (dlyah) для (for) (too-rees´-tah) туриста. If вы choose ехать на машине, вот a few key слов.

(shohs-syeh´) **шоссе** (main road) ______

(dah-roh´-gah) **дорога** (road) **в Петербург** ______

(oo´-lee-tsah) **улица** (street) ______

(mah-shee´-nah)(nah-prah-kaht´) **машина напрокат** (rental car) ______

(byoo-roh´) (prah-kah´-tah) **бюро проката** (car rental agency) ______

(ahv-tah-stahn´-tsee-yah) **автостанция** (service station) ______

Вот четыре очень important opposites.

Санкт-Петербург - Москва		
(aht-hoh´-deet) **Отходит** (departs)	**Поезд No.**	(pree-dyoht´) **Придёт** (arrives)
0:41	50	12:41
7:40	19	19:40
12:15	10	0:15
14:32	4	2:32
21:40	22	9:40

(pree-yezd´) **приезд** (arrival) ______

(aht-prahv-lyeh´-nee-yeh) **отправление** (departure) ______

(ee-nah-strahn´-nee) **иностранный** (foreign) ______

(myest´-nee) **местный** (domestic/internal) ______

Let's learn the basic travel verbs. Follow the same pattern **вы** have in previous steps.

(lee-tyet´) **лететь** = to fly

______

(prah´-veet) **править** = to drive

______

(zah-kah´-zih-vaht) **заказывать** = to reserve/ order

______

(pree-yez-zhaht´) **приезжать** = to arrive

______

(oo-yez-zhaht´) **уезжать** = to leave

______

(dyeh´-laht) **делать** = to make

______

(ah-pahz´-dih-vaht) **опаздывать** = to be late

______

(dyeh´-laht) (pyair-yeh-sahd´-koo) **делать пересадку** = to make a transfer

______

(oo-klah´-dih-vaht) **укладывать** = to pack

______

(pree-hah-deet´) **приходить** = to arrive (trains, buses, ships)

______

(aht-hah-deet´) **отходить** = to depart (trains, buses, ships)

______

Т

- ☐ **старт** *(start)*. . . . . start ______
- ☐ **студент** *(stoo-dyent)*. . . . . student ______
- ☐ **суп** *(soup)*. . . . . soup ______
- ☐ **табак** *(tah-bahk)*. . . . . tobacco ______
- ☐ **такси** *(tahk-see)*. . . . . taxi ______

С these verbs, **вы** are ready for any trip anywhere. **Вы** should have no problem **с** these verbs. Just remember the basic "plug-in" formula **вы** have already learned. Use that knowledge to translate the following thoughts **на русский** (into). **Ответы внизу.**

1. I fly to Russia. ____________________
2. I transfer in Moscow. ____________________
3. He arrives in Yalta. ____________________
4. We leave tomorrow. ____________________
5. We reserve tickets to Kiev. ____________________
6. They drive to Novgorod. ____________________
7. Where is the train to Odessa? ____________________
8. How can I fly to Russia? ____________________

____

Вот some **новые** *(noh´-vih-yeh)* **слова для** *(dlyah)* **поездки** *(pah-yezd´-kee)*. As always, write out **слова и** practice the sample sentences out loud.

(plaht-for´-mah)
платформа
platform

____

Извините. Где платформа номер два?

(vahk-zahl´)
вокзал
train station

____

Извините. Где вокзал?

(air-oh-drohm´)
аэродром
airport

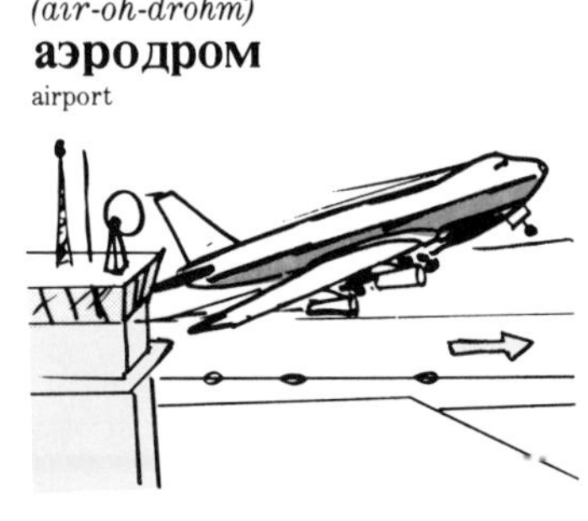

____

Извините. Где аэродром?

ОТВЕТЫ

1. Я лечу в Россию.
2. Я делаю пересадку в Москве.
3. Он приезжает в Ялту.
4. Мы уезжаем завтра.
5. Мы заказываем билеты в Киев.
6. Они правят в Новгород.
7. Где поезд в Одессу?
8. Как я могу лететь в Россию?

(bahnk)
банк
bank

____

Извините. Где банк?

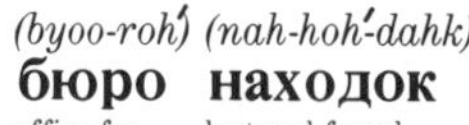

(byoo-roh) (nah-hoh-dahk)
бюро находок
office for lost-and-found

____

Извините. Где бюро находок?

(rah-spee-sah-nee-yeh)
расписание поездов
timetable

Санкт-Петербург - Москва		
(aht-hah-deet) Отходит departs	Поезд No.	*(pree-dyoht)* Придёт arrives
0:41	50	12:41
7:40	19	19:40
12:15	10	0:15
14:32	4	2:32
21:40	22	9:40

____

Извините. Где расписание поездов?

(zahn-yah-tah)
занято ______________________________
occupied
(svah-bohd-nah)
свободно ______________________________
free
(vah-gohn)
вагон ______________________________
compartment/wagon
(myes-tah)
место ______________________________
seat/place

Это место занято? ______________________________

Это место свободно? ______________________________

(vah-gohn) (zahn-yaht)
Этот вагон занят? ______________________________
this

(svah-bohd-yen)
Этот вагон свободен? ______________________________

Practice writing out the following **вопросы.** It will help you **позже** *(pohzh-yeh)* (later).

Извините. Где туалет? ______________________________

(vah-gohn-res-tah-rahn)
Извините. Где вагон-ресторан? ______________________________
dining compartment

(zahl) (ah-zhee-dahn-ee-yah)
Где зал ожидания? ______________________________
waiting room

Где окно номер восемь? ______________________________
window

(mohzh-nah) (koo-reet)
Можно курить? ______________________________
is it possible to smoke

НЕ КУРИТЬ! ______________________________
no smoking

- ☐ **театр** *(tee-ah-ter)* . . . . theater ______________
- ☐ **телевизор** *(tee-lee-vee-zar)* . . . . television ______________
- ☐ **телеграмма** *(tee-lee-grahm-mah)* . . . . . telegram ______________ **Т**
- ☐ **телескоп** *(tee-lee-skope)* . . . . telescope ______________
- ☐ **телефон** *(tee-lee-fohn)* . . . . telephone ______________

Increase your travel **слова** by writing out **слова внизу и** practicing the sample sentences out loud. Practice asking **„где"** questions.

в ______________________ (to)
Где поезд в Москву?

(vreh'-mee-nee) **времени** ______________________ (time)
У меня мало времени.

(poot) **путь** ______________________ (line/route)
Где путь номер семь?

(sprah'-vahch-nah-yeh)(byoo-roh') **справочное бюро** ______________________ (information bureau)
Где...?

(kah'-myair-ah)(hrahn-yen'-ee-yah) **камера хранения** ______________________ (left-luggage office)
Где...?

(tah-mohzh'-nyah) **таможня** ______________________ (customs)
Где таможня?

(nah-seelsh'-cheek) **носильщик** ______________________ (porter)
Где носильщик?

(kahs'-sah) **касса** ______________________ (tickets/cashier)
Где касса?

Practice these **слова** every day. **Вы** will be surprised **как** *(chahs'-tah)* **часто** (often) **вы** will use them.

Вы *(mohzh'-yet-yeh)* **можете** (can) *(prah-chee-taht')* **прочитать** (read) the following paragraph?

> **Вы теперь в** *(aah mahl yoht'ych)* **самолёте и вы** *(lee teet'yeh)* **летите** (fly) **в Россию.** *(oo)(vahs)* **У вас** (you have) **есть** *(dyen'gee)* **деньги** (you do, don't you?), **билеты,** *(pahs'-port)* **паспорт** (passport), *(vee'-zah)* **виза** (visa) **и** *(cheh-mah-dahn')* **чемодан** (suitcases). **Теперь вы** *(too-reest')* **турист. Вы** *(pree-yed'-yet-yeh)* **приедете** (arrive) **завтра в пять часов в Россию.** *(schahst-lee'-vah-vah)* **Счастливого** *(poo-tee')* **пути!**

В России, there are **два** main types of **поезда.** *(pree'-gah-rahd-nee-yeh)* **Пригородные** (suburban) **поезда,** called *(eh-lek-treech'-kee)* **„электрички,"** provide the main transportation from *(pree'-gah-rah-dahv)* **пригородов** (suburbs) to *(tsen'-trah)* **центра** (center) *(goh'-rah-dah)* **города** ((of) city). *(myezh-doo-gah-rohd'-nee-yeh)* **Междугородные** (inter-city/long distance) **поезда** travel longer distances, *(myezh'-doo)* **между** (between) *(gah-rah-dah'-mee)* **городами** (cities). If **вы** *(poot-yeh-shest-voo-yet-yeh)* **путешествуете** (travel) **из Москвы в Петербург, или из Москвы во Владивосток, вы** may want to catch *(skoh'-ree)* **скорый** (express) **поезд** that travels faster **и** makes no intermediate stops.

Some **поезда** have **вагоны-рестораны и** some **поезда** have *(spahl'-nee-yeh)* **спальные** (sleeping) **вагоны** (wagons). All this will be indicated on your *(rah-spee-sah'-nee-yeh)* **расписание** (timetable), but remember **вы** *(znah'-yet-yeh)* **знаете** (know) **как** to ask things like this.

Practice your possible **вопросы** combinations by writing out the following samples.

Где *(spahl'-nee)* **спальный** (sleeping) **вагон** (compartment/wagon)**?** ______________________

Где *(boof-yet')* **буфет** (snack car)**?** ______________________

Т

- ☐ **теннис** *(tyen'-nees)* .... tennis ______________
- ☐ **три** *(tree)* .... three ______________
- ☐ **томат** *(tah-maht')* .... tomato ______________
- ☐ **тост** *(toast)* .... toast ______________
- ☐ **турист** *(too-reest')* .... tourist ______________

What about inquiring about the price of (beel-yet'-tohv) **билетов?** (tickets) **Вы** (mohzh'-yet-yeh) **можете** (can) ask **вопросы.**

(beel-yet') (tahsh-kyent') **Сколько стоит билет в Ташкент?** ____________________

(ahd-nohm') (nah-prahv-lyeh'-nee-ee) **В одном направлении** (one-way) ____________ (too-dah') (ahb-raht'-nah) **туда и обратно** (there and back) ____________

(ah-des'-soo) **Сколько стоит билет в Одессу?** ____________________

(mahsk-voo') **Сколько стоит билет в Москву?** ____________________

(ahb-raht'-nah) **Туда и обратно?** ____________________

What about times of (aht-prahv-lyeh'-nee-yah) **отправления** (departures) **и** (pree-bih'-tee-yah) **прибытия?** (arrivals) **Вы** (toh'-zheh) **тоже можете** ask these **вопросы.**

(kahg-dah') **Когда** (when) **я** (mah-goo') **могу** (can) (yek'-haht) **ехать** (go) **на поезде в** (tahsh-kyent') **Ташкент?** ____________________

Когда я могу (lee-tyet') **лететь на** (sah-mahl-yoht'-yeh) **самолёте в Москву?** ____________________

Когда я могу лететь на самолёте (voh) **во** (vlah-dee-vah-stohk') **Владивосток?** ____________________

Когда (pree-dyoht') **придёт** (arrives) **поезд из** (from) (ree'-gee) **Риги?** (Riga) ____________________

Когда придёт поезд из (bah-koo') **Баку?** (Baku) ____________________

Вы have just arrived. **Вы теперь на** (at) (vahk-zahl'-yeh) **вокзале.** **Вы** (hah-teet'-yeh) **хотите** (want) **ехать** (to go) **в Ташкент?** **В** (kee'-yev) **Киев?** (Kiev) **В Москву?** Well, tell that to the person at **окна** (window) selling **билеты.**

Я (hah-choo') **хочу** (pah-yek'-haht) **поехать в** (nohv'-gah-rahd) **Новгород.** ____________ ____________________

Я хочу поехать в (yahl'-too) **Ялту.** (Yalta) ____________________

Я хочу поехать в (ah-des'-soo) **Одессу.** (Odessa) ____________________

Когда я (mah-goo') **могу ехать на поезде в Одессу?** ____________________

Сколько стоит билет в Одессу? ____________________

Я хочу купить билет в Одессу. ____________________

(ahb-raht'-nah) **Туда и обратно?** ____________________

(mnyeh) **Мне** (I need) (noozh'-nah) **нужно** (sdyeh'-laht) **сделать** (to make) (pyair-yeh-sahd'-koo) **пересадку?** (a transfer) ____________ (spah-see'-bah) **Спасибо.** ____________

С this practice, **вы** are off **и** running. These travel **слова** will make your holiday twice as enjoyable **и** at least three times as easy. Review these **новые слова** by doing the crossword puzzle (nah) **на странице** 77. Practice drilling yourself on this step by selecting other locations **и** asking your own **вопросы** about **поездах,** *(poh-yez-dahk)* **автобусах** *(ahv-toh-boo-sahk)* **или самолётах** *(sah-mahl-yoh-tahk)* that go there. Select **новые слова из** *(eez)* from **словаря** *(slah-var-yah)* dictionary **и** practice asking questions that begin **с**

ГДЕ **КОГДА** **СКОЛЬКО** **КАК ЧАСТО** **или** making statements like

Я хочу поехать в Смоленск.
Я хочу купить билет.

ACROSS

1. to arrive
4. platform
7. station
9. excuse me
12. main road
13. compartment/wagon
14. to eat
15. one
17. thank-you
19. arrival
20. eastern
22. cat
23. customs
25. under
27. fast
29. domestic/internal
30. to order/reserve
32. street
33. bank
34. motorcycle

DOWN

2. restaurant
3. to go/to ride
4. traveler
5. schedule
6. airport
8. or
10. tomorrow
11. over
15. departure
16. left
18. mail/post office
21. to open
24. porter
25. to drink
26. give!
28. taxi
29. menu
31. toilet

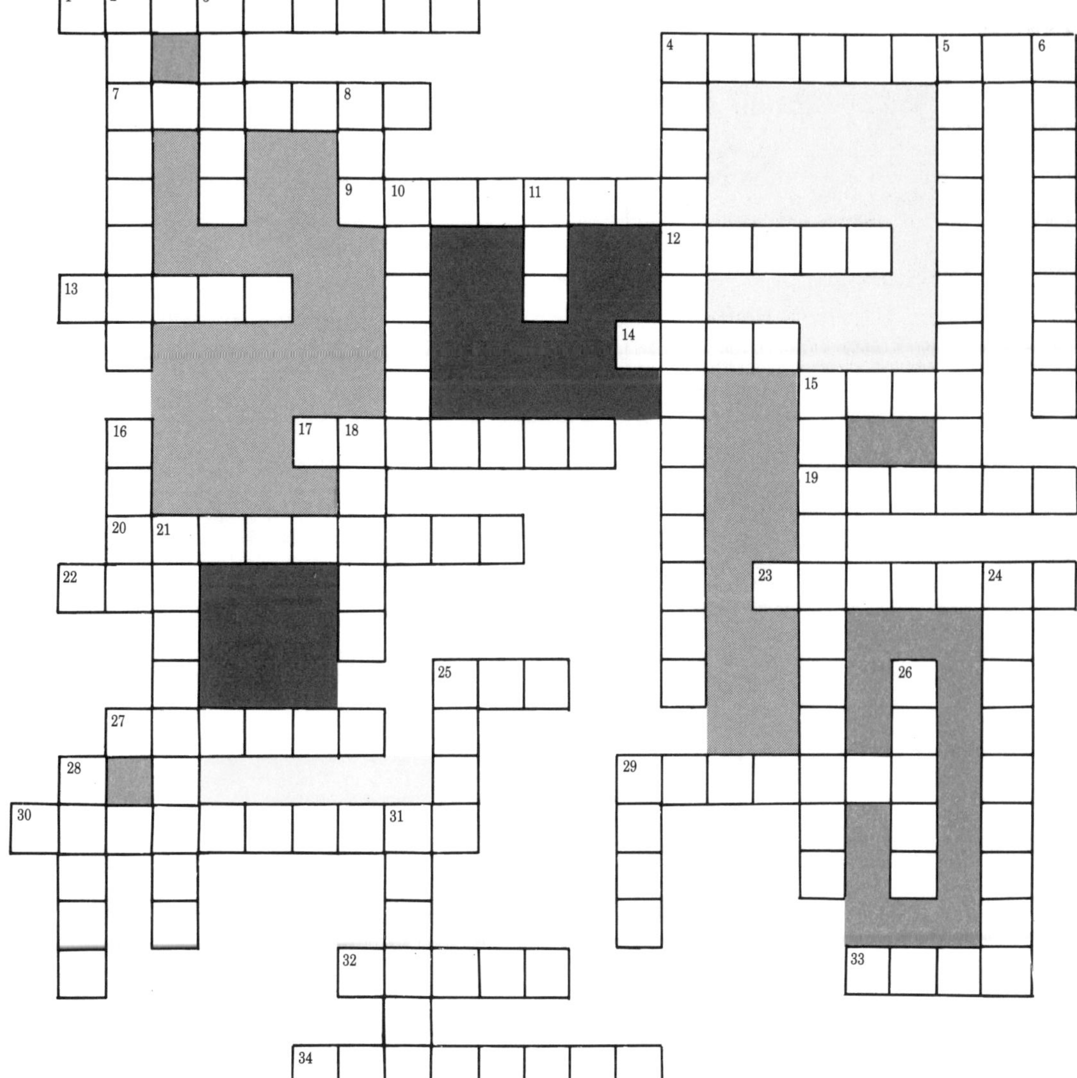

ACROSS

1. приезжать
4. платформа
7. станция
9. извините
12. шоссе
13. вагон
14. есть
15. один
17. спасибо
19. приезд
20. восточный
22. кот
23. таможня
25. под
27. быстро
29. местный
30. заказывать
32. улица
33. банк
34. мотоцикл

DOWN

2. ресторан
3. ехать
4. путешественник
5. расписание
6. аэродром
8. или
10. завтра
11. над
15. отправление
16. лево
18. почта
21. открывать
24. носильщик
25. пить
26. дайте
28. такси
29. меню
31. туалет

Step 18

Вы теперь в России *(oo)* у *(vahs)* вас [you have] есть номер. Вы *(gah-lohd´-nih)* голодны [hungry]. Вы *(hah-teet´-yeh)* хотите *(yest)* есть [to eat]. Где *(hah-roh´-shee)* хороший [good] *(res-tah-rahn´)* **ресторан?** First of all, there are different types of places to eat. Let's learn them.

(res-tah-rahn´) **ресторан**	= the most expensive and fancy of **русских** restaurants—frequently a dinner-and-dance establishment
(stah-loh´-vah-yah) **столовая**	= generally self-service, similar to a cafeteria **или** canteen
(boof-yet´) **буфет**	= a snack bar generally found in **гостиницах,** theaters, *(moo-zyay´-yahk)* **музеях и** stations
(bar) **бар**	= exactly that, a place **где** drinks are served
(kahf-yeh´) **кафе**	= similar to a restaurant serving meals through the evening

There are some **рестораны** whose names are indicative of the foods they serve.

(shahsh-leech´-nah-yah) **шашлычная**	= where they serve *(shahsh-leek´)* **шашлык** (shashlik, kebabs)
(pee-rohzh´-kah-vah-yah) **пирожковая**	= **где** they serve *(pee-rohzh-kee´)* **пирожки** (pastries, small cakes)
(bleen-nah´-yah) **блинная**	= **где** they serve *(blee-nih´)* **блины** (pancakes)
(pyel-myen´-nah-yah) **пельменная**	= **где они** serve *(pyel-myeh´-nee)* **пельмени** (pelmeni, dumplings)
(zah-koo´-sahch-nah-yah) **закусочная**	= **где они** serve *(zah-koo´-skee)* **закуски** (snacks)

Try them all. Experiment. **Теперь вы** have found *(hah-roh´-shee)* **хороший** *(res-tah-rahn´)* **ресторан. Вы** *(vhoh´-deet-yeh)* **входите** [enter] **в ресторан и** *(nah-hoh´-deet-yeh)* **находите** [find] *(myes´-tah)* **место** [seat]. Sharing *(stoh-lih´)* **столы** [tables] **с** others is a common **и** *(oh´-chen)* **очень** [very] pleasant *(ah-bih´-chay)* **обычай** [custom]. If **вы** *(vee´-deet-yeh)* **видите** [see] a vacant *(stool)* **стул** [chair], just be sure to ask

Извините. Это место *(zahn´-yah-tah)* **занято** [occupied]**?**

If *(vahm)* **вам** *(noozh´-nah)* **нужно** [you need] **меню,** catch the attention of *(ah-fee-tsee-ahnt´)* **официант** [waiter] **и** say

Официант! *(die´-teh)* **Дайте мне меню,** *(pah-zhah´-loo-stah)* **пожалуйста.**

- ☐ **февраль** *(fyev-rahl´)* .... February
- ☐ **фильм** *(feelm)* .... film
- ☐ **фотограф** *(fah-toh´-grahf)* .... photographer
- ☐ **Франция** *(frahn´-tsee-yah)* .... France
- ☐ —where they speak **по-французски** *(pah-frahn-tsoo´-skee)*

ф

В России, there are **три** main meals to enjoy every day, plus **кофе** (kohf'-yeh) **и** perhaps pastry **для** (dlyah) for the tired traveler late in **днём** (dnyohm) afternoon.

завтрак (zahv'-trahk)	=	breakfast …	can mean much more than **чай или кофе, хлеб, масло, и** jam. It may include ham **и яйца** (yigh'-tsah) eggs, **сыр** (seer) cheese **или сосиски** (sah-see'-skee) sausages. Check serving times before **вы** retire for the night.
обед (ah-byed')	=	mid-day meal …	generally served from 14:00 to 16:00. For most people, this is the main meal of the day.
ужин (oo'-zheen)	=	evening meal …	generally served from 19:00 to 22:30; frequently, after 22:30, only cold meals are served.

If **вы** look around you **в русском ресторане, вы** will see that some **русские обычаи** (ah-bih'-chah-ee) customs are different from ours. **Хлеб** (hlyeb) bread may be set directly on the tablecloth, elbows are often rested **на** (nah) **столе и** please **не** forget to mop up your **соус** (soh'-oos) sauce **с** your **хлебом** (hlyeh'-bahm). Before beginning your **обед** (ah-byed'), be sure to wish those sharing your table **„Приятного аппетита."** (pree-yaht'-nah-vah) (ahp-peh-tee'-tah) enjoy your meal. If your **официант** asks if **вы** enjoyed your **обед** (ah-byed'), a smile **и** a **„Да, спасибо,"** will tell him that **вы** did.

Теперь, it may be breakfast time at home, **но** (noh) but **вы в России и** it is 20:00. Most **русские рестораны** (res-tah-rah'-nih) post **меню** outside **или** inside. Ask to see **меню** before being seated so **вы знаете** (znah'-yet-yeh) know what type of **обеды** (ah-byeh'-dih) meals **и цены** (tsyeh'-nih) prices **вы** will encounter inside. Most **рестораны** offer a special meal of the day. This is a complete **обед** (ah-byed') meal at a fair **цене** (tsyen-yeh') price. Be forewarned that frequently **не** all items **в меню** are available. So have a second **и** third choice in mind.

In addition, there are the following main categories **в меню.**

- ☐ **фрукт** *(frookt)* .... fruit
- ☐ **футбол** *(foot-bohl')* .... soccer, football
- ☐ **царь** *(tsar)* .... czar, tsar
- ☐ **цирк** *(tseerk)* .... circus
- ☐ **Чили** *(chee'-lee)* .... Chile

Ц ______________

Ч ______________

(zah-koo'-skee) **закуски**	appetizers
(soop) **суп**	soup
(yigh'-tsah) **яйца**	eggs
(rih'-bah) **рыба**	fish dishes
(myah'-sah) **мясо**	meat dishes
(ptee'-tsah) (deech) **птица и дичь**	poultry and game
(oh'-vahsh-chee) **овощи**	vegetables
(sah-laht') **салат**	salad
(dyes-yairt') **десерт**	dessert
(slahd'-kah-yeh) (bloo'-dah) **сладкое блюдо**	sweets
(frook'-tih) (seer) **фрукты или сыр**	fruit or cheese
(pee-rohzh'-nih-yeh) **пирожные**	pastries, small cakes
(nah-peet'-kee) **напитки**	beverages

Most **рестораны** have standard **меню.** Don't expect to get a separate wine list—it is usually printed on **меню.** Service can be slow, so be prepared to wait between courses. **Теперь** for a preview of delights to come . . . At the back of this *(knee'-gee)* **книги, вы** will find a sample **русское меню.** Read **меню** *(see-vohd'-nyah)* **сегодня** (today) **и** learn **новые слова! Когда вы** are ready to leave, cut out **меню,** fold it **и** carry it in your pocket, wallet **или** purse.

- ☐ **шарф** *(sharf)* . . . . scarf
- ☐ **Швеция** *(shveh'-tsee-yah)* . . . . Sweden
- ☐—where they speak **по-шведски** *(pah-shved'-skee)*
- ☐ **штат** *(shtaht)* . . . . state
- ☐ **шторм** *(shtorm)* . . . . storm

Ш

In addition, learning the following should help you to identify what kind of meat **или** poultry **вы** *(hah-teet'-yeh)* **хотите** *(zah-kah'-zih-vaht)* **заказывать** (to order) **и как** it will be prepared.

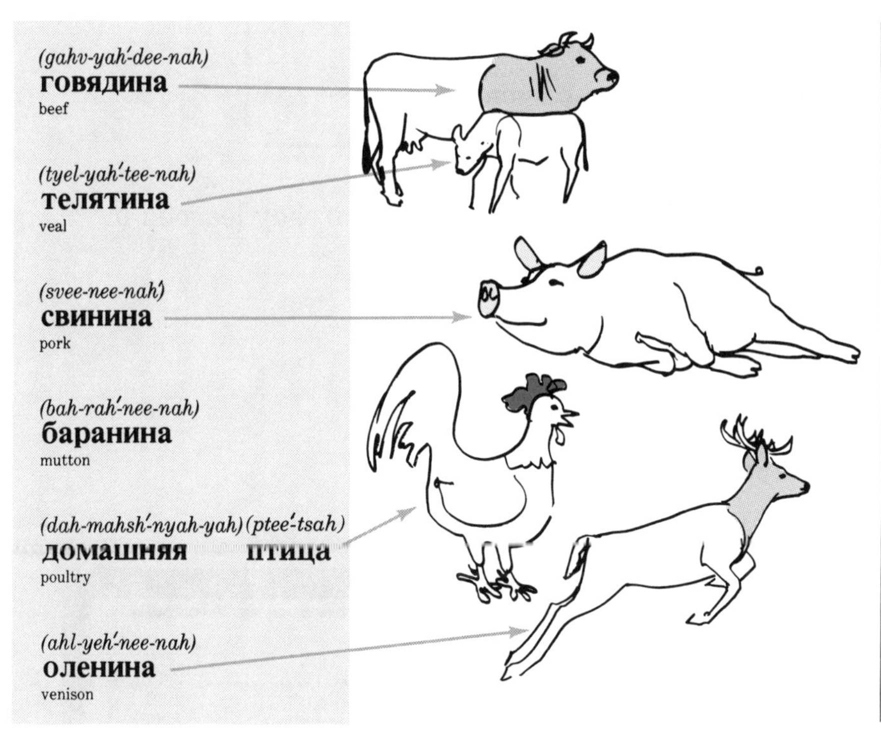

(aht-var-noh'-yeh) **отварное** = boiled

(zhar'-yeh-nah-yeh) **жареное** = roasted/fried

(toosh-yoh'-nah-yeh) **тушёное** = stewed

(zahp-yeh-chyon'-nah-yeh) **запечённое** = baked

(nah-too-rahl'-nee) **натуральный** = grilled

(far-shee-roh'-vahn-nee) **фаршированный** = stuffed

Вы will also get *(oh'-vahsh-chee)* **овощи** (vegetables) with your *(ahb-yeh'-dahm)* **обедом** (meal) **и** perhaps **салат.** One day at an open-air *(rin'-kyeh)* **рынке** (market) will teach you *(nahz-vah'-nee-yah)* **названия** (names) for all the different kinds of *(ah-vahsh-chay')* **овощей и** *(frook'-tahv)* **фруктов,** (fruit) plus it will be a delightful experience for you. **Вы** *(mohzh'-yet-yeh)* **можете** always consult your menu guide at the back of *(knee'-gee)* **книги** if **вы** forget the correct **название. Теперь вы** have decided what **вы** *(hah-teet'-yeh)* **хотите** (want) *(yest)* **есть** (to eat) **и** *(ah-fee-tsee-ahnt')* **официант** arrives.

- ☐ **экватор** *(ek-vah'-tar)*........................ equator
- ☐ **экзамен** *(ek-zah'-myen)*........................ exam
- ☐ **экономика** *(ek-ah-noh'-mee-kah)*............ economics
- ☐ **экспресс** *(ek-spres')*........................ express
- ☐ **эра** *(air'-ah)*........................ era

Э

Не forget to treat yourself to **русским десертом.** You would not want to miss out on trying the following **десерт.**

(kees-yel') **кисель** jello-type dessert	*(mah-roh'-zheh-nah-yeh)* **мороженое** ice cream
(pee-rohg') **пирог** tart	*(roh'-mah-vah-yah) (bah'-bah)* **ромовая баба** cake steeped in rum

After completing your *(ah-byed')* **обед,** call *(ah-fee-tsee-ahn'-tah)* **официанта и** pay just as **вы** have already learned in Step 16:

(die'-teh) *(pah-zhah'-loo-stah)*
Дайте счёт, пожалуйста.

Внизу is a sample **меню** to help you prepare for your holiday.

РЕСТОРАН „МОСКВА"

ОБЕДЕННОЕ МЕНЮ

ХОЛОДНЫЕ ЗАКУСКИ

Икра (caviar)	руб. 5-85
Салат мясной (meat salad)	1-35
Салат с крабами (crab salad)	1-10
Осетрина (sturgeon)	1-10

СУПЫ

Борщ украинскнй (borsch)	-45
Щи (cabbage soup)	-51
Грибной суп (mushroom soup)	-56
Уха (fish soup)	-61

САЛАТЫ

Салат из помидоров (tomato salad)	-52
Салат из огурцов (cucumber salad)	-49
Салат из капусты с яблоками (cabbage-and-apple salad)	-59

ГОРЯЧИЕ БЛЮДА

Бефстроганов (beef Stroganoff)	3-77
Котлеты (chops)	2-60
Судак в белом вине (perch in white wine)	2-85
Осетрина жареная с помидорами (fried sturgeon with tomatoes)	2-91
Курица жареная с грибами (fried chicken with mushrooms)	2-65

СЛАДКИИ БЛЮДА

Компот из свежих абрикос (compote of fresh apricots)	-65
Лимонный мусс (lemon mousse)	-85
Мороженое из ягод (berry ice cream)	-95
Кисель с мороженым (jello with ice cream)	-85

НАПИТКИ

Чай (tea)	-20
Кофе (coffee)	-22
Белое вино (white wine)	-90
Красное вино (red wine)	-90
Пиво (beer)	-85
Молоко (milk)	-50
Лимонад (lemonade)	-45

Ресторан работает с 9 час. до 23 час. 30

- ☐ **эскалатор** *(es-kah-lah'-tor)* .... escalator
- ☐ **январь** *(yahn-var')* .... January
- ☐ **Япония** *(yah-poh'-nee-yah)* .... Japan
- ☐ —where they speak **по-японски** *(pah-yah-pohn'-skee)*
- ☐ **яхта** *(yahk'-tah)* .... yacht

Я

(zahv'-trahk)
Завтрак is a little different because it can vary from a light continental breakfast to a
breakfast

hearty breakfast of eggs **или** cold cuts **или** vegetables. **Внизу** is a sample of what **вы**

(mohzh'-yet-yeh) *(oo'-trahm)*
можете expect to greet you **утром.**
in morning

СТОЛОВАЯ „ОКТЯБРЬСКАЯ“

Доброе Утро!

Яйца

омлет с сыром (cheese) .... -85

взбитая яичница (scrambled eggs) .... -69

яичиница-глазунья (eggs fried) .... -59

Мясо

сосиски (sausages) .... -90

колбаса (cold cuts) .... -89

ветчина жареная (ham fried) .... -93

Напитки

чай с лимоном .... -20

чай с вареньем .... -20

кофе чёрный .... -20

кофе с молоком .... -20

апельсиновый сок (orange juice) .... -30

какао .... -20

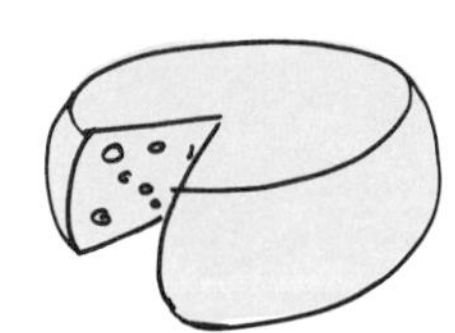

И...

сыр (cheese) .... -35

пирожные .... -28

булочки (rolls) .... -15

масло .... -03

варенье .... -02

блинчики с вареньем .... -85

Вот a few special greetings **по-русски.**

- ☐ **С Рождеством Христовым!** *(rahzh-dyest-vohm' hrees-toh'-vim)* .... Merry Christmas!
- ☐ **С Новым Годом!** *(noh'-vim goh'-dahm)* .... Happy New Year!
- ☐ **С Днём Рождения!** *(dnyohm rahzh-dyeh'-nee-yah)* .... Happy Birthday!
- ☐ **Поздравления!** *(pahz-drahv-lyeh'-nee-yah)* .... Congratulations!

Step 19

What is different about **телефоне** *(tee-lee-fohn'-yeh)* **в России? Вы** never notice such things until **вы** want to use them. Be warned **теперь** that **телефоны** *(tee-lee-foh'-nih)* **в России** are much less numerous than **в США** *(shah)* **или в Канаде.** Nevertheless, **телефон** allows you to call **друзьям,** *(drooz-yahm)* friends, reserve **билеты** *(beel-yeh'-tih)* **в театр,** *(tee-ah'-ter)* **на балет** *(bahl-yet)* **и концерт,** *(kohn-tsairt)* make emergency calls, check on the hours of a **музея,** *(moo-zyeh'-yah)* rent **машину** *(mah-shee'-noo)* car **и** all those other things which **нам** *(nahm)* we need **нужно** *(noozh'-nah)* **сделать** to do on a daily basis. It also gives you a certain amount of freedom **когда вы можете** *(mohzh'-yet-yeh)* **позвонить** *(pahz-vah-neet)* phone on your own.

Having **телефон в гостинице не** as common **в России** as **в США.** That means that **вам** *(vahm)* **нужно** *(noozh'-nah)* **знать** *(znaht)* to know **как** to find **телефон: на почте,** *(poach'-teh)* **на** *(nah)* **улице,** *(oo'-lee-tseh)* street **в баре** *(bar'-yeh)* bar **и** in the lobby of **гостиницы.**

Вот русский телефон-автомат.

So far, so good. **Теперь,** let's read the instructions for using **телефон.** This is one of those moments when you realize,

Я не в США.
Я не в Канаде.
Я не в Англии.

So let's learn how to operate **телефон.**

(een-strook´-tsee-ee)
Инструкции look complicated but actually are not—some of these **слова вы** should be able
instructions

(een-strook´-tsee-ee)
to recognize already. Let's learn the others. **Вот как инструкции** might go.

ТЕЛЕФОН-АВТОМАТ

1. Pick up the receiver.
2. Drop **две копейки** into the slot.
3. Wait for the dial tone **и** dial **номер.**

These are free telephone calls:

Бесплатно Вызываются

(pah-zhar´-nah-yah) (ah-hrah´-nah) **Пожарная охрана** fire **01**	**Скорая помощь** emergency medical help **03**
(mee-lee´-tsee-yah) **Милиция** police **02**	**Служба газа** heating gas service **04**

(ahn-glee´-skee) **Английский**		*(roos´-skee)* **Русский**	*(ahn-glee´-skee)* **Английский**		*(roos´-skee)* **Русский**
telephone	=	*(tee-lee-fohn´)* **телефон**	public telephone booth	=	**телефон-автомат**
to telephone	=	*(pahz-vah-neet´)* **позвонить**	telephone book	=	*(tee-lee-fohn´-nah-yah)* **телефонная книга**
operator	=	*(tee-lee-fah-neest´)* **телефонист**	telephone conversation	=	*(rahz-gah-vor´)* **разговор по телефону**

Вы не можете звонить other cities from **телефон-автомат.** To call another city
can

(poach'-too)
вам нужно идти на почту или звонить телефонисту из гостиницы.
you need to go operator

На почте tell **телефонисту „Мне нужно позвонить в США.“** Do not be surprised if **вы** have to pay for your call in advance. Sometimes it is even necessary to order your call a day in advance.

When answering **телефон, вы** pick up (troob'-koo) **трубку** (receiver) **и** say, (ahl-loh') **Алло. Это** ______________________. (your name)

When saying goodbye, you say **„До свидания“** or **„До завтра.“** (until tomorrow) (voht) **Вот** some sample (dee-ah-loh'-gee) **диалоги** (dialogues) (tee-lee-foh'-noo) **по телефону.** Write them in the blanks **внизу.**

(yah) **Я** (pahz-vah-neet') **хочу позвонить** (to call) **в** (mahs-kohv'-skee) **Московский** (Moscow) (oo-nee-vyair-see-tyet') **Университет.** (university) ______________________

(hah-choo') **Я хочу позвонить** (to call) **в** (chee-kah'-goh) **Чикаго.** (Chicago) ______________________

Я хочу позвонить (bah-ree'-soo) **Борису** (Boris) **в** (nohv'-gah-rahd) **Новгород.** (Novgorod) ______________________

Я хочу позвонить (eh-lyen'-yeh) **Елене в** (bah-koo') **Баку.** (Baku) ______________________

Я хочу позвонить в (air-oh-floht') **Аэрофлот в** (air-ah-port') **Аэропорт.** ______________________

Я хочу позвонить в (lohn'-dahn) **Лондон.** ______________________

Где телефон-автомат? (public telephone) ______________________

Где телефонная книга? (book) ______________________

(moy) **Мой** (my) (nohm'-yair) **номер 344-21-89.** ______________________

(vahsh) **Ваш** (your) **номер** (number) **телефона** (telephone)**,** (pah-zhah'-loo-stah) **пожалуйста?** ______________________

Номер телефона гостиницы (of hotel) (ahk-tyah'-ber-skah-yah) **„Октябрьская,“ пожалуйста?** ______________________

Вот another possible **диалог.** Pay close attention to **слова и как** they are used.

(ee-vahn') **Иван:**	**Алло. Это Иван Иванович** *(ee-vah'-nah-veech)*. **Я хочу поговорить** *(pah-gah-vah-reet')* (to speak) **с Анной** *(ahn'-noy)* **Петровной.**
(syek-ryair-tar') **Секретарь:**	**Одну** (one) **минуту, пожалуйста. Извините, но линия** *(lee'-nee-yah)* (line) **занята** *(zahn-yah-tah')* (busy).
Иван:	**Повторите** *(pahv-tah-reet'-yeh)* (repeat), **пожалуйста. Я мало** *(mah'-lah)* (a little) **говорю по-русски.**
	Говорите (speak) **медленно** *(myed'-lyen-nah)* (slowly).
Секретарь:	**Извините, но линия занята.**
Иван:	**Ох. Спасибо. До свидания.**

И still another possibility...

(kaht'-yah) **Катя:**	**Мне нужен** *(noozh'-yen)* **номер телефона доктора Петровича** *(pee-troh'-vee-chah)* **в Иркутске, пожалуйста.**
(tee-lee-fah-neest') **Телефонист:**	**Номер** *(nohm'-yair)* **254-43-96.**
Катя:	**Повторите номер, пожалуйста.**
Телефонист:	**Номер 254-43-96.**
Катя:	**Большое спасибо. До свидания.**
Телефонист:	**Пожалуйста. До свидания.**

Вы теперь ready to use any **телефон в России.** Just take it **медленно** *(myed'-lyen-nah)* (slowly) **и** speak clearly.

Не forget that **вы можете** *(mohzh'-yet-yeh)* (can) ask...

Сколько *(skohl'-kah)* **стоит** *(stoy'-eet)* **позвонить** *(pahz-vah-neet')* (to call) **в Ригу** *(ree'-goo)* (Riga)?

____

Сколько стоит позвонить в США *(shah)* (U.S.A.)?

____

Сколько стоит позвонить в Киев *(kee'-yev)* (Kiev)?

____

Сколько стоит позвонить в Англию?

____

Remember that **вам** *(vahm)* (you need) **нужна** *(noozh-nah')* **мелочь** *(myeh'-lahch)* (change) **для телефона.**

Step 20

An excellent means of transportation **в России** is **метро** *(myeh-troh)* (subway). Both **в Петербург и в Москве, метро** is an extensive system with express lines to the suburbs. **Трамвай** *(trahm-vy)* (streetcar/trolley) is also a good means of transportation, plus **вы можете** see your surroundings **на трамвае** *(trahm-vah-yeh)*. **Какие** *(kah-kee-yeh)* (what kind of) **слова** (words) **нужны** *(noozh-nih)* (necessary) **для** a traveler **на** (on) **метро** *(myeh-troh)* (subway), **на автобусе, на трамвае** *(trahm-vah-yeh)* **или в такси?**

Let's learn them by practicing them aloud **и** then by writing them in the blanks below.

(myeh-troh) **метро**	*(trahm-vy)* **трамвай**	*(ahv-toh-boos)* **автобус**
метро, метро ______	______	______

(ahs-tah-nohv-kah) **остановка** = stop ______

остановка автобуса *(ahv-toh-boo-sah)* = bus stop ______

(lee-nee-yah) **линия** = line ______

(kahs-sah) **касса** = ticket machine ______

остановка трамвая *(trahm-vah-yah)* = trolley stop ______

(stahn-tsee-yah) **станция метро** = metro station ______

Let's also review the "transportation" verbs at this point. Yes, both **„уезжать"** *(oo-yez-zhaht)* and **„уходить"** *(oo-hah-deet)* can mean "to leave." Don't worry about it, just be aware of it.

(oo-yez-zhaht) **уезжать** = to leave (by vehicle) ______

(oo-hah-deet) **уходить** = to leave (on foot) ______

(pree-yez-zhaht) **приезжать** = to arrive ______

(pree-hah-deet) **приходить** = to arrive ______

Maps displaying the various **линии** *(lee'nee-ee)* lines **и остановки** *(ahs-tah-nohv'kee)* stops are generally posted inside **станции** *(stahn'tsee-ee)* **метро.** Almost every **карта Москвы и Петербурга** has **метро** map included. **Линии** are color-coded to facilitate reading. **Метро в Москве** has over 50 **станций** *(stahn'tsee-ee)* **и** is famous for its elaborate stations with mosaics, chandeliers, paintings **и** sculptures. To enter **метро, вам нужно** to drop a token into the turnstile at **входа.** entrance Other than having foreign words, the Russian **метро** functions just like **метро в США, в Канаде или в Англии.** Locate your destination, select the correct line **и** hop on board. See **карту внизу.**

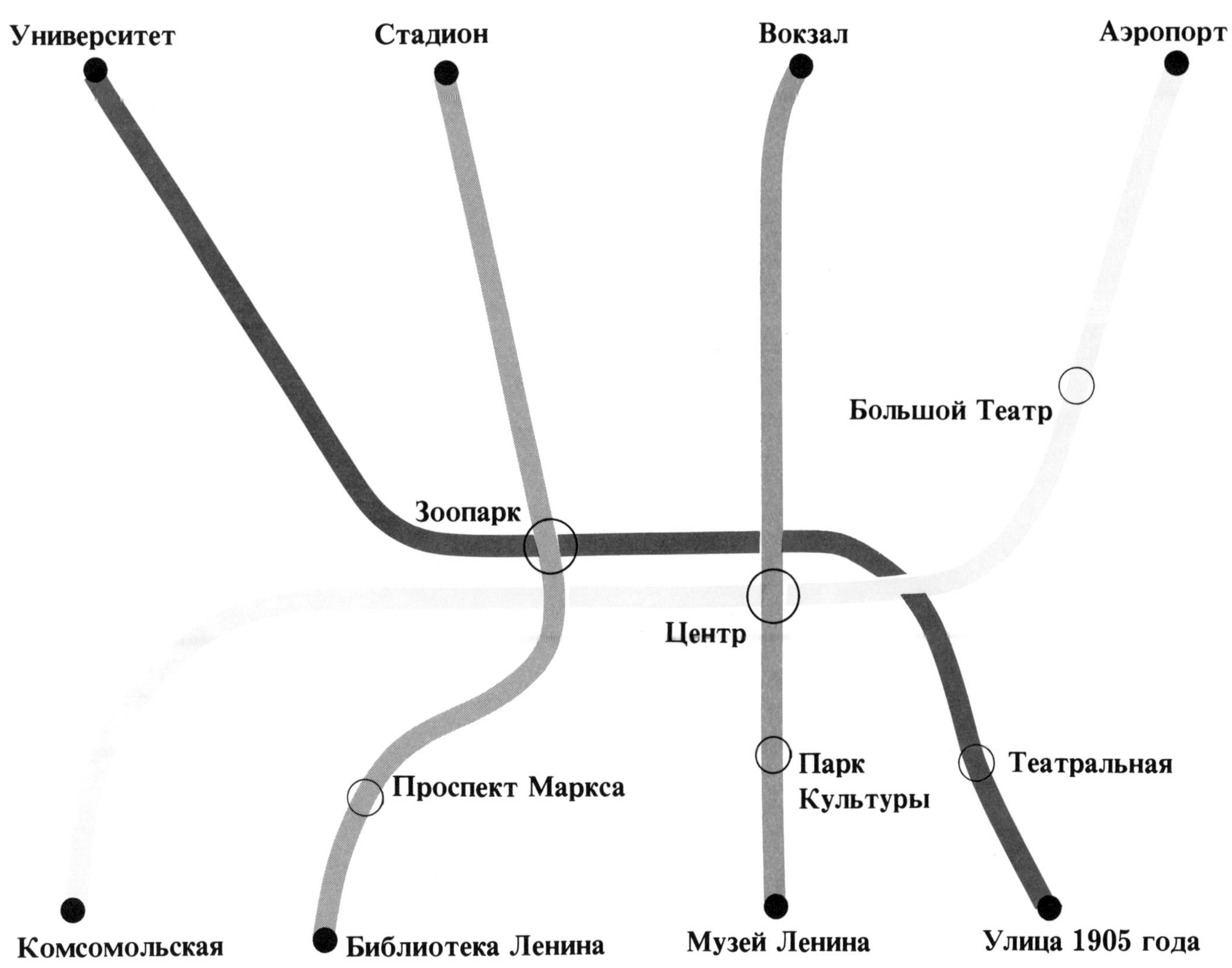

The same basic set of **слова и вопросы** will see you through traveling **на метро, на автобусе, на трамвае, на машине и** even **на поезде.**

Naturally, the first **вопрос** is **„где.“**

Где станция Метро?

(ahs-tah-nohv'-kah)
Где остановка автобуса?

(trahm-vah'-yah)
Где остановка трамвая?

(stah-yahn'-kah)
Где стоянка такси?

Practice the following basic **вопросы** out loud **и** then write them in the blanks below.

1. **Где станция Метро?** ______________________________

   Где остановка автобуса? ______________________________

   Где стоянка такси? ______________________________

2. **Как** (how) **часто** *(chahs'-tah)* (often) **ходит** *(hoh'-deet)* (goes) **автобус номер 36?** ______________________________

   Как часто ходит трамвай *(trahm-vy')* **номер 20?** ______________________________

   Как часто ходит поезд? *(poh'-yezd)* (train) ______________________________

3. **Когда** *(kahg-dah')* **отходит** *(aht-hoh'-deet)* (leaves) **автобус номер восемь?** ______________________________

   Когда отходит трамвай номер три? ______________________________

   Когда отходит поезд в центр? *(tsen'-ter)* (city center) ______________________________

4. **Идёт** *(ee-dyoht')* **автобус до Большого Театра?** ______________________________

   Идёт трамвай до Зоопарка? ______________________________

   Идёт поезд до Гостиницы Метрополь? ______________________________

5. **Сколько стоит билет на Метро?** ______________________________

   Сколько стоит билет на автобус? ______________________________

   Сколько стоит билет на поезд? ______________________________

   Сколько стоит билет на трамвай? ______________________________

Теперь that **вы** have gotten into the swing of things, practice the following patterns aloud substituting **„автобус“** for **„метро“** and so on.

1. Где я могу купить билет на Метро? На автобус? На поезд?
(mah-goo) can; buy

2. Когда отходит поезд в Университет? В Гостиницу Петербург? В Аэропорт? В Зоопарк? В Центр? В Театр? В Музей Ленина?
(aht-hoh'-deet) leaves; (oo-nee-vyair-see-tyet) university; (tsen'-ter) city center

3. Где станция метро „Проспект Маркса"?

Где станция метро „Библиотека Ленина"?

Где остановка автобуса номер 17?
(ahs-tah-nohv'-kah)

Где остановка трамвая номер 11?

Где станция метро „Университет"?

Где станция метро „Аэропорт"?

Где остановка автобуса восемь?

Где станция метро „Вокзал"?

Read the following very typical conversation **и** write it in the blanks **направо.**

Которая линия для университета? ____________________
(kah-toh'-rah-yah) which; (dlyah)(oo-nee-vyair-see-tyeh'-tah)

Красная линия до университета. ____________________
(krahs'-nah-yah) red

Как часто? ____________________
how; (chahs'-tah) often

Каждые пять минут. ____________________
(kahzh'-dih-yeh) every

Мне нужно сделать пересадку? ____________________
do I; (noozh'-nah) need; (sdyeh'-laht) to make; (pyair-yeh-sahd'-koo) transfer

Да, у зоопарка вам нужно сделать пересадку. ____________________
(vahm) you; need; (sdyeh'-laht) (pyair-yeh-sahd'-koo)

Сколько времени занимает до университета? ____________________
(skohl'-kah) how much; (vreh'-mee-nee) time; takes

Двадцать минут. ____________________

Сколько стоит билет до университета? ____________________

Пять копеек. ____________________
(kah-pyeh'-eek)

Вы можете translate the following thoughts **на русский? Ответы внизу.**

1. Where is the subway station? ______
2. What does a ticket cost to the university? ______
3. How often does the bus go to the airport? ______
4. Where can I buy a ticket for the subway? ______
5. Where is the bus stop? ______
6. Where is the exit? ______
7. Do I need to transfer? ______
8. Where do I need to transfer? ______

Here are **три** more verbs.

(stee-raht)
стирать = to wash/clean (clothes)

(tyair-yaht)
терять = to lose

(zah-nee-mah-yet)
занимает = it takes

______ ______ ______

Вы знаете the basic "plug-in" formula, so translate the following thoughts **с** these new verbs. **Ответы тоже внизу.**

1. I wash the jacket. ______
2. You wash the clothes. ______
3. It takes 20 minutes to the Kremlin. ______
4. By car it takes three hours to Odessa. ______

ОТВЕТЫ

1. **Где станция Метро?**
2. **Сколько стоит билет до университета?**
3. **Как часто ходит автобус в аэропорт?**
4. **Где я могу купить билет на Метро?**
5. **Где остановка автобуса?**
6. **Где выход?**
7. **Мне нужно сделать пересадку?**
8. **Где мне нужно сделать пересадку?**

---

1. **Я стираю жакет.**
2. **Вы стираете одежду.**
3. **Занимает двадцать минут до Кремля.**
4. **На машине занимает три часа до Одессы.**

Продавать (prah-dah-vaht') [to sell] и Покупать (pah-koo-paht') [to buy]

Shopping abroad is exciting. The simple everyday task of buying **литр** (leetr) [liter] **молока** (mah-lah-kah') [milk] **или яблоко** (yah'-blah-kah) [apple] becomes a challenge that **вы** (vwee) should **теперь** be able to meet quickly **и** easily. Of course, **вы** will purchase **сувениры** (soov-yeh-nee'-rih) [souvenirs], **марки и открытки,** but **не** (nee) forget those many other **вещи** (vesh'-chee) [things] ranging from shoelaces to **аспирина** that **вы** might need unexpectedly. **Вы знаете** (znah'-yet-yeh) [do you know] the difference **между** (myezh'-doo) [between] **книжным** (kneezh'-nim) [book] **магазином** (mah-gah-zee'-nahm) [store] **и почтой? Нет.** Let's learn about the different **отделах** (aht-dyeh'-lahk) [shops] **и магазинах** [stores] **в России. Внизу карта** of a section of **Москвы.**

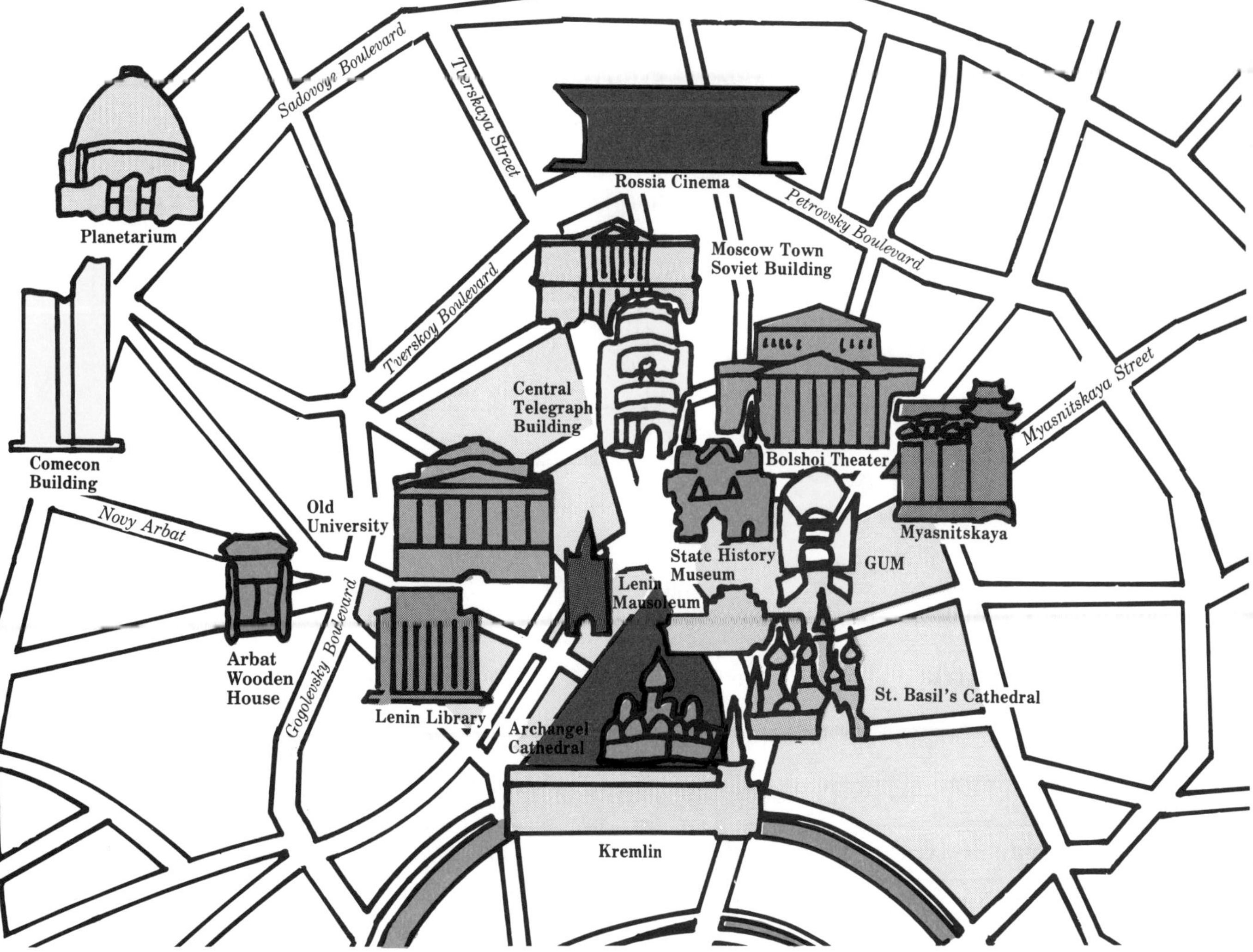

Sadovoye Boulevard
Tverskaya Street
Rossia Cinema
Petrovsky Boulevard
Planetarium
Moscow Town Soviet Building
Tverskoy Boulevard
Central Telegraph Building
Bolshoi Theater
Myasnitskaya Street
Comecon Building
Novy Arbat
Old University
Myasnitskaya
State History Museum
GUM
Lenin Mausoleum
Arbat Wooden House
Gogolevsky Boulevard
St. Basil's Cathedral
Lenin Library
Archangel Cathedral
Kremlin

На [on] the following **странице,** there are all types of **магазинов** (mah-gah-zee'-nof) **вы** might find **в России.** Be sure to fill in the blanks **под** [under] **картинками** (kar-teen'-kah-mee) **с названиями** (nahz-vah'-nee-yah-mee) [names] **магазинов.**

(boo'-lahch-nah-yah)
булочная, **где**
bakery
можно *(koo-peet')* **купить** *(hlyeb)* **хлеб**
one can, buy, bread

(myahs-noy') **мясной** *(mah-gah-zeen')* **магазин, где**
butcher shop
(mohzh'-nah) **можно купить** *(myah'-sah)* **мясо**
meat

(prahch'-yech-nah-yah)
прачечная, **где**
laundry
можно *(stee-raht')* **стирать** *(ah-dyezh'-doo)* **одежду**
wash, clothes

(kahf-yeh')
кафе, где
cafe
можно *(peet)* **пить кофе**
drink

(skahb-yah-noy') **скобяной** *(mah-gah-zeen')* **магазин, где**
hardware store
можно купить *(bah-tar-yeh'-yoo)* **батарею**
battery

(ahp-tyeh'-kah)
аптека, **где**
pharmacy
можно купить *(ahs-pee-reen')* **аспирин**
aspirin

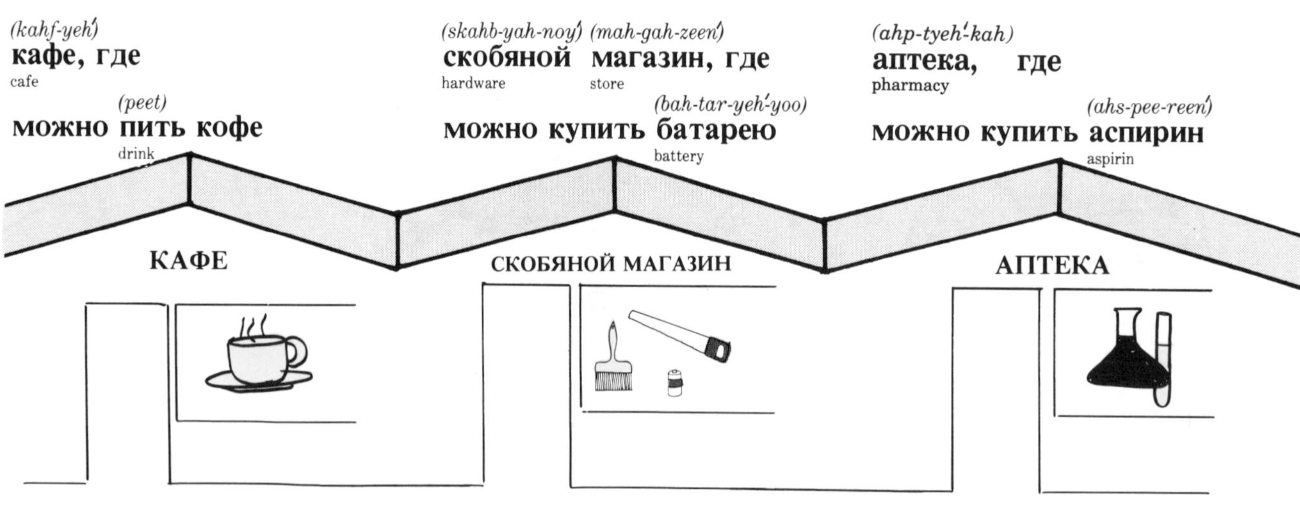

(tsveh-tohch'-nih)
цветочный **магазин,**
flower shop
где можно купить
(tsveh-tih')
цветы

(tah-bahch'-nih)
табачный магазин,
tobacco store
где можно купить
табак и *(see-gar-yeh'-tih)* **сигареты**
cigarettes

(kahn-deet'-yair-skah-yah)
кондитерская, **где**
candy store
можно купить *(kahn-fyeh'-tih)* **конфеты**
candy
(shah-kah-lahd')
и шоколад
chocolate

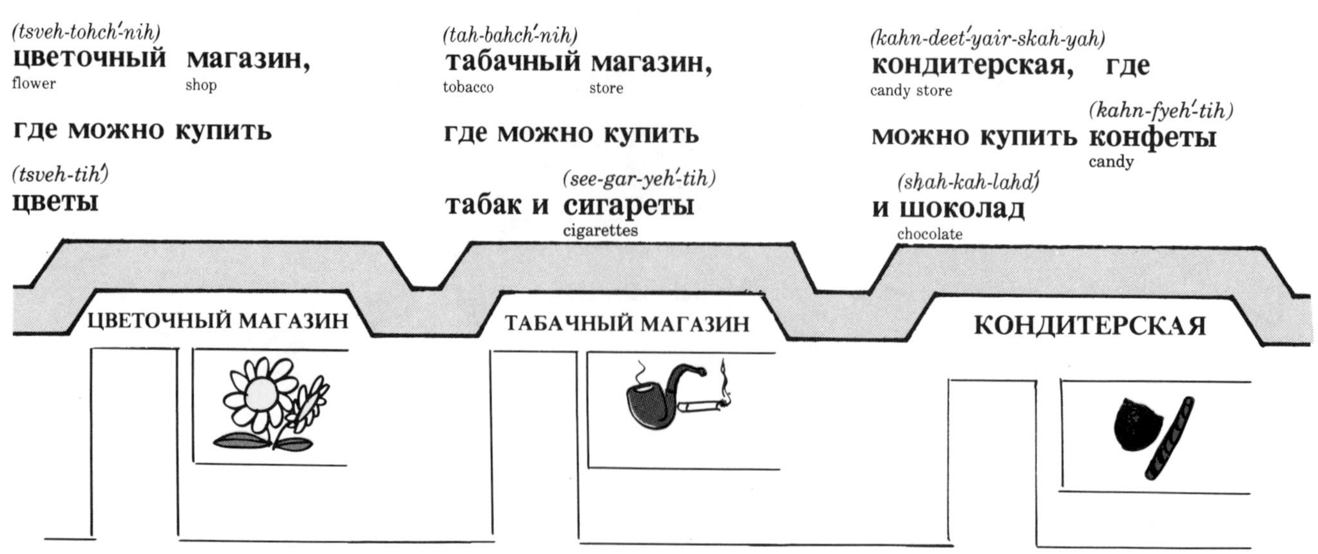

(mah-lohch'-nah-yah)
молочная, где
dairy
(mah-lah-koh')
можно купить молоко
milk

(boo'-lahch-nah-yah)
булочная, где
pastry shop
(mohzh'-nah) *(pryah'-nee-kee)*
можно купить пряники
pastries

(ah-vahsh-chnoy') *(mah-gah-zeen')*
овощной магазин, где
greengrocer's
(oh'-vahsh-chee)
можно купить овощи
vegetables

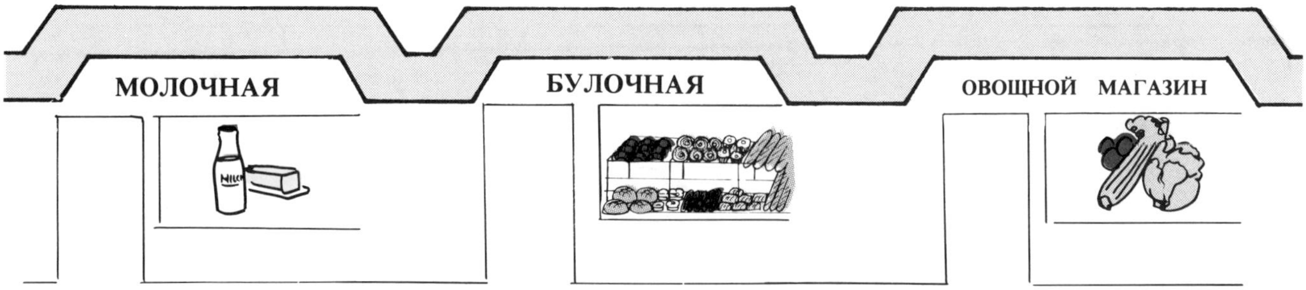

МОЛОЧНАЯ

БУЛОЧНАЯ

ОВОЩНОЙ МАГАЗИН

________________ ________________ ________________

(stah-yahn'-kah)
стоянка, где
parking lot
(stah'-veet)
можно ставить
park/put
(mah-shee'-noo)
машину
car

(pah-reek-mahk'-yairs-kah-yah)
парикмахерская,
hairdresser
(stree-goot')
где стригут
cut
(voh'-lah-sih)
волосы
hair

(ah-tyel-yeh')
ателье, где
tailor
(part-noy') *(shyoht)*
портной шьёт
tailor sews
(ah-dyezh'-doo)
одежду
clothes

СТОЯНКА

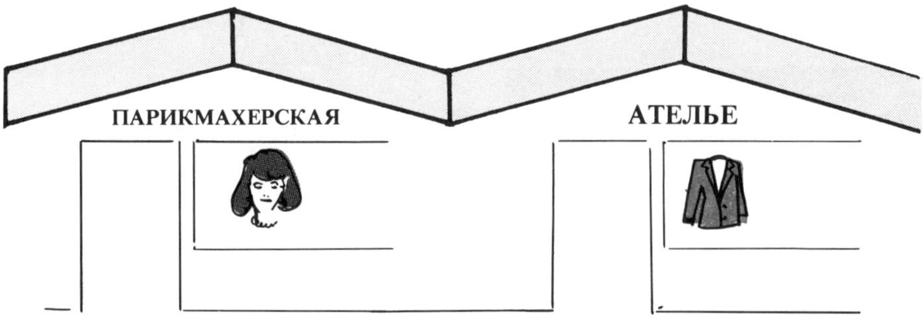

ПАРИКМАХЕРСКАЯ

АТЕЛЬЕ

________________ ________________ ________________

(poach'-tah)
почта, где
post office

можно купить

марки

(aht-dyel-yen'-ee-yeh) *(mee-lee'-tsee-ee)*
отделение милиции,
police station
(ny-tee')
где можно найти
find
(mee-lee'-tsee-yoo)
милицию
police

(bahnk)
банк, где
bank
(ahb-myen-yaht')
можно обменять
exchange
(dyen'-gee)
деньги
money

________________ ________________ ________________

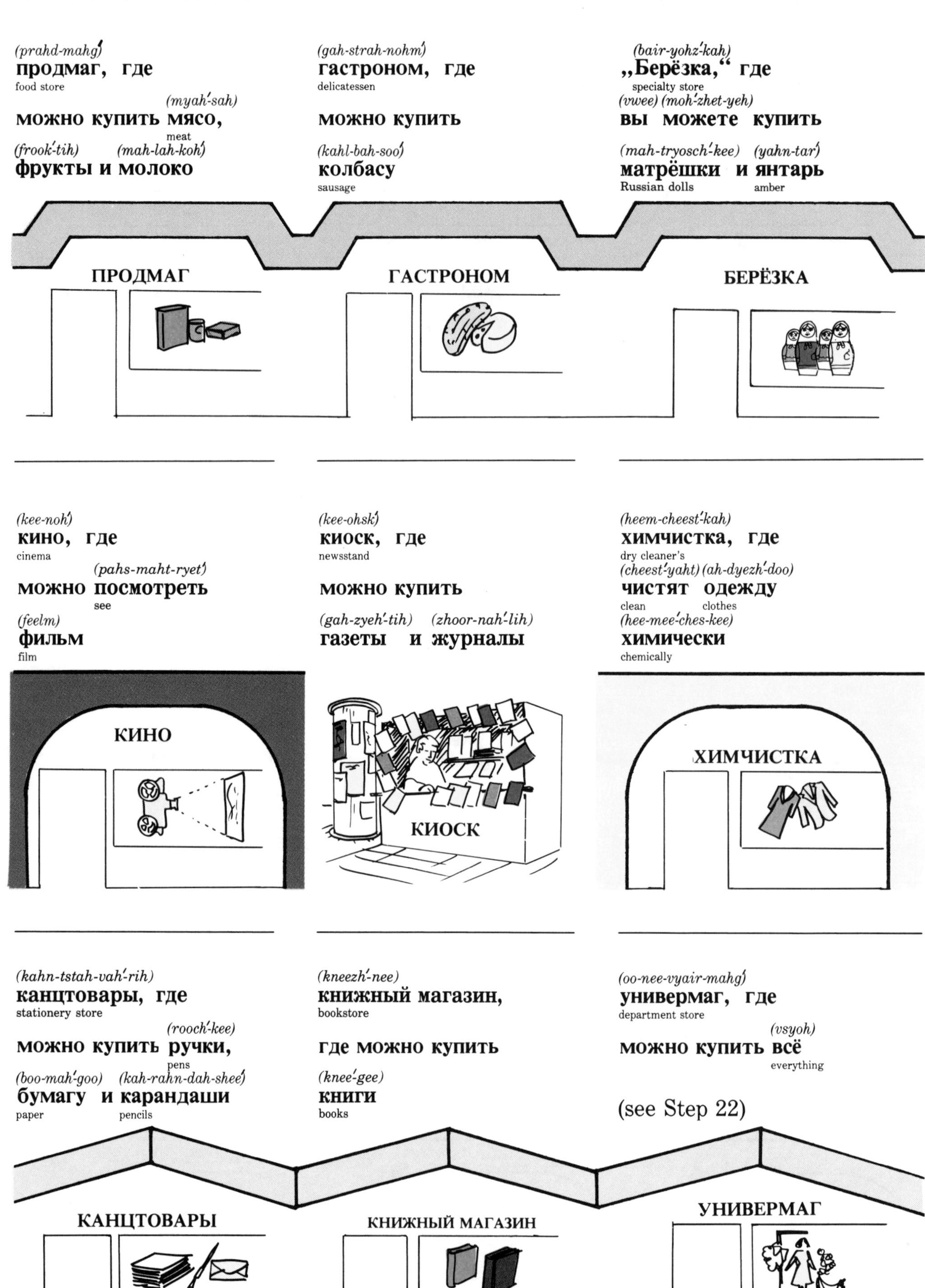

(prahd-mahg)
продмаг, где
food store
(myah-sah)
можно купить мясо,
meat
(frook-tih) (mah-lah-koh)
фрукты и молоко

(gah-strah-nohm)
гастроном, где
delicatessen
можно купить
(kahl-bah-soo)
колбасу
sausage

(bair-yohz-kah)
„Берёзка," где
specialty store
(vwee) (moh-zhet-yeh)
вы можете купить
(mah-tryosch-kee) (yahn-tar)
матрёшки и янтарь
Russian dolls amber

(kee-noh)
кино, где
cinema
(pahs-maht-ryet)
можно посмотреть
see
(feelm)
фильм
film

(kee-ohsk)
киоск, где
newsstand
можно купить
(gah-zyeh-tih) (zhoor-nah-lih)
газеты и журналы

(heem-cheest-kah)
химчистка, где
dry cleaner's
(cheest-yaht) (ah-dyezh-doo)
чистят одежду
clean clothes
(hee-mee-ches-kee)
химически
chemically

(kahn-tstah-vah-rih)
канцтовары, где
stationery store
(rooch-kee)
можно купить ручки,
pens
(boo-mah-goo) (kah-rahn-dah-shee)
бумагу и карандаши
paper pencils

(kneezh-nee)
книжный магазин,
bookstore
где можно купить
(knee-gee)
книги
books

(oo-nee-vyair-mahg)
универмаг, где
department store
(vsyoh)
можно купить всё
everything

(see Step 22)

(rih′-nahk)
рынок, где
market

можно купить

фрукты и овощи

(foh-toh-mah-gah-zeen′)
фотомагазин,
camera supplies

где можно купить

(foh-toh-plyohn′-kee)
фотоплёнки
film

(byen-zah-kah-lohn′-kah)
бензоколонка,
service station

где можно купить

(byen-zeen′)
бензин
gas/petrol

(byoo-roh′) (poot-yeh-shest′-vee)
бюро путешествий
travel agency

где можно купить

(sah-mahl-yoht′)
билеты на самолёт

(chah-sih′)
часы, где

можно купить

часы

(rib′-nee) (rih′-nahk)
рыбный рынок,
fish market

где можно

(rih′-boo)
купить рыбу

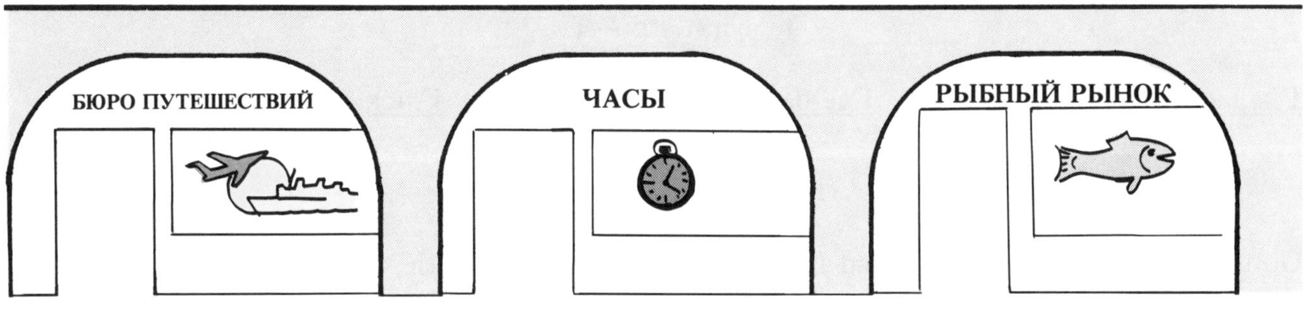

Магазины are generally **открыты** *(aht-krih′-tih)* (open) **с 8-ми до 20-ти часов. Днём** *(dnyohm)* **с 13-ти до 14-ти магазины закрыты** *(zah-krih′-tih)* (closed) for lunch. To make one stop for food, go to a **„гастроном."** *(gah-strah-nohm′)* Within this store **вы** will find many small **отделы** *(aht-dyeh′-lih)* (shops)**: хлебный** *(hlyeb′-nee)*, **кондитерский** *(kahn-deet′-yair-skee)*, **молочный** *(mah-lohch′-nee)*, **мясной** *(myahs-noy′)* **и фруктовый** *(frook-toh′-vee)*. **В гастрономе вы не можете купить овощей. Овощи** are sold **на рынках** (markets)**.**

Is there anything else which **вы** will want to know about Russian stores? **Да.** Look at **картинку на** next **странице.**

(eh-tahzh)
4. **четвёртый этаж**

3. **третий этаж**

2. **второй этаж**

1. **первый этаж**

While **в Москве вы** will probably want to visit **ГУМ,** *(goom)* short for **„Государственный** *(gah-soo-darst'-vyen-nee)* **Универсальный Магазин."** *(oo-nee-vyair-sahl'-nee)* **ГУМ** sells everything **от чемоданов до телевизоров.**

Теперь вы know the names for **русских магазинов,** let's practice shopping.

I. First step—**Где?**

Где молочная? **Где банк?** **Где кино?**

Go through **магазины** introduced in this step **и** ask, **„где"** with each **магазине.**

Где булочная? *(boo'-lahch-nah-yah)* **Где прачечная?** *(prahch'-yech-nah-yah)*

Где кафе? **Где аптека?**

II. Next step—tell them what **вы** are looking for, need **или хотите!**

1) **Мне нужно...** ____________________

2) **У вас есть...?** ____________________
do you have

3) **Я хочу...** ____________________

(kah-rahn-dahsh)
Мне нужно купить карандаш.

(oo) (vahs) (yest)
У вас есть карандаш?
do you have

Я хочу купить карандаш.

(kee-loh) (yah-blahk)
Мне нужно кило яблок.
kilo apples

У вас есть кило яблок?
apples

Я хочу купить кило яблок.

Go through the glossary at the end of **этой** *(this)* **книги и** select **двадцать** *(dvahd-tset)* **слов.** Drill the above patterns **с этими** *(these)* **двадцатью словами.** Don't cheat. Drill them **сегодня** *(see-vohd-nyah)*. **Теперь,** take **двадцать** *(dvahd-tset)* more **слов из** your glossary **и** do the same.

III. Next step—find out сколько *(skohl-kah)* это стоит *(stoy-eet)*.

Сколько это стоит? ______________________________________

Сколько стоит карандаш?

(aht-krit-kah)
Сколько стоит открытка?

Сколько стоит марка?

Сколько стоит карта?
map

Сколько стоит кило яблок?

(ah-pyel-see-nahv)
Сколько стоит кило апельсинов ?
oranges

(myah-sah)
Сколько стоит кило мяса?
meat

(chahsh-kah)
Сколько стоит чашка чая?
cup tea

Using these same **слова** that **вы** selected above, drill **эти** *(these)* **вопросы тоже.**

IV. If вы не знаете *(znah-yet-yeh; know)* где to find something, вы можете спросить *(sprah-seet; ask)*

(mah-goo)
Где я могу купить аспирин?

(ahch-kee)
Где я могу купить очки?

Once **вы** find what **вы** would like, **говорите,** *(gah-vah-reet-yeh; say)*

Я хочу это, пожалуйста.

Или if **вы** would not like it,

Я не хочу этого *(that)*, **спасибо.**

Теперь, вы are all set to shop for anything!

Step 22

(oo-nee-vyair-sahl'-nee) Универсальный *(mah-gah-zeen')* Магазин
department store

At this point, **вы** should just about be ready for your **поездки** (trip). **Вы** have gone shopping for those last-minute odds 'n ends. Most likely, the store directory at your local **универсальный** *(oo-nee-vyair-sahl'-nee)* (department) **магазин** (store) did not look like the one **внизу. Вы** already know **много слов и вы можете** guess at **много** others. **Вы знаете что „женщина“** *(zhen'-shchee-nah)* is Russian for "woman" so if **вам нужно** something for a woman, **вы** would probably look **на втором** *(vtah-rohm')* (second) **этаже,** *(eh-tahzh-yeh')* (floor) wouldn't you?

Этаж			
7. этаж	Булочная Кафе Спиртные напитки	Вино Фрукты Овоши Мясо	Дичь Домашняя птица Мороженая
6. этаж	Кровати Полотно Зеркала	Мебель Лампы Ковры	Картины Электроприборы
5. этаж	Посуда Хрусталь Фарфор	Ножевые изделия Кухонные приборы	Ключи Керамика
4. этаж	Книги Телевизоры Игрушки Радио	Табак Газеты Журналы Ресторан	Детская мебель Музыкальные инструменты Писчебумажный отдел Пластинки
3. этаж	Косметика Бельё Платки	Детский отдел Детские туфли Купальные костюмы	Антикварные вещи Фотографические аппараты
2. этаж	Женская одежда Женские шляпы Женские туфли	Мужская одежда Мужские шляпы Мужские туфли	Носки Пояса Зонтики
1. этаж	Духи Конфеты Часы Перчатки	Кожаные вещи Юверлирные изделия Рабочие инструменты Спортивные принадлежности	Запчасти автомобиля Принадлежности туалета Карты

Let's start a checklist **для поездки** (trip). Besides **одежды** *(ah-dyezh'-dih)*, **что вам нужно?**

(pahs'-port)
паспорт

(beel-yet')
билет

(cheh-mah-dahn')
чемодан

(soom'-kah)
сумка

(boo-mahzh'-neek)
бумажник

(dyen'-gee)
деньги

(foh-toh-ahp-pah-raht')
фотоаппарат

(foh-toh-plyohn'-kah)
фотоплёнка

Take the next **восемь** labels **и** label **эти вещи** *(seh-vohd'-nyah)* **сегодня.** Better yet, assemble them **в углу** of your **дома.**

Вы *(poot-yeh-shest'-voo-yet-yeh)* **путешествуете** *(zee-moy')* **зимой или летом? Не** forget...

(koo-pahl'-nee) *(kahst-yoom')*
купальный костюм
swimsuit

(sahn-dah'-lee-ee)
сандалии
sandals

Не forget the basic toiletries either!

(mwee'-lah)
мыло
soap

(zoob-nah'-yah) *(shchoht'-kah)*
зубная щётка
toothbrush

(zoob-nah'-yah) *(pahs'-tah)*
зубная паста
toothpaste

(breet'-vah)
бритва
razor

(dyeh-zah-dah-rahnt')
дезодорант
deodorant

(gryeb'-yen)
гребень
comb

For the rest of **вещи** let's start with the outside layers **и** work our way in.

(pahl-toh)
пальто ____________________ ☐
overcoat

(plahshch)
плащ ____________________ ☐
raincoat

(zohn-teek)
зонтик ____________________ ☐
umbrella

(pyair-chaht-kee)
перчатки ____________________ ☐
gloves

(shlah-pah)
шляпа ____________________ ☐
hat

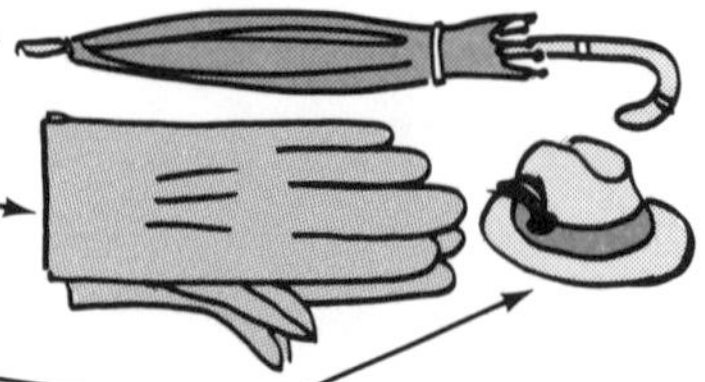

(sah-pah-gee)
сапоги ____________________ ☐
boots

(too-flee)
туфли ____________________ ☐
shoes

(nah-skee)
носки ____________________ ☐
socks

(chool-kee)
чулки ____________________ ☐
stockings

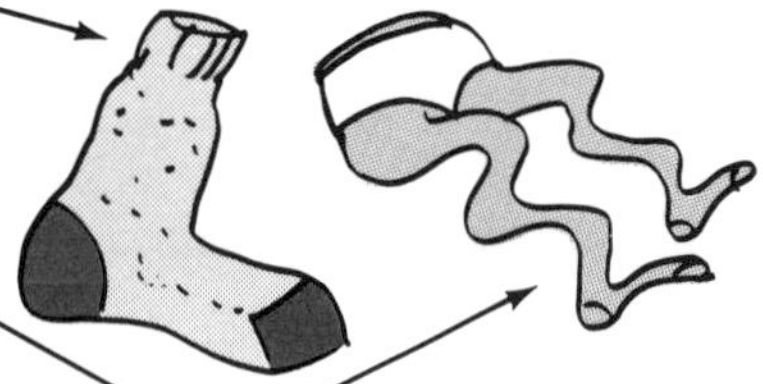

Take the next **семнадцать** labels **и** label **эти** (these) **вещи.** Check **и** make sure that **они** **чистые** *(chees-tih-yeh)* (clean) **и** ready **для** **поездки** *(pah-yezd-kee)* (trip). Be sure to do the same **с** the rest of **вещами** *(vesh-chah-mee)* that **вы** pack. Check them off on this list as **вы** organize them. From now on, **у** *(oo)* (you) **вас** *(vahs)* (have) **„зубная паста"** *(zoob-nah-yah) (pahs-tah)* **и не** "toothpaste."

(pee-zhah-mah)
пижама ____________________ ☐

(nahch-nah-yah)(roo-bahsh-kah)
ночная рубашка ____________________ ☐

(koo-pahl-nee) (hah-laht)
купальный халат ____________________ ☐
bathrobe

(bahsh-mah-kee)
башмаки ____________________ ☐
slippers

(koo-pahl-nee) (hah-laht) (bahsh-mah-kee) (moh-goot) (vahs) (plyah-zheh)
Купальный халат и башмаки могут (can) double **для вас** (you) **на** (at) **пляже.** (beach)

Having assembled **эти вещи, вы** (these) are ready **поехать** (*pah-yek'-haht*, to go). On the following pages, you'll find a Russian-English glossary and an English-Russian glossary. Refer to them when you need help with any unfamiliar words. **Удачи!** (*oo-dah'-chee*) **Счастливого** (*schahst-lee'-vah-vah*) **пути!** (*poo-tee*) (have a good trip)

GLOSSARY

Russian-English

А

абрикос ... apricot
август ... August
авиапочта ... airmail
авиация ... aviation
Австралия ... Australia
автобиография ... autobiography
автобус ... bus
автограф ... autograph
автомат ... automat
автомобиль ... car
автор ... author
автостанция ... service station
агент ... agent
адвокат ... advocate, lawyer
адрес ... address
Азия ... Asia
академия ... academy
аккуратн/ый, -ая, -ое; -ые ... neat
акробат ... acrobat
акт ... act
актёр ... actor
акцент ... accent
алгебра ... algebra
алкоголь ... alcohol
алло ... hello
Америка ... America
американец ... American man
американка ... American woman
Англия ... England
  по-английски ... in English
анекдот ... anecdote, joke
антенна ... antenna
антибиотики ... antibiotics
апельсин ... orange (fruit)
аппетит ... appetite
апрель ... April
аптека ... drugstore
арена ... arena
арест ... arrest
армия ... army
аспирин ... aspirin
астронавт ... astronaut
ателье ... tailor's
атлет ... athlete
аэродром, аэропорт ... airport

Б

бабушка ... grandmother
багаж ... baggage
базар ... bazaar
бал ... ball (dance)
балалайка ... balalaika
балерина ... ballerina
балет ... ballet
балкон ... balcony
банан ... banana
банк ... bank
бар ... bar (restaurant)
баранина ... mutton
баржа ... barge
барьер ... barrier
бас ... bass (voice)
баскетбол ... basketball
батарея ... battery
башмаки ... slippers
беден ... poor
без ... minus, without
бел/ый, -ая, -ое; ые ... white
бензин ... gas/petrol
„Берёзка"
  ... "Beriozka" (hard-currency store)
билет ... ticket
бинокль ... binoculars
бланк ... blank (form)
богат ... rich
бокс ... boxing
болен ... sick
больш/ой, -ая, -ое; -ые ... big, large
больше ... more
бомба ... bomb
борщ ... borsch (beet soup)
брат ... brother
брать ... to take
бритва ... razor
бронза ... bronze
брюнет (-ка) ... brunette
будет ... will be
будильник ... alarm clock
булочная ... bakery, pastry shop
бульвар ... boulevard
бумага ... paper
бумажник ... wallet
был ... was
быстро ... fast
бюро ... bureau, office

В

в ... in
важно ... important
ваза ... vase
вальс ... waltz
вам нужно ... you need
ванная ... bathroom
ваш, ваша, ваше; ваши ... your
веранда ... veranda
весна ... spring
весной ... in spring
ветрено ... windy
вечер ... evening
вещи ... things
видеть ... to see
вилка ... fork
вино ... wine
витамин ... vitamin
внизу ... downstairs, below
вода ... water
водка ... vodka
вокзал ... train station
волейбол ... volleyball
вопрос ... question
восемь ... eight
восемнадцать ... eighteen
восемьдесят ... eighty
восемьсот ... eight hundred
воскресенье ... Sunday
восток ... east
восточн/ый, -ая, -ое; -ые ... eastern
вот ... here is
врач ... doctor
время ... time
  Сколько времени? ... What time is it?
всё ... everything
вторник ... Tuesday
второй этаж ... second floor
вход ... entrance
  входа нет ... do not enter
входить ... to enter
вчера ... yesterday
вы ... you
высок/ий, -ая, -ое; -ие ... high, tall
выход ... exit
выходить ... to go out, to exit

Г

газ ... natural gas
газета ... newspaper
  газетчик ... newspaper man
галерея ... gallery
гараж ... garage
гастроном ... delicatessen, grocery store
где ... where
география ... geography
геология ... geology
  геолог ... geologist
геометрия ... geometry
гид ... guide
гимнастика ... gymnastics
гитара ... guitar
говорить ... to speak, to say
говядина ... beef
год ... year
голоден ... hungry
горы ... mountains
горяч/ий, -ая, -ее; -ие ... hot
гостиная ... living room
гостиница ... hotel, inn
градусы ... degrees
грамм ... gram
гранит ... granite
гребень ... comb
громко ... loudly
группа ... group
гусь ... goose

Д

да ... yes
дайте мне ... give me
дама ... lady, woman
дата ... date
два, две ... two
двадцать ... twenty
двенадцать ... twelve
дверь ... door
девять ... nine
девятнадцать ... nineteen
девяносто ... ninety
дед ... grandfather
дезодорант ... deodorant
декабр ... December
делать ... to do, to make
  я делаю ... I do, I make
делать пересадку
  ... to make a transfer (on bus, subway, etc.)
делегат ... delegate
день ... day
деньги ... money
десять ... ten
  десяти ... ten from
дети, детей ... children
дешёв/ый, -ая, -ое; -ые ... inexpensive
джаз ... jazz
джин ... gin
диагноз ... diagnosis
диаграмма ... diagram, blueprint
диалоги ... dialogues
диван ... divan, couch
дизель ... diesel
диплом ... diploma
дипломат ... diplomat
директор ... director
дискуссия ... discussion
длинн/ый, -ая, -ое; -ые ... long
для ... for
до ... until
доброе утро ... good morning
добрый вечер ... good evening
добрый день .. good day, good afternoon
дождь ... raining
доктор ... doctor
документ ... document
доллар ... dollar
дом ... house
домашняя птица ... poultry
дорога ... road

дорог/ой, -ая, -ое; -ие .... expensive
до свидания.................. goodbye
дочь .... daughter
драма .... drama
друзья........................ friends
душ .... shower
дядя .... uncle

Е

еврей .... Jewish man
еврейка .... Jewish woman
есть .... to eat
ехать............... to go (by vehicle)

Ж

жакет .... woman's jacket
жарен/ый, -ая, -ое; -ые .....roasted, fried
жарко .... hot
ждать .... to wait for
желе .... jelly
женщина .... woman
  женщины .... women
жёлт/ый, -ая, -ое; -ые ....yellow
жить .... to live, to reside
журнал .... magazine

З

за .... behind
завтра .... tomorrow
завтрак...................... breakfast
заказывать......... to order, to reserve
закрыто .... closed
занавес .... curtain
занят, -а, -о; -ы .... busy
запад.......................... west
  западн/ый, -ая, -ое; -ые .... western
запеченн/ый, -ая, -ое; -ые .... baked
звонок........................ doorbell
здесь .... here
здоров .... healthy
здравствуйте .... hello
зелён/ый, -ая, -ое; -ые .... green
зеркало .... mirror
зима.......................... winter
зимой .... in winter
знать .... to know
зовут .... is called
  меня зовут ....I am called/my name is
зона........................... zone
зонтик .... umbrella
зоопарк.......................... zoo
зубная паста .... toothpaste
зубная щётка............... toothbrush

И

и .... and
идти .... to go (on foot)
  я иду .... I go
  он/она идёт.............he/she goes
из..................... out of, from
извините .... excuse me
изучать.......................to learn
  я изучаю .... I learn
икра.......................... caviar
или.............................. or
импортн/ый, -ая, -ое; -ые ...... imported
имя.......................... name
Индия .... India
индустриальн/ый, -ая, -ое; -ые
.... industrial
инженер .... engineer

иностранн/ый, -ая, -ое; -ые ...... foreign
инспектор.................... inspector
институт .... institute
инструктор.................. instructor
инструкции .... instructions
инструмент................. instrument
интеллигент .... intellectual
интервью .... interview
интерес .... interest
интернациональн/ый, -ая, -ое; -ые
.... international
информация .... information
искать .... to look for
  я ищу .... I look for
Исландия .... Iceland
Испания .... Spain
  по-испански .... in Spanish
история .... history
Италия .... Italy
  по-итальянски .... in Italian
июль .... July
июнь .... June

К

к себе .... pull (the doors)
кабина .... cabin, booth
кабинет .... study
каждые .... every
как .... how
  Как дела?
  .... How are things?/How are you?
какая, какие............. what kind of
какао .... cocoa
календарь.................... calendar
камера........................ camera
Канада .... Canada
канал.......................... canal
канарейка..................... canary
кандидат .... candidate
канцтовары .... stationery store
капитал .... capital (money)
карандаш .... pencil
карта .... map
картина, картинка .... picture
касса
  .... cash register, box office,
  ticket machine
кассир .... cashier
католик .... Catholic man
католичка .... Catholic woman
кило .... kilo
километр .... kilometer
кино .... cinema
киоск .... newsstand
класс......................... class
классик .... classic
клоун .... clown
книга .... book
книжный магазин............ bookstore
ковёр .... carpet
когда .... when
колбаса...................... sausage
коллекция .... collection
комедия .... comedy
комната .... room
компас .... compass
композитор .... composer
конверт .... envelope
конференция .... conference
концерт .... concert
коньяк .... cognac
копейки, копеек .... kopecks
корзина .... basket
коричнев/ый, -ая, -ое; -ые .... brown
короткий, -ая, -ое; -ие .... short
кот............................ cat
который, -ая, -ое; -ые .... which

кофе .... coffee
краб .... crab
красив/ый, -ая, -ое; -ые .... pretty
красн/ый, -ая, -ое; -ые .... red
Кремль .... Kremlin
кровать........................ bed
кто .... who
Куба .... Cuba
купальный костюм .... swimsuit
купальный халат .... bathrobe
купить .... to buy
кухня .... kitchen

Л

лаборатория .... laboratory
лампа .... lamp
лево .... left
  налево .... to the left
лет........................... years
лететь .... to fly
  я лечу .... I fly
лето .... summer
летом .... in summer
лимон .... lemon
лимонад .... lemonade
линия .... line
литература .... literature
литр .... liter
ложка .... spoon
любить .... to love
люди .... people

М

магазин........................ store
май .... May
маленький, -ая, -ое; ие .... small
мало .... little
марка .... stamp
март .... March
масло .... butter
масса.......................... mass
мастер....................... master
математика .... mathematics
материя .... material
матрёшки .... Russian dolls
матч .... match (game)
мать......................... mother
машина................ machine (car)
  машина напрокат .... rental car
медаль........................ medal
медик .... medic
медицина .... medicine
медленно .... slow, slowly
медь.................... copper coins
между .... between
мелодия .... melody
мелочь .... change (coins)
меню .... menu
местн/ый, -ая, -ое; -ые.....domestic, local
месяцы .... months
металл........................ metal
метод .... method
метро .... metro, subway
механик .... mechanic
микрофон................. microphone
милиция .... police
миллион .... million
миниатюра................ miniature
минут .... minutes
миссия .... mission
митинг .... meeting
много .... a lot, many
модель....................... model
мой, моя, моё; мои .... my
молод/ой, -ая, -ое; -ые........... young

молоко .... milk
молочная .... dairy
момент .... moment
монеты .... coins
Москва .... Moscow
мотор .... motor
мотоцикл .... motorcycle
мочь .... to be able to/can
мужчина .... man
  мужчины .... men
музей .... museum
музыка .... music
мусульманин .... Moslem man
мусульманка .... Moslem woman
мы .... we
мыло .... soap
мясо .... meat
мяч .... ball

Н

на .... on, into
наверху .... upstairs
над .... over
название .... name
налево .... to the left
напишите .... write out
направо .... to the right
например .... for example
натуральн/ый, -ая, -ое; -ые .... grilled
нация .... nation
начинается .... begins
не .... not, no
неделя .... week
нейлон .... nylon
несерьёзн/ый, -ая, -ое; -ые .... not serious
нет .... no
низк/ий, -ая, -ое; -ие .... low
никель .... nickel
нов/ые, -ая, -ое; -ые .... new
нож .... knife
ноль .... zero
номер .... hotel room, number
норма .... norm, standard
нормальн/ый, -ая, -ое; -ые .... normal
нос .... nose
носки .... socks
ночь .... night
ночная рубашка .... nightshirt
ноябрь .... November
нужно .... need
  мне нужно .... I need
нуж/ен, -на, -но; -ны .... necessary

О

обменять .... to exchange
обед .... meal, dinner
овощи .... vegetables
овощной .... greengrocer's
одежда .... clothes
одеяло .... blanket
один .... one
одиннадцать .... eleven
окно .... window
октябрь .... October
оленина .... venison
олимпиада .... Olympics
он .... he
она .... she
они .... they
опаздывать .... to be late
опера .... opera
оплатить .... to pay
опоздал .... late
оранжев/ый, -ая, -ое; -ые .. orange (color)
органист .... organist
оркестр .... orchestra
осень .... autumn
осенью .... in autumn
остановка .... stop
  остановка автобуса .... bus stop
  остановка трамвая .... trolley stop
отварн/ой, -ая, -ое; -ые .... boiled
ответы .... answers
отделение милиции .... police station
отделы .... shops, departments
отель .... hotel
отец .... father
открытка .... postcard
открыто .... open
отправление .... departure
от себя .... push (the doors)
отходить
.... to depart (trains, buses, ships)
офицер .... officer
официальн/ый, -ая, -ое; -ые .... official
официант .... waiter
официантка .... waitress
очень .... very
очки .... eyeglasses

П

павильон .... pavilion
пакет .... package
пальто .... overcoat
пансионат .... pension, boarding house
парад .... parade
парикмахерская .... hairdresser
парк .... park
парламент .... parliament
партия .... party
паспорт .... passport
пассажир .... passenger
перед .... in front of
перец .... pepper
перо .... pen
перчатки .... gloves
Петербург .... Petersburg
пианист .... pianist
пиво .... beer
пижама .... pajamas
пикник .... picnic
пилот .... pilot
писать .... to write
письмо .... letter
пить .... to drink
платформа .... platform
плащ .... raincoat
плита .... stove
плохо .... bad
пляж .... beach
по .... on
повторять .... to repeat
погода .... weather
под .... under
подвал .... basement
подушка .... pillow
поезд .... train
поездка .... trip
пожалуйста .... please, you're welcome
пожар .... fire
позвонить .... to telephone, to call
позиция .... position
полиция .... police
половина .... half
полотенца .... towels
показывать .... to show
покупать .... to buy
понедельник .... Monday
понимать .... to understand
порт .... port
портрет .... portrait
посылать .... to send
посылка .... package
потолок .... ceiling
потом .... then
почему .... why
почта .... mail, post office
почтовое отделение .... post office
почтовый ящик .... mailbox
поэт .... poet
правильно .... correct
править .... to drive
право .... right
  направо .... to the right
православная .... Orthodox woman
православный .... Orthodox man
практика .... practice
прачечная .... laundry
приезд .... arrival
приезжать .... to arrive
примеры .... examples
приходить
.... to arrive (trains, buses, ships)
программа .... program
прогресс .... progress
продавать .... to sell
продмаг .... food store
продукт .... product
проект .... project
профессия .... profession
профессор .... professor
процент .... percent
прямо .... straight ahead
пряники .... pastries
путешественник .... traveler
путешествовать .... to travel
пятнадцать .... fifteen
пять .... five
пятьдесят .... fifty
пятьсот .... five hundred
пятница .... Friday

Р

радио .... radio
разговор по телефону
.... telephone conversation
размер .... size
  Который размер? .... Which size?
ракета .... rocket
ранг .... rank
рапорт .... report
расписание .... schedule
револьвер .... revolver
революция .... revolution
регистрация .... registration
рекорд .... record
религия .... religion
ресторан .... restaurant
родители .... parents
родственники .... relatives
розов/ый, -ая, -ое; -ые .... pink
Россия .... Russia
рубль/рубли .... ruble/rubles
русский .... Russian
  по-русски .... in Russian
  русские .... Russians
ручка .... pen
рыбный рынок .... fish market
рыба .... fish
рынок .... market
рядом с .... next to

С

с .... with
сад .... garden
салат .... salad
салфетка .... napkin

самовар . . . . . samovar
самолёт . . . . . airplane
сандалии . . . . . sandals
сапоги . . . . . boots
свинина . . . . . pork
сдача . . . . . change
север . . . . . north
северн/ый, -ая, -ое; -ые . . . . . northern
сегодня . . . . . today
сезон . . . . . season
секретарь . . . . . secretary
секунда . . . . . second
семинар . . . . . seminar
семнадцать . . . . . seventeen
семь . . . . . seven
семьдесят . . . . . seventy
семья . . . . . family
сентябрь . . . . . September
серебро . . . . . silver coins
сер/ый, -ая, -ое; -ые . . . . . gray
сестра . . . . . sister
сигара . . . . . cigar
сигарета . . . . . cigarette
симфония . . . . . symphony
син/ий, -яя, -ее; -ие . . . . . blue
сколько . . . . . how much
  Сколько времени? . . . . What time is it?
словарь . . . . . dictionary
слово . . . . . word
слон . . . . . elephant
снег . . . . . snow
собака . . . . . dog
советский, -ая, -ое; -ие . . . . . Soviet
  Советский Союз . . . . . Soviet Union
соль . . . . . salt
сорок . . . . . forty
спальня . . . . . bedroom
спасибо . . . . . thank you
спать . . . . . to sleep
спокойной ночи . . . . . good night
спросить . . . . . to ask
  я спрашиваю . . . . . I ask
среда . . . . . Wednesday
ставить . . . . . to put, to park
стадион . . . . . stadium
стакан . . . . . glass
станция . . . . . station
  станция метро . . . . . metro station
стар/ый, -ая, -ое; -ые . . . . . old
  старейш/ий, -ая, -ее; -ие . . . . . oldest
старт . . . . . start
стена . . . . . wall
стирать . . . . . to wash (clothes)
сто . . . . . one hundred
стоит . . . . . costs
стол . . . . . table
столовая . . . . . dining room
стоянка . . . . . parking lot, taxi stand
страница . . . . . page
студент . . . . . student
стул . . . . . chair
суббота . . . . . Saturday
сувениры . . . . . souvenirs
сумка . . . . . purse
суп . . . . . soup
Счастливого пути! . . . . Have a good trip!
счёт . . . . . bill
сын . . . . . son

Т

табак . . . . . tobacco
такси . . . . . taxi
там . . . . . there
тарелка . . . . . plate
театр . . . . . theater
телевизор . . . . . television
телеграмма . . . . . telegram
телескоп . . . . . telescope
телефон . . . . . telephone
телефон-автомат . . . . . public telephone
телятина . . . . . veal
температура . . . . . temperature
теперь . . . . . now
терять . . . . . to lose
тётя . . . . . aunt
тихо . . . . . softly
тогда . . . . . then
тоже . . . . . also
толст/ый, -ая, -ое; -ые . . . . . thick
только . . . . . only
томат . . . . . tomato
тонк/ий, -ая, -ое; -ие . . . . . thin
тост . . . . . toast
трамвай . . . . . street car, trolley
три . . . . . three
тридцать . . . . . thirty
тринадцать . . . . . thirteen
триста . . . . . three hundred
трубка . . . . . receiver (telephone)
туалет . . . . . toilet
туман . . . . . fog
турист . . . . . tourist
туфли . . . . . shoes
тушён/ый, -ая, -ое; -ые . . . . . stewed
тысяча . . . . . one thousand

У

у вас есть . . . . . you have
у меня есть . . . . . I have
у нас есть . . . . . we have
угол . . . . . corner
удачи . . . . . good luck
уезжать . . . . . to leave
  я уезжаю . . . . . I leave
указания . . . . . directions
укладывать . . . . . to pack
  я укладываю . . . . . I pack
улица . . . . . street
умывальник . . . . . washstand
универмаг . . . . . department store
универсальны магазин
  . . . . . department store
университет . . . . . university
утро . . . . . morning

Ф

фаренгейт . . . . . Fahrenheit
фаршированный, -ая, -ое; -ые . . . . stuffed
февраль . . . . . February
фильм . . . . . film (movie)
фотоаппарат . . . . . camera
фотограф . . . . . photographer
фотомагазин . . . . . camera store
фотоплёнка . . . . . film (photographic)
Франция . . . . . France
  по-французски . . . . . in French
фрукты . . . . . fruit
футбол . . . . . soccer, football

Х

химически . . . . . chemically
химчистка . . . . . dry cleaner's
хлеб . . . . . bread
холодильник . . . . . refrigerator
холодн/ый, -ая, -ое; -ые . . . . . cold
хорошо . . . . . good
  не хорошо . . . . . not good
  хорошо сидит . . . . . it fits well
хочу . . . . . (I) want
  я хочу пить . . . . . I am thirsty

Ц

царь . . . . . czar, tsar
цвет . . . . . color
цветок . . . . . flower
Цельсий . . . . . Celsius
центр . . . . . city center
церковь . . . . . church
цирк . . . . . circus

Ч

чай . . . . . tea
час . . . . . (one) o'clock, hour
  Который час? . . . . . What time is it?
часто . . . . . often
часы . . . . . clock, watch
чашка . . . . . cup
чемодан . . . . . suitcase
чёрн/ый, -ая, -ое; -ые . . . . . black
четверг . . . . . Thursday
четверть . . . . . a quarter (toward)
четыре . . . . . four
четырнадцать . . . . . fourteen
числа . . . . . numbers
чист/ый, -ая, -ое; -ые . . . . . clean
читать . . . . . to read
  я читаю . . . . . I read
что . . . . . what
чулки . . . . . stockings

Ш

шарф . . . . . scarf
Швеция . . . . . Sweden
  по-шведски . . . . . in Swedish
шестнадцать . . . . . sixteen
шесть . . . . . six
шестьдесят . . . . . sixty
шкаф . . . . . wardrobe, cupboard
школа . . . . . school
шляпа . . . . . hat
шоссе . . . . . main road
штат . . . . . state
шторм . . . . . storm
шьёт . . . . . sews

Э

экватор . . . . . equator
экзамен . . . . . exam
экономика . . . . . economics
экспресс . . . . . express
эра . . . . . era
эскалатор . . . . . escalator
этаж . . . . . floor (of building)
этот, эта, это/эти . . . . . that, this
  Это всё . . . . . That's all.

Ю

юг . . . . . south
южн/ый, -ая, -ое; -ые . . . . . southern

Я

я I
яблоко . . . . . apple
язык . . . . . language, tongue
январь . . . . . January
янтарь . . . . . amber
Япония . . . . . Japan
яхта . . . . . yacht

GLOSSARY

English-Russian

A

academy .... академия
accent .... акцент
acrobat .... акробат
act .... акт
actor .... актёр
address .... адрес
agent .... агент
airmail .... авиапочта
airplane .... самолёт
airport .... аэродром, аэропорт
alarm clock .... будильник
alcohol .... алкоголь
algebra .... алгебра
a lot .... много
also .... тоже
amber .... янтарь
America .... Америка
American man .... американец
American woman .... американка
and .... и
answers .... ответы
antenna .... антенна
antibiotics .... антибиотики
appetite .... аппетит
apple .... яблоко
apricot .... абрикос
April .... апрель
arena .... арена
army .... армия
arrest .... арест
arrival .... приезд
arrive (inf.) .... приезжать
arrive (trains, buses, ships), inf.
.... приходить
Asia .... Азия
ask (inf.) .... спросить
I ask .... я спрашиваю
aspirin .... аспирин
astronaut .... астронавт
athlete .... атлет
August .... август
aunt .... тётя
Australia .... Австралия
author .... автор
autobiography .... автобиография
autograph .... автограф
automat .... автомат
autumn .... осень
in autumn .... осенью
aviation .... авиация

B

bad .... плохо
bag .... сумка
baggage .... багаж
baked .... запечённ/ый, -ая, -ое; -ые
bakery .... булочная
balalaika .... балалайка
balcony .... балкон
ball (dance) .... бал
ball .... мяч
ballerina .... балерина
ballet .... балет
banana .... банан
bank .... банк
bar (restaurant) .... бар
barge .... баржа
barrier .... барьер
basement .... подвал
basket .... корзина
basketball .... баскетбол
bass (voice) .... бас
bathrobe .... купальный халат
bathroom .... ванная

battery .... батарея
bazaar .... базар
be able to (inf.) .... мочь
beach .... пляж
bed .... кровать
bedroom .... спальня
beef .... говядина
beer .... пиво
begins .... начинается
behind .... за
below .... внизу
"Beriozka" (hard-currency store)
.... „Берёзка"
between .... между
big .... больш/ой, -ая, -ое; -ые
bill .... счёт
binoculars .... бинокль
black .... чёрн/ый, -ая, -ое; -ые
blank (form) .... бланк
blanket .... одеяло
blue .... син/ий, -яя, -ее; -ие
boiled .... отварн/ой, -ая, -ое; -ые
bomb .... бомба
book .... книга
bookstore .... книжный магазин
booth .... кабина
boots .... сапоги
borsch (beet soup) .... борщ
boulevard .... бульвар
boxing .... бокс
box office .... касса
bread .... хлеб
breakfast .... завтрак
bronze .... бронза
brother .... брат
brown .... коричнев/ый, -ая, -ое; -ые
brunette .... брюнет (ка)
bureau .... бюро
bus .... автобус
bus stop .... остановка автобуса
busy .... занят, -а, -о; -ы
butter .... масло
buy (inf.) .... покупать, купить

C

calendar .... календарь
camera .... фотоаппарат, камера
camera store .... фотомагазин
Canada .... Канада
canal .... канал
canary .... канарейка
candidate .... кандидат
capital (money) .... капитал
car .... автомобиль, машина
rental car .... машина напрокат
carpet .... ковёр
cashier .... кассир
cash register .... касса
cat .... кот
Catholic man .... католик
Catholic woman .... католичка
caviar .... икра
ceiling .... потолок
Celsius .... Цельсий
chair .... стул
change (coins) .... мелочь
change (from a transaction) .... сдача
chemically .... химически
children .... дети, детей
church .... церковь
cigar .... сигара
cigarette .... сигарета
cinema .... кино

circus .... цирк
city center .... центр
class .... класс
classic .... классик
clean .... чист/ый, -ая, -ое; -ые
clock .... часы
closed .... закрыто
clothes .... одежда
clown .... клоун
cocoa .... какао
coffee .... кофе
cognac .... коньяк
coins .... монеты
cold .... холодн/ый, -ая, -ое; -ые
collection .... коллекция
color .... цвет
comb .... гребень
comedy .... комедия
compass .... компас
composer .... композитор
concert .... концерт
conference .... конференция
copper coins .... медь
corner .... угол
correct .... правильно
costs .... стоит
couch .... диван
crab .... краб
Cuba .... Куба
cup .... чашка
cupboard .... шкаф
curtain .... занавес
czar .... царь

D

dairy .... молочная
date .... дата
daughter .... дочь
day .... день
December .... декабрь
degrees .... градусы
delegate .... делегат
deodorant .... дезодорант
depart (trains, buses, ships), inf.
.... отходить
departments .... отделы
department store
.... универмаг, универсальный магазин
departure .... отправление
diagnosis .... диагноз
diagram .... диаграмма
dialogues .... диалоги
dictionary .... словарь
diesel .... дизель
dining room .... столовая
dinner .... обед
diploma .... диплом
diplomat .... дипломат
directions .... указания
director .... директор
discussion .... дискуссия
do (inf.) .... делать
I do .... я делаю
doctor .... доктор, врач
document .... документ
dog .... собака
dollar .... доллар
domestic .... местн/ый, -ая, -ое; -ые
door .... дверь
doorbell .... звонок
downstairs .... внизу
drama .... драма
drink (inf.) .... пить
drive (inf.) .... править
drugstore .... аптека
dry cleaner's .... химчистка

E

east .... восток
eastern .... восточн/ый, -ая, -ое; -ые
eat (inf.) .... есть
economics .... экономика
eight .... восемь
eighteen .... восемнадцать
eight hundred .... восемьсот
eighty .... восемьдесят
elephant .... слон
elevator .... лифт
eleven .... одиннадцать
engineer .... инженер
England .... Англия
in English .... по-английски
enter (inf.) .... входить
do not enter .... входа нет
entrance .... вход
envelope .... конверт
equator .... экватор
era .... эра
escalator .... эскалатор
evening .... вечер
every .... каждые
everything .... всё
exam .... экзамен
examples .... примеры
exchange (inf.) .... обменять
excuse me .... извините
exit .... выход
exit (inf.) .... выходить
expensive .... дорог/ой, -ая, -ое; -ие
express .... экспресс
eyeglasses .... очки

F

Fahrenheit .... Фаренгейт
family .... семья
fast .... быстро
father .... отец
February .... февраль
fifteen .... пятнадцать
fifty .... пятьдесят
film (movie) .... фильм
film (photographic) .... фотоплёнка
fire .... пожар
fish .... рыба
fish market .... рыбный рынок
five .... пять
five hundred .... пятьсот
floor (of building) .... этаж
flower .... цветок
flowers .... цветы
fly (inf.) .... лететь
I fly .... я лечу
fog .... туман
food store .... продмаг
for .... для
foreign .... иностранн/ый, -ая, -ое; -ые
for example .... например
fork .... вилка
forty .... сорок
four .... четыре
fourteen .... четырнадцать
France .... Франция
in French .... по-французски
Friday .... пятница
fried .... жарен/ый, -ая, -ое; -ые
friends .... друзья
from .... из
fruit .... фрукты

G

gallery .... галерея
garage .... гараж
garden .... сад
gas (natural) .... газ
gasoline .... бензин
geography .... география
geologist .... геолог
geology .... геология
geometry .... геометрия
gin .... джин
give me .... дайте мне
glass .... стакан
gloves .... перчатки
go (by vehicle), inf. .... ехать
go (on foot), inf. .... идти
I go .... я иду
he/she goes .... он/она идёт
good .... хорошо
not good .... не хорошо
it fits well .... хорошо сидит
good afternoon .... добрый день
goodbye .... до свидания
good day .... добрый день
good evening .... добрый вечер
good luck .... удачи
good morning .... доброе утро
good night .... спокойной ночи
goose .... гусь
go out (inf.) .... выходить
gram .... грамм
grandfather .... дед
grandmother .... бабушка
granite .... гранит
gray .... сер/ый, -ая, -ое; -ые
green .... зелён/ый, -ая, -ое; -ые
greengrocer's .... овощной
grilled .... натуральн/ый, -ая, -ое; -ые
grocery store .... гастроном
group .... группа
guide .... гид
guitar .... гитара
gymnastics .... гимнастика

H

hairdresser .... парикмахерская
half .... половина
hat .... шляпа
have (I have) .... у меня есть
you have .... у вас есть
we have .... у нас есть
Have a good trip! ... Счастливого пути!
he .... он
healthy .... здоров
hello (on the telephone) .... алло
hello .... здравствуйте
here .... здесь
here is .... вот
highway .... шоссе
history .... история
hot (air temperature) .... жарко
hot (to the touch)
.... горяч/ий, -ая, -ее; -ие
hotel .... гостиница, отель
hour/o'clock .... час
a quarter (to) .... четверть
house .... дом
how .... как
How are things?/How are you?
.... Как дела?
how much .... сколько
hundred (one) .... сто
hungry .... голоден

I

I .... я
Iceland .... Исландия
important .... важно
imported .... импортн/ый, -ая, -ое; -ые
in .... в
India .... Индия
industrial
.... индустриальн/ый, -ая, -ое; -ые
inexpensive .... дешёв/ый, -ая, -ое; -ые
information .... информация
in front of .... перед
inspector .... инспектор
institute .... институт
instructions .... инструкции
instructor .... инструктор
instrument .... инструмент
intellectual .... интеллигент
interest .... интерес
international
.... интернациональн/ый, -ая, -ое; -ые
interview .... интервью
into .... на
Italian .... Италия
in Italian .... по-итальянски

J

jacket (woman's) .... жакет
January .... январь
Japan .... Япония
jazz .... джаз
jelly .... желе
Jewish man .... еврей
Jewish woman .... еврейка
joke .... анекдот
July .... июль
June .... июнь

K

kilo .... кило
kilometer .... километр
kitchen .... кухня
knife .... нож
know (inf.) .... знать
kopecks .... копейки, копеек
Kremlin .... Кремль

L

laboratory .... лаборатория
lady .... дама
lamp .... лампа
language .... язык
late (be), inf. .... опаздывать
I am late .... опоздал
laundry .... прачечная
lawyer .... адвокат
learn (inf.) .... изучать
I learn .... я изучаю
leave (inf.) .... уезжать
I leave .... я уезжаю
left .... лево
to the left .... налево
lemon .... лимон
lemonade .... лимонад
letter .... письмо
line .... линия
liter .... литр
literature .... литература
little .... мало
live (inf.) .... жить
living room .... гостиная
local .... местн/ый, -ая, -ое; -ые
long .... длинн/ый, -ая, -ое; -ые
look for (inf.) .... искать
I look for .... я ищу
lose (inf.) .... терять
loudly .... громко
love (inf.) .... любить
low .... низк/ий, -ая, -ое; -ие

M

magazine.....................журнал
mail.........................почта
mailbox..............почтовый ящик
make (inf.)....................делать
 I make....................я делаю
man.........................мужчина
many........................много
map..........................карта
March........................март
market.......................рынок
mass.........................масса
master.......................мастер
match (game)..................матч
material.....................материя
mathematics...............математика
May..........................май
meal.........................обед
meat.........................мясо
mechanic....................механик
medal........................медаль
medic........................медик
medicine....................медицина
meeting.....................митинг
melody......................мелодия
men.........................мужчины
menu.........................меню
metal........................металл
method.......................метод
metro........................метро
 metro station.........станция метро
microphone................микрофон
milk.........................молоко
million.....................миллион
miniature.................миниатюра
minus........................без
minutes......................минут
mirror......................зеркало
mission.....................миссия
model........................модель
moment.......................момент
Monday...................понедельник
money........................деньги
months.......................месяцы
more.........................больше
morning......................утро
Moscow......................Москва
Moslem man.................мусульманин
Moslem woman...............мусульманка
mother.......................мать
motor........................мотор
motorcycle..................мотоцикл
mountains....................горы
museum.......................музей
music........................музыка
mutton.....................баранина
my.................мой, моя, моё; мои

N

name (for people; first name)....имя
 I am called/my name is..меня зовут
name (for things)...........название
napkin.....................салфетка
nation.......................нация
neat.........аккуратн/ый, -ая, -ое; -ые
necessary........нуж/ен, -на, -но; -ны
need.........................нужно
 I need...................мне нужно
new.............нов/ый, -ая, -ое; -ые
newspaper....................газета
 newspaper man...............газетчик
newsstand....................киоск
next to.....................рядом с
nickel.......................никель
night........................ночь
nightshirt...........ночная рубашка
nine.........................девять
nineteen................девятнадцать
ninety.....................девяносто
no...........................не, нет
norm.........................норма
normal.......нормальн/ый, -ая, -ое; -ые
north........................север
northern.......северн/ый, -ая, -ое; -ые
nose.........................нос
not..........................не
November.....................ноябрь
now..........................теперь
number.......................номер
numbers......................числа
nylon........................нейлон

O

October......................октябрь
office.......................бюро
officer......................офицер
official.....официальн/ый, -ая, -ое; -ые
often........................часто
old.............стар/ый, -ая, -ое; -ые
oldest........старейш/ий, -ая, -ее; -ие
Olympics....................олимпиада
on (for telephone, radio, T.V.).....по
on...........................на
one..........................один
only.........................только
open.........................открыто
opera........................опера
or...........................или
orange (color)
..............оранжев/ый, -ая, -ое; -ые
orange (fruit)...............апельсин
orchestra....................оркестр
order (inf.)...............заказывать
organist.....................органист
Orthodox man...............православный
Orthodox woman.............православная
out of.......................из
over.........................над
overcoat.....................пальто

P

pack (inf.)................укладывать
 I pack.................я укладываю
package................пакет, посылка
page.........................страница
pajamas......................пижама
paper........................бумага
parade.......................парад
parents......................родители
park (inf.)..................ставить
park.........................парк
parking lot..................стоянка
parliament...................парламент
party........................партия
passenger....................пассажир
passport.....................паспорт
pastries.....................пряники
pastry shop..................булочная
pavilion.....................павильон
pay (inf.)...................оплатить
pen......................ручка, перо
pencil.......................карандаш
pension (guest house)......пансионат
people.......................люди
pepper.......................перец
percent......................процент
Petersburg...................Петербург
photographer.................фотограф
pianist......................пианист
picnic.......................пикник
picture..............картина, картинка
pillow.......................подушка
pilot........................пилот
pink...........розов/ый, -ая, -ое; -ые
plate........................тарелка
platform.....................платформа
please.......................пожалуйста
poet.........................поэт
police...............милиция, полиция
police station......отделение милиции
poor.........................беден
pork.........................свинина
port.........................порт
portrait.....................портрет
position.....................позиция
postcard.....................открытка
post office..почта, почтовое отделение
poultry..................домашняя птица
practice.....................практика
pretty.........красив/ый, -ая, -ое; -ые
product......................продукт
profession...................профессия
professor....................профессор
program......................программа
progress.....................прогресс
project......................проект
pull (the doors).............к себе
purse........................сумка
push (the doors).............от себя
put (inf.)...................ставить

Q

question.....................вопрос

R

radio........................радио
rain.........................дождь
raincoat.....................плащ
rank.........................ранг
razor........................бритва
read (inf.)..................читать
 I read.......................я читаю
receiver (telephone).........трубка
record.......................рекорд
red............красн/ый, -ая, -ое; -ые
refrigerator.................холодильник
registration.................регистрация
relatives....................родственники
religion.....................религия
repeat (inf.)................повторять
report (official)............рапорт
reserve (inf.)...............заказывать
reside (inf.)................жить
restaurant...................ресторан
revolution...................революция
revolver.....................револьвер
rich.........................богат
right........................право
 to the right................направо
road.........................дорога
roasted..........жарен/ый, -ая, -ое; -ые
rocket.......................ракета
room.........................комната
ruble/rubles.................рубль/рубли
Russia.......................Россия
Russian (language)...........русский
 in Russian..................по-русски
Russians.....................русские
Russian stacked dolls........матрёшки

S

salad........................салат
salt.........................соль
samovar......................самовар
sandals......................сандалии
Saturday.....................суббота
sausage......................колбаса
say (inf.)...................говорить
scarf........................шарф

schedule .... расписание
school .... школа
season .... сезон
second .... секунда
second floor .... второй этаж
secretary .... секретарь
see (inf.) .... видеть
sell (inf.) .... продавать
seminar .... семинар
send (inf.) .... посылать
September .... сентябрь
serious .... серьёзн/ый, -ая, -ое; -ые
  not serious
  .... несерьёзн/ый, -ая, -ое; -ые
service station .... автостанция
seven .... семь
seventeen .... семнадцать
seventy .... семьдесят
sews .... шьёт
she .... она
shoes .... туфли
short .... коротк/ий, -ая, -ое; -ие
show (inf.) .... показывать
shower .... душ
sick .... болен
silver coins .... серебро
sister .... сестра
six .... шесть
sixteen .... шестнадцать
sixty .... шестьдесят
size .... размер
sleep (inf.) .... спать
slippers .... башмаки
slow .... медленно
slowly .... медленно
small .... маленьк/ий, -ая, -ое; -ие
snow .... снег
soap .... мыло
soccer .... футбол
socks .... носки
softly .... тихо
son .... сын
soup .... суп
south .... юг
southern .... южн/ый, -ая, -ое; -ые
souvenirs .... сувениры
Soviet .... советский, -ая, -ое; -ие
  Soviet Union .... Советский Союз
Spain .... Испания
  in Spanish .... по-испански
speak (inf.) .... говорить
spoon .... ложка
spring .... весна
  in spring .... весной
stadium .... стадион
stamp .... марка
start .... старт
state .... штат
station (metro) .... станция
stationery store .... канцтовары
stewed .... тушён/ый, -ая, -ое; -ые
stockings .... чулки
stop (bus, trolley, etc.) .... остановка
store .... магазин
storm .... шторм
stove .... плита
straight ahead .... прямо
street .... улица
street car .... трамвай
  street car stop .... остановка трамвая
student .... студент
study .... кабинет
stuffed .... фаршированн/ый, -ая, -ое; -ые
subway .... метро
suitcase .... чемодан
summer .... лето
  in summer .... летом
Sunday .... воскресенье
Sweden .... Швеция
  in Swedish .... по-шведски
swimsuit .... купальный костюм
symphony .... симфония

T

table .... стол
tailor's .... ателье
take (inf.) .... брать
tall .... высок/ий, -ая, -ое; -ие
taxi .... такси
taxi stand .... стоянка
tea .... чай
telegram .... телеграмма
telephone .... телефон
  public telephone .... телефон-автомат
  telephone conversation
  .... разговор по телефону
telephone (inf.) .... позвонить
telescope .... телескоп
television .... телевизор
temperature .... температура
ten .... десять
  ten from .... десяти
thank you .... спасибо
that .... этот, эта, это; эти
  That's all. .... Это всё.
theater .... театр
then .... потом, тогда
there .... там
they .... они
thick .... толст/ый, -ая, -ое; -ые
thin .... тонк/ий, -ая, -ое; -ие
things .... вещи
thirteen .... тринадцать
thirty .... тридцать
this .... этот, эта, это; эти
thousand (one) .... тысяча
three .... три
three hundred .... триста
Thursday .... четверг
ticket .... билет
ticket machine .... касса
time .... время
  What time is it?
  .... Сколько времени? Который час?
toast .... тост
tobacco .... табак
today .... сегодня
toilet .... туалет
tomato .... томат
tomorrow .... завтра
toothbrush .... зубная щётка
toothpaste .... зубная паста
tourist .... турист
towels .... полотенца
train .... поезд
  train station .... вокзал
transfer (on bus, subway, etc.), inf.
  .... делать пересадку
travel (inf.) .... путешествовать
traveler .... путешественник
trip .... поездка
trolley .... трамвай
  trolley stop .... остановка трамвая
tsar .... чарь
Tuesday .... вторник
twelve .... двенадцать
twenty .... двадцать
two .... два, две

U

umbrella .... зонтик
uncle .... дядя
under .... под
understand (inf.) .... понимать
university .... университет
until .... до
upstairs .... наверху

V

vase .... ваза
veal .... телятина
vegetables .... овощи
venison .... оленина
veranda .... веранда
very .... очень
vitamin .... витамин
vodka .... водка
volleyball .... волейбол

W

waiter .... официант
wait for (inf.) .... ждать
waitress .... официантка
wall .... стена
wallet .... бумажник
waltz .... вальс
want (I want) .... хочу
  I am thirsty .... я хочу пить
wardrobe .... шкаф
was .... был
wash (clothes), inf. .... стирать
washstand .... умывальник
watch .... часы
water .... вода
we .... мы
weather .... погода
Wednesday .... среда
week .... неделя
west .... запад
western .... западн/ый, -ая, -ое; -ые
what .... что
  what kind of .... какая, какие
  What time is it? .... Сколько времени?
when .... когда
where .... где
which .... котор/ый, -ая, -ое; -ые
  Which size? .... Который размер?
white .... бел/ый, -ая, -ое; -ые
who .... кто
why .... почему
will be .... будет
window .... окно
windy .... ветрено
wine .... вино
winter .... зима
  in winter .... зимой
with .... с
without .... без
woman .... женщина, дама
women .... женщины
word .... слово
write (inf.) .... писать
write out .... напишите

Y

yacht .... яхта
year .... год
years .... лет
yellow .... жёлт/ый, -ая, -ое; -ые
yes .... да
yesterday .... вчера
you .... вы
you need .... вам нужно
young .... молод/ой, -ая, -ое; -ые
your .... ваш, ваша, ваше; ваши
you're welcome .... пожалуйста

Z

zero .... ноль
zone .... зона
zoo .... зоопарк

DRINKING GUIDE

This guide is intended to explain the variety of beverages available to you while in Russia. It is by no means complete. Some of the experimenting has been left up to you, but this should get you started. One asterisk indicates a brand name, while two asterisks indicate a regional variety.

ГОРЯЧИЕ НАПИТКИ (hot drinks)

чай с лимоном ... tea with lemon
чай с вареньем ... tea with jam
чай с молоком ... tea with milk
чай с мёдом ... tea with honey

Чай was traditionally made in a samovar, **самовар.** A very strong tea was made in a teapot, which was kept warm on top of the samovar. A small portion of the tea was poured into a cup and diluted with hot water from the samovar.

кофе ... coffee
  кофе с молоком ... coffee with milk
  чёрный кофе ... black coffee
  кофе по-восточному ... Turkish coffee
  кофе-гляссе ... coffee with ice cream
какао ... cocoa

ХОЛОДНЫЕ НАПИТКИ (cold drinks)

молоко ... milk
  фруктовый коктейль ... milkshake
  кефир ... sour milk (usually topped with sugar)
  ряженка ... thick, sour milk
кисель ... sour-fruit drink
лимонад ... lemonade
байкал ... cola drink
*** пепси-кола** ... Pepsi-Cola
квас ... kvass

Квас is a dark, non-alcoholic beverage made from yeast and black bread. Although it is not sold in restaurants, it is readily available from street vendors.

минеральная вода ... mineral water
*** Нарзан**
*** Ессентуки**
*** Боржоми**

You'll find that most mineral waters in Russia are domestic, bottled from natural spring-water from the Caucasus.

фруктовый сок ... fruit juice
  апельсиновый сок ... orange juice
  яблочный сок ... apple juice
  виноградный сок ... grape juice
  клюквенный морс ... cranberry juice
  сливовый сок ... prune juice
  абрикосовый сок ... apricot juice
  гранатовый сок ... pomegranate juice
  персиковый сок ... peach juice
  томатный сок ... tomato juice

Don't miss a chance to sample Russian fruit juices. They are delicious. You'll find juice bars in the larger grocery stores.

ПИВО (beer)

светлое пиво ... light beer
тёмное пиво ... dark beer
*** Московское**
*** Ленинградское**
*** Двойное золотое**
*** Рижское**

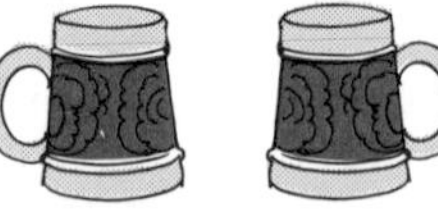

Пиво is available in restaurants, but if you're visiting during the summer, you'll want to visit the streetside beer stalls.

СПИРТНЫЕ НАПИТКИ (alcohol)

Both **спиртные напитки** and **вино** can be purchased by the bottle or by weight. A shot is 50 grams and a glass of wine is approximately 150 grams.

водка ... vodka
*** Экстра**
*** Столичная**
*** Русская**
*** Пшеничная**
*** Смирновская**
*** Охотничья**

Коньяк ... cognac
****Армянский коньяк** ... Armenian cognac
****Грузинский коньяк** ... Georgian cognac

виски ... whiskey
джин ... gin
ром ... rum
аперитив ... aperitif
ликёр ... liqueur

ВИНО (wine)

красное вино ... red wine
****Алазанская долина** ... Georgian wine
****Мукузани** ... Georgian wine
белое вино ... white wine
****Цинандали** ... Georgian wine
розовое вино ... rosé wine
вермут ... vermouth
портвейн ... port
херес ... sherry
шампанское ... champagne
  сухое шампанское ... dry champagne
  полу-сухое шампанское ... semi-dry champagne
  сладкое шампанское ... sweet champagne
  полу-сладкое шампанское ... semi-sweet champagne
*** Игристое**
*** Золотое**

Russian champagne and **вино** from Georgia are considered to be some of the finest wines in the world. They are rated for their quality on a star system: seven stars indicates a superlative wine, while one star indicates a wine of lesser quality.

CUT ALONG DOTTED LINE, FOLD AND TAKE WITH YOU

Салат (salad)

салат из белых грибов	white-mushroom salad
салат столичный	meat-and-vegetable salad
винегрет	vinaigrette of vegetables
соус винегрет	vinaigrette
соус фруктово-ягодный	berry, fruit sauce

Десерт (dessert)

мороженое	ice cream
ванильное мороженое	vanilla ice cream
шоколадное мороженое	chocolate ice cream
кисель	jello-style dessert
компот	compote
крем	whipped cream
пудинг	pudding
рисовый пудинг	rice pudding
лимон с сахаром	lemon with sugar
яблоки в вине	apples in wine
шоколадный соус	chocolate sauce
торт	torte, cake
кекс	muffin
пирог	pie
пряники	cookies
пирожные	pastries, small cakes
печенье	pastries, biscuits
коржики	shortcakes

Фрукты (fruit)

апельсин	orange
арбуз	watermelon
банан	banana
виноград	grapes
вишни	cherries
грейпфрут	grapefruit
груша	pear
дыня	melon
земляника	strawberries
дыня	cantaloupe
лимон	lemon
малина	raspberries
персик	peach
чёрная смородина	blackberries
яблоко	apple
ягоды	berries

FOLD HERE

Птица и Дичь (poultry and game)

курица/цыплята	chicken
гусь	goose
утка	duck
индейка	turkey
рябчик	hazel grouse
тетерев	black grouse
куропатка	partridge
вальдшнеп	woodcock
бекас	snipe
чирок	teal
перепел	quail
кролик	rabbit
оленина	venison
цыплята жареные	fried chicken
куриные крокеты	chicken croquettes
белое мясо курицы	breast of chicken
котлеты по-киевски	chicken Kiev

Овощи (vegetables)

баклажаны	eggplant
горох	peas
грибы	mushrooms
капуста	cabbage
красная капуста	red cabbage
цветная капуста	cauliflower
картофель	potatoes
картофель жареный	fried potatoes
картофель отварной	boiled potatoes
картофель пюре	mashed potatoes
картофель в сметане	potatoes in sour cream
кукуруза	corn
лук	onions
морковь	carrots
перец	pepper/green pepper
перец горький	pimentos
петрушка	parsley
помидоры	tomatoes
редиска	radishes
репа	turnips
свёкла	beets
шпинат	spinach

(pree-yaht'-nah-vah) (ahp-peh-tee'-tah)
Приятного аппетита!

FOLD HERE

Меню

menu

Завтрак? Обед? Или Ужин?

отварное	boiled
жареное	roasted
тушёное	stewed
запеченное	baked
фаршированный	stuffed
на вертеле	grilled on a skewer
в сметане	in a sour cream sauce
в томате	in a tomato sauce
паровой	steamed
мало прожаренный	rare
не сильно прожаренный	medium
хорошо прожаренный	well-done

Что мне нужно? (what do I need?)

масло	butter
сахар	sugar
варенье	jam
мёд	honey
соль	salt
перец	pepper
уксус	vinegar
растительное масло	oil
оливковое масло	olive oil
горчица	mustard
соус	sauce, gravy
сыр	cheese
вода	water
лед	ice
майонез	mayonnaise
сливки	cream
сметана	sour cream
кефир	sour milk
творог	cottage cheese

Закуски (appetizers)

икра	caviar
икра грибная	mushroom caviar
красная икра	red caviar
чёрная икра	black caviar
сардины	sardines
сельдь	herring
креветки	shrimp
балык	smoked sturgeon
сосиски	sausages
колбаса	cold cuts
копчёная колбаса	smoked cold cuts
паштет	pâté
студень	aspic
форшмак	potato-and-meat hash
бутерброды открытые	open-faced sandwiches
бутерброды закрытые	sandwiches

Хлеб (bread and dough dishes)

чёрный хлеб	black bread
белый хлеб	white bread
ржаной хлеб	rye bread
пшеничный хлеб	wheat bread
булочки	rolls
блины	pancakes
блины с маслом и сметаной	pancakes with butter and sour cream
пельмени	small dumplings
каша	buckwheat, cereal
манная каша	farina
пирожки	baked, stuffed dumplings
кулебяка	breaded fish loaf
рис	rice
макароны	macaroni
пирог с грибами	mushroom pie
пирог с капустой	cabbage pie
пирог с луком	onion pie
пирог с мясом	meat pie

Яйца (eggs)

яйца вкрутую	hard-boiled eggs
яйца всмятку	soft-boiled eggs
яичница	fried eggs
взбитая яичница	scrambled eggs
фаршированные яйца	stuffed eggs
яйца с икрой	eggs with caviar

FOLD HERE

Суп (soup)

борщ	borsch
борщ со свининой	borsch with pork
щи	cabbage soup
щи суточные	sauerkraut soup
уха	fish soup
лапша	noodle soup
молочная лапша	milk soup with noodles
суп-грибной	mushroom soup
суп-овощной	vegetable soup
суп-пюре из овощей	vegetable purée
суп молочный с овощами	cream-of-vegetable soup
суп из фасоли	bean soup
суп картофельный	potato soup
суп гороховый	pea soup
солянка	spicy, thick soup
рисовый суп	rice soup
бульон	bouillon
бульон с яйцом	bouillon with an egg
бульон с фрикадельками	bouillon with meatballs
рассольник	kidney-and-cucumber soup

Рыба (fish dishes)

треска	cod
камбала	flounder
карп	carp
лосось	salmon
кета	Siberian salmon
щука	pike
раки	crayfish
краб	crab
окунь	perch
судак	pike perch
палтус	halibut
форель	trout
осетрина	sturgeon
осетрина в томате	sturgeon in tomato sauce
осетрина под маринадом	pickled sturgeon
севрюга	type of sturgeon
осетрина „фри“	fried sturgeon
судак „фри“	fried pike perch

Мясо (meat dishes)

баранина	mutton
ветчина	ham
говядина	beef
свинина	pork
телятина	veal

FOLD HERE

Мясо (meat dishes)

бараньи котлеты	lamb chops
ветчина жареная	fried ham
колбаса жареная	fried sausages
мозги жареные	fried brains
телятина жареная	roast veal
мясо жареное в сметане с луком	meat roasted in sour cream and onions
ростбиф	roast beef
поджарка	roast pork
бефстроганов	beef Stroganoff
бифштекс	beefsteak
рагу	stew
говядина тушеная	beef stew
говядина в сухарях	breaded beef
рулет	meatloaf
гуляш	goulash
котлеты	chopped beef
шашлык	shashlik, kebabs
долма	stuffed grape leaves
голубцы мясные	stuffed cabbage
котлеты свиные отбивные	breaded pork chops
котлеты отбивные из баранины	breaded lamb chops
котлеты натуральные из баранины	grilled lamb chops
шницель	breaded veal cutlet
язык	tongue
печёнка	liver
сосиски	sausages
бекон	bacon
битки/биточки	meatballs
почки	kidneys
купаты	spicy pork sausage
плов	pilaf

Салат (salad)

салат из фруктов	fruit salad
салат из огурцов	cucumber salad
салат из помидоров	tomato salad
салат из фасоли	bean salad
салат из редиса	radishes with sour cream
салат картофельный	potato salad
салат из капусты с яблоками	cabbage-and-apple salad

(yah) *(zah-kah'-zih-vah-yoo)* **я заказываю**	*(yah)* *(yeh'-doo)* **я еду**
(yah) *(pah-koo-pah'-yoo)* **я покупаю**	*(yah)* *(pree-yez-zhy'-yoo)* **я приезжаю**
(yah) *(ee-zoo-chah'-yoo)* **я изучаю**	*(yah)* *(vee'-zhoo)* **я вижу**
(yah) *(pahv-tar-yah'-yoo)* **я повторяю**	*(yah)* *(zhee-voo')* **я живу**
(yah) *(pah-nee-mah'-yoo)* **я понимаю**	*(yah)* *(zhdoo)* **я жду**
(yah) *(gah-vah-ryoo')* **я говорю**	*(yah)* *(eesh-choo')* **я ищу**

I go (by vehicle)	I order/reserve
I arrive	I buy
I see	I learn
I live/reside	I repeat
I wait for	I understand
I look for	I speak/say

(yah) (yem) **я ем**	*(yah) (prah-dah-yoo')* **я продаю**
(yah) (pyoo) **я пью**	*(yah) (pah-sih-lah'-yoo)* **я посылаю**
(yah) (hah-choo') **я хочу**	*(yah) (splyoo)* **я сплю**
(mnyeh) (noozh'-nah) **мне нужно**	*(yah) (zvah-nyoo')* **я звоню**
(men-yah') (zah-voot') **меня зовут...**	*(die'-teh) (mnyeh)* **дайте мне**
(oo) (men-yah') (yest) **у меня есть**	*(yah) (pee-shoo')* **я пишу**

I sell	I eat
I send	I drink
I sleep	I want
I phone	I need
give me…	my name is…
I write	I have

(yah) *(pah-kah'-zih-vah-yoo)* **я показываю**	*(yah)* *(lee-choo')* **я лечу**
(yah) *(plah-choo')* *(zah)* **я плачу за**	*(yah)* *(prahv'-lyoo)* **я правлю**
(yah) *(znah'-yoo)* **я знаю**	*(yah)* *(oo-yez-zhah'-yoo)* **я уезжаю**
(yah) *(mah-goo')* **я могу**	*(yah)* *(dyeh'-lah-yoo)* **я делаю**
(yah) *(chee-tah'-yoo)* **я читаю**	*(yah)* *(dyeh'-luh-yoo)* *(pyair-yeh-sahd'-koo)* **я делаю пересадку**
(yah) *(poot-yeh-shest'-voo-yoo)* **я путешествую**	*(yah)* *(oo-klah'-dih-vah-yoo)* **я укладываю**

I fly	I show
I drive	I pay for
I leave	I know
I do/make	I can
I make a transfer	I read
I pack	I travel

(poh'-yezd) (ah-pahz'-dih-vah-yet)

Поезд опаздывает.

(yah) (zah-krih-vah'-yoo)

я закрываю

(poh'-yezd) (pree-hoh'-deet) (v')

Поезд приходит в...

(yah) (aht-krih-vah'-yoo)

я открываю

(poh'-yezd) (aht-hoh'-deet) (v')

Поезд отходит в...

(yah) (ee-doo')

я иду

(yah) (stee-rah'-yoo)

я стираю

(yah) (lyoob-lyoo')

я люблю

(yah) (tyair-yah'-yoo)

я теряю

(yah) (sprah'-shee-vah-yoo)

я спрашиваю

(yah) (rah-boh'-tah-yoo)

я работаю

(yah) (nah-chee-nah'-yoo)

я начинаю

I close

The train is late.

I open

The train arrives at…

I go (on foot)

The train departs at…

I like

I wash/clean

I ask

I lose

I begin

I work

(zah-nee-mah'-yet) **занимает**	*(eez-vee-neet'-yeh)* **извините**
(skohl'-kah) (eh'-tah) (stoy'-eet) **Сколько это стоит?**	*(ee-dyoht') (dohzhd)* **Идёт дождь.**
(kahk) (dee-lah') **Как дела?**	*(ee-dyoht') (snyeg)* **Идёт снег.**
(doh) (svee-dahn'-yah) **До свидания!**	*(see-vohd'-nyah)* **сегодня**
(pah-zhah'-loo-stah) **пожалуйста**	*(zahv'-trah)* **завтра**
(spah-see'-bah) **спасибо**	*(vchee-rah')* **вчера**

excuse me	it takes
It is raining.	How much does this cost?
It is snowing.	How are things/ How are you?
today	good bye!
tomorrow	please/you're welcome
yesterday	thank you

(zdah-rohv´) (bohl´-yen) **здоров - болен**	(tohl´-stah-yah) (tohn´-kah-yah) **толстая - тонкая**
(hah-rah-shoh´) (ploh´-hah) **хорошо - плохо**	(nahd) (pohd) **над - под**
(gar-yah´-chah-yah) (hah-lohd´-nah-yah) **горячая - холодная**	(lyeh´-vah) (prah´-vah) **лево - право**
(tee´-hah) (grohm´-kah) **тихо - громко**	(myed´-lyen-nah) (bis´-trah) **медленно - быстро**
(kah-roht´-kah-yah) (dleen´-nah-yah) **короткая - длинная**	(vwee-soh´-kah-yah) (neez´-kah-yah) **высокая - низкая**
(vwee-soh´-kah-yah) (mah´-lyen-kah-yah) **высокая - маленькая**	(stah´-ree) (mah-lah-doy´) **старый - молодой**

thick - thin

healthy - sick

above - below

good - bad

left - right

hot - cold

slow - fast

softly - loudly

high - low

short - long

old - young

tall/high - small

(dah-rah-gah'-yah) *(dyeh-shyoh'-vah-yah)* **дорогая - дешёвая**	*(yah)* **я**
(bah-gaht') *(byed'-yen)* **богат - беден**	*(ohn)* **он**
(mnoh'-gah) *(mah'-lah)* **много - мало**	*(ah-nah)* **она**
(aht-krih'-tah) *(zah-krih'-tah)* **открыто - закрыто**	*(mwee)* **мы**
(slahd'-kee) *(kees'-lee)* **сладкий - кислый**	*(vwee)* **вы**
(bahl-shoy') *(mah'-lyen-kee)* **большой - маленький**	*(ah-nee)* **они**

Sunset
Proof-of-Purchase
ISBN 0-944502-46-6

I	expensive-inexpensive
he	rich - poor
she	a lot - a little
we	open - closed
you	sweet - sour
they	big - small